Giving Circles

Philanthropic and Nonprofit Studies
Dwight F. Burlingame and David C. Hammack, *editors*

ANGELA M. EIKENBERRY

Giving Circles

Philanthropy, Voluntary
Association, and Democracy

INDIANA UNIVERSITY PRESS
Bloomington and Indianapolis

This book is a publication of

Indiana University Press
601 North Morton Street
Bloomington, IN 47404-3797 USA

http://iupress.indiana.edu

Telephone orders   800-842-6796
Fax orders   812-855-7931
Orders by e-mail   iuporder@indiana.edu

The paper used in this publication meets the minimum requirements of American National Standard for Information Sciences—Permanence of Paper for Printed Library Materials, ANSI Z39.48-1984.

Manufactured in the United States of America

Library of Congress Cataloging-in-Publication Data

Eikenberry, Angela M.
  Giving circles : philanthropy, voluntary association, and democracy / Angela M. Eikenberry.
    p. cm. — (Philanthropic and nonprofit studies)
  Includes bibliographical references and index.
    ISBN 978-0-253-35319-1 (cloth : alk. paper) — ISBN 978-0-253-22085-1 (pbk. : alk. paper) 1. Charities—United States. 2. Public-private sector cooperation—United States. 3. Voluntarism—United States. 4. Humanitarianism—United States. I. Title.
    HV91.H382 2009
    361.70973—dc22

                                                                            2008044987

1 2 3 4 5 14 13 12 11 10 09

*This book is dedicated
to Griff and Ella.*

Contents

Preface

One of the things that just occurred to me . . . is that it's really quite democratic to be able to do this sort of thing at your own pace and in your own way.

—Giving circle member

Ever since Robert Putnam published his admonition that Americans are increasingly "bowling alone," there has been revived attention in the United States to community. Our image of society has increasingly become one of individualism, fragmentation, and deterioration of social ties. The common wisdom is that people no longer want to participate in traditional civic and voluntary institutions. The work I present in this book, along with work done by others in recent years on the emergence of new avenues of citizen participation, mobilization, and expression, show that this perceived erosion in community and civic participation may actually be a change in *how* people participate in community and civic life today. Giving circles are one example of a "new" form of organization and mode of participation enabling citizens to fulfill a desire to take a more active role in the larger community, but in their own way.

Giving circles typically involve individuals pooling money and other resources and then deciding together where to give these away. Through regular meetings and events, they also serve to educate members about community issues, engage them in voluntary efforts, provide social opportunities, and maintain donor independence from any particular charity. Giving circles are growing in popularity, especially among women, people of color, and people of more modest means in the United States and beyond. While some might argue that giving circles are merely a new way to describe an age-old phenomenon, compared with other modern philanthropic mechanisms such as foundations, federated giving programs, or check-writing, giving circles seem to be something different, indicative of new efforts to "democratize philanthropy." The problem is that very little reliable research has examined the giving circle movement and its outcomes and implications for democratic governance.

Who participates in giving circles? What motivates members to join and give in this collective fashion? How do giving circles actually function? What impacts do giving circles have on members? How do they affect the individuals and organizations they fund? What are the larger societal impacts of giving circles? These questions are some of the main concerns of this book, which comes out of nearly five years of research based on more than forty-five interviews with giving circle participants and staff, philanthropic professionals working with giving circles, and nonprofit professionals who have received funding from giving circles; analysis of hundreds of documents and news articles; data from surveys and case studies; and the literature on voluntary associations and philanthropy. This is supplemented with my own observations as a member of two giving circles. Indeed, I came to this topic because of my participation in the Omaha Venture Group (OVG). I discovered that this giving circle was part of a larger movement and that the giving circle movement was part of larger societal shifts in the way that people participate in communities today.

Beyond attempting to portray the dimensions of the giving circle movement, this book is also concerned with the role of philanthropy and voluntary association in a democratic society. Giving circles have emerged at the nexus of several social, political, and economic trends that have led to shifts in voluntarism and the way people relate to community in the midst of government cutbacks, devolution, and privatization, which coincide with a drive for increasing reliance on voluntary institutions to address community needs (what I call a shift to "governance beyond the state"). In this context, I examine the question of the best role for voluntary action in a democratic society. Can philanthropy and voluntary association act as laboratories for democracy in the context of governance beyond the state? Can philanthropy and voluntary association adequately address social needs and solve community problems? This book examines the degree to which giving circles might enhance the civic education and participation of its members while solving problems in an environment of governance beyond the state. It also explores the context out of which giving circles have emerged and the implications of changes in philanthropy and voluntary associations for democratic governance.

I find that what may be democratic for a member of the giving circle as donor and participant does not necessarily translate into democratic outcomes for the larger society, especially in the context of governance beyond the state. Although voluntarism can enhance members' ability to participate in their community and enable them to be more fully human,[1] it cannot be relied upon to adequately address deep-seated problems in communities or do enough to provide for basic social welfare needs in society. Indeed, the more that we rely on voluntarism to address basic community needs—and demand that voluntarism be held to high standards of democratic accountability in providing for these needs—the less democratic voluntarism may become. Voluntary associations and philanthropists will contribute most to democracy if they are allowed the freedom to do as they wish while the state is made strong enough to develop and enforce a system of fundamental rights, protect zones of freedom within which associational life grows, and support citizens with enough basic income and services to ensure that they do not become dependent upon one or a few associations for their life necessities.[2] What is needed in American society (and elsewhere) today is a serious discussion about the appropriate role of philanthropy, voluntary association, and government in creating a "good society."

This book is intended for at least three groups of readers: nonprofit professionals and philanthropists who maintain the philanthropic system through their work and resources, public servants who create and implement public policy, and citizens who guide and receive benefits from the voluntary system and governance structure. It contributes to an emerging body of literature that challenges basic assumptions about philanthropy's and voluntary associations' benefits to society, which is of growing importance in an environment where politicians and others continue to call for a larger role for these institutions in securing our everyday welfare. Although my intention in this book is to uncover assumptions about the potential for philanthropy and voluntary association to enhance democracy and meet needs in the community, I also hope that it will reveal the ways in which they might be tools for social change and improving quality of life. In understanding the limitations of philanthropy and voluntary association, we can better understand their potential advantages and how to enhance them.

Acknowledgments

Several sections of this book are drawn from articles that have appeared in academic journals and collections of essays. I am grateful to the journals and publishers for permission to use selections from these publications. I would also very much like to thank several individuals for their support, encouragement, and constructive criticism. Thanks first to Anne Khademian and Max Stephenson for being the first to review the book prospectus and providing me with feedback that greatly influenced my thinking about how to frame the story of this book. Joyce Rothschild gave me not only substantive feedback on the prospectus but also crucial tips on how to sell the idea to a publisher. It worked! Her mentoring and friendship have made all the difference. The other mentor to whom I owe a good deal is my dissertation advisor and now colleague, Dr. Richard C. Box. I also owe a debt of gratitude to many people who encouraged me along the way, especially Patricia Mooney Nickel, Thomasina Borkman, John Bartle, Jessica Bearman, Daria Teutonico, Andrea Pactor, and my dissertation committee members: Drs. Christine Reed, Jay White, and Ann Coyne. Special thanks also to the good folks who made this all happen at the Indiana University Press, including the reviewers and editors. Thanks also to Courtney Jensen and Glen Orr for their research assistance. Finally, this book would certainly not have happened without the support of my wonderful husband, Griff Elder, and our family members who supported us as we moved across country twice while I worked on this book and raised the smartest toddler and now preschooler one will ever run across.

Giving Circles

Introduction: Giving Circles and Democratic Governance

The New River Valley Change Network is a group of a dozen individuals—mostly women, university students and others with varying backgrounds and experiences—who meet once a month in Blacksburg, Virginia, to give away money they collectively contribute to a fund held at their local community foundation. Each member donates about $10 a month or $100 a year. The members decide together, through a consensus decision-making process, where to give their money. They like to fund small organizations and endeavors that might lead to social change. The group occasionally invites community experts and activists to their meetings to find out about projects or organizations in need of funding. So far, the group has mainly supported one small organization that works with university students to provide hands-on, grassroots efforts to meet community needs in a variety of areas, including addressing the household needs of low-income individuals, assisting nonprofits with collecting donated items and maintenance projects, assistance to home-bound older adults, community beautification, and historic preservation.

Washington Womenade raises money by holding frequent potluck dinners where attendees donate $35 to a fund that provides financial assistance to individuals who need help paying for prescriptions, utility bills, rent, food, and the like. Membership in the group is fairly loose; "members" show up when they can and the focus of their time together is highly social. In 2002, *Real Simple* magazine did a story on Washington Womenade, leading to the independent creation of more than 40 Womenade groups across the country. This article also inspired Marsha Wallace to start Dining for Women, now a national network of more than 177 small groups located across the country in which women meet for dinner on a monthly basis and pool the funds they would have spent eating out to support international grassroots programs helping women around the world.

Social Venture Partners (SVP) Seattle, one of twenty-four SVP affiliates in the United States, Canada, and Japan, asks members to commit approximately $5,000 annually for two years to participate in the group. SVP Seattle chooses organizations to receive grants through a rigorous process conducted by a grants committee. They fund in the areas of early childhood development, K–12 education, out-of-school time, early learning advocacy and policy, and the environment. The group follows a venture philanthropy philosophy that emphasizes long-term relationships with funding recipients, the provision of seed capital and organizational advice, and close tracking of funding recipients' progress and effectiveness.[1] Most SVP Seattle Partners also donate their time to the organizations they fund to help with capacity building efforts.

The groups described above—called giving circles—are a few examples of a rapidly growing movement in the United States and elsewhere. They involve individuals pooling their resources to support organizations and individuals of mutual interest. More than this, they are independent voluntary associations that frequently include social, educational, and engagement opportunities for members, connecting participants to their communities and to one another. It is impossible to say how many giving circles exist because of their grassroots and emergent nature. In 2005, with the help of the Forum of Regional Associations of Grantmakers' New Ventures in Philanthropy Initiative, I located about 200 giving circles in the United States and Canada. In 2007, we have been able to identify nearly 600 giving circles in the United States, Canada, Japan, South Africa, and the United Kingdom. There is a strong indication that many more exist and will continue to emerge.[2]

On the surface, giving circles seem very much like voluntary groups that have been a staple of the American landscape; one can see similarities in women's clubs and Kiwanis, Rotary, or the Junior League, for example. Many of us are very likely members of a group that meets regularly or have friends or family members who have participated in a book club or a church group. What makes giving circles different is the environment in which they have emerged and in which they operate: a philanthropic sector that is increasingly modernized and where voluntary associations are losing numbers and their grassroots natures rapidly (see chapter 2). They are also unique in that their express purpose is to give away money and other resources for community betterment.[3] Giving circles represent a transformation in the way we (ordinary citizens) are attempting to address community problems through giving and volunteering. They also represent one way in which collective grassroots philanthropy and voluntary association manifest themselves in the "new philanthropy" environment.[4]

The New Philanthropy and the Changing Shape of Civic Engagement

Many claim a new era has begun in American philanthropy.[5] This new philanthropy is different from "traditional" or "modern" philanthropy in several ways. Modern philanthropy, dominant throughout the last century, has been driven by the actions of large institutions such as charitable foundations and federated giving programs (such as the United Way) and characterized by professionalization, fragmentation across sector lines, and distance between the donor and the funding recipient and/or client. It also focuses on the "demand" side of philanthropy. In contrast, the new philanthropy appears to be guided by individual donors, some of whom emphasize collaboration across groups and sectors, partner with funding recipients, and use hands-on, unconventional modes of giving and volunteering that focus on grassroots, often entrepreneurial problem solving. This new philanthropy focuses on the donor-driven "supply" side of philanthropy.[6] Indicative of this shift in focus are what some have called "new and emerging donors," who seek to be more engaged in results-driven ways of giving or "investing" in organizations and individuals.[7] Some giving circles have emerged as a tool for these types of donors to be more engaged in their giving and in their communities. Simultaneously, the new philanthropy consists of another element that appears to run counter to increased engagement. This element is one in which individuals want to be *less* engaged in their giving and community, either because they do not have enough time to be fully engaged in giving and volunteering but want to do something to contribute to society betterment, or because they want more control over their everyday lives and the way they participate or do not participate in community activities. Some giving circles, such as Womenade or Dining for Women, provide an *alternative* to more and long-term engagement in communities, such as the type of engagement found in traditional voluntary associations.[8]

The new philanthropy reflects larger social changes.[9] Ulrich Beck, for example, describes society today as increasingly characterized by the dissolution of traditional parameters and "variation and differentiation of lifestyles and forms of life, opposing the thinking behind the traditional categories of large-group societies."[10] That is, we increasingly live in a posttraditional society (see chapter 3). Part of the reaction by individuals to this shift has been to seek out more engagement in community but in ways that match their personal interests, that they can control, and that they can manage in the context of their hectic lives. Cobb believes the emergence of the new philanthropy has been in response to several of these trends as well as socioeconomic factors such as technological innovation, the creation of large new fortunes, the dominance of market ideology, new demographics (particularly the growing disparity between rich and poor), and government retrenchment.[11]

The giving circle movement is but one example of new forms of organization and modes of participation becoming increasingly prominent in such an environment. Scholars have documented the significant emergence of small, informal self-help and support groups in recent decades.[12] These small groups include Bible study groups, therapy groups, book discussion groups, study circles, money clubs, and so on. In a broad-based national study, Wuthnow found that 40 percent of the American adult population claimed to be involved in "a small group that meets regularly and provides caring and support for those who participate in it." These small groups seem to attract people who are fed up with large-scale institutions and prefer instead to help themselves. The small group movement, according to Wuthnow, is rooted in a breakdown of traditional support structures—neighborhoods and family—and in a continuing desire for community. It "has emerged as a serious effort to combat forces of fragmentation and anonymity in our society."[13]

Simultaneously, some have recently documented the appearance of what can be called "network associations" or looser, more informal, and personal forms of association, emerging in the United States and elsewhere.[14] Within this type of association, engagement is directed toward concrete problem solving in everyday life more so than the performance of government institutions or large-scale bureaucracy. Individuals see it as natural that they have the right and power to cope with day-to-day political problems on their own terms and in their own way; they are not interested in engagement that is full-time and for life as did previous generations.[15] Wuthnow writes that "instead of cultivating lifelong ties with their neighbors, or joining organizations that reward faithful long-term service, people [increasingly] come together around specific needs and to work on projects that have definite objectives."[16] Traditional "voluntary associations have become optional."[17]

Thus changes in philanthropy and voluntary association—in particular the emergence of giving circles—reflect larger trends in society and provide an informative framework for understanding the cross-cutting tensions concerning the role that voluntarism can or should play in a democratic society. Giving circles are described by some as "democratizing philanthropy" and creating social capital, yet little empirical evidence exists about who participates in giving circles, what they do, and what the impacts of their participation are on society.[18] Beyond studies on specific types of giving circles,[19] case studies for use in the classroom,[20] organizational evaluations,[21] and reports or manuals for philanthropic practitioners to help them promote and create giving circles,[22] little research has been done to understand giving circles and their broader impacts. The work in this book provides a comprehensive picture of the giving circle movement in the United States and analyzes its impacts on voluntarism and democracy. As supposedly highly democratic philanthropic mechanisms, giving circles offer a unique opportunity to understand the ways in which philanthropy and voluntary association may or may not contribute to democratic governance, especially in the context of governance beyond the state.

Giving Circles, Democracy, and Governance beyond the State

There has been a growing interest around the world in the connections between civil society, voluntary association, and democracy.[23] Several scholars, beginning in the early 1990s, have created, debated, and fine-tuned various normative theories of associational democracy.[24] Many see voluntary associations "as [a] means of unburdening the state and revitalizing small-scale, functionally delineated arenas of democratic decision making."[25] Several associational democrats propose that associations—in particular, voluntary associations— play a more central role in addressing collective problems, including implementing what have long been considered *public* social welfare policies. Paul Hirst suggests, for example, that voluntary associations should be "an alternative to top-down bureaucracy in the competent provision of services," where the "state becomes a secondary, but vitally necessary, public power that ensures peace between associations and protects the rights of individuals."[26] While there has been a good deal of theoretical discussion about the normative hopes and critiques of associational democracy, there has been little empirical data to help us understand the practical potentials and dilemmas of associational democracy in this context. A study of giving circles provides much needed empirical data in this regard.

The call for a more central role for voluntary institutions emerged in the context of what some see as a shift from an age of *government* to one of *governance*.[27] That is, a shift from state-centered action to one of governance beyond the state, where "third parties, often nonprofits . . . deliver social services and generally act in the name of the state."[28] This environment has been described variously as "government by proxy," the "shadow state," the "hollow state," "third-party government," and "network governance."[29] It involves privatizing, devolving, and rolling back the state. While this shift to governance beyond the state is not exactly new, it is "increasingly regarded as an effective and legitimate form of societal governance," a form of societal governance that arguably utilizes "publicly regulated self-governance of [non-governmental] groups for the creation and enforcement of *collective obligations.*"[30]

The move to govern beyond the state is part of a larger neoliberal policy agenda—emerging most clearly when Ronald Reagan famously proclaimed in his 1981 inaugural address that "government is not the solution to our problem"—that has advocated for lower taxes, fewer social welfare subsidies, and more private and individualistic approaches to addressing social problems. The driving force behind this neo-liberal model is an assumption that political and economic life is a matter of individual freedom and initiative. Accordingly, a free-market society and a minimal state are key objectives achieved through the extension of the market to more and more areas of life with a state stripped of excessive involvement in the economy and provision of opportunities.[31] While there has been little actual "cutting back" of government in the past few decades, "what has changed is that the growth of the size of the state has been halted" and the "private side of America's hybrid system of social benefits has been eroding as corporations eliminate and restructure benefits to cut costs and encourage self-reliance."[32] In effect, this lack of growth in social spending by government and the private sector indicates that the welfare state and private institutions are less of a force for security and stability; that is, "welfare provisions have not kept up with the need for them," according to Esping-Anderson.[33] This erosion has occurred at the same time that political leaders have increasingly looked to private institutions for the means to "replace" public social programs.[34] In this context, voluntarism has taken center stage, offered as a utopian "middle way" by which we can achieve both liberty and fraternity, maintain individual rights, and meet social needs.[35] George H. W. Bush's "thousand points of light," Bill Clinton's "charitable choice amendment," and George W. Bush's "faith-based initiative" are all manifestations of this drive to link voluntary action to smaller government, to encourage voluntarism as a replacement for state-sponsored collective action.[36]

The main focus of this book, beyond documenting the giving circle landscape, is to extend a discussion about the role of voluntary association in society more directly into the realm of philanthropy (and thus into issues of resource distribution) and consider the impacts of philanthropy and voluntary association within this governance beyond the state environment. It does this by addressing two major questions of importance to democratic theory and governance: What do giving circles, supposedly highly democratic forms of philanthropy and voluntary association, contribute to the civic education and participation of members? And what do giving circles reveal about the capacity of voluntary associations and philanthropy to meet social needs and solve community problems in an environment of governance beyond the state?

Democracy is understood here in both its procedural and substantive sense—emphasizing the importance of citizen participation and deliberation in the public sphere and the ability of citizens to understand each other and come to some notion of the common good.[37] The first aspect, supported by participatory democratic theorists such as Aristotle, Rousseau, John Stuart Mill, Pateman, and Habermas, is based on the belief that direct participation in governance is vital for creating a virtuous, engaged, and deliberative citizenry and democratic society. In this regard, participation not only ensures greater government responsiveness, trust, and accountability but "the practice of active citizenship . . . has value in its own right. Because it draws on and develops the highest human capacities."[38] The idea of substantive democracy has been considered by scholars and practitioners since ancient Athens. Aristotle, though not condoning pure equality, believed extremes of wealth served to undermine the stability of democracy and led to oligarchy or tyranny.[39] Rousseau also wrote that "only a broad similarity in economic conditions can prevent major differences of interest from developing into organized factional disputes which would undermine hopelessly the establishment of a general will."[40] These notions of democracy will be discussed in more detail in chapter 1.

Thus the work in this book extends into the empirical realm analysis of what Putnam sees as the two levels of democratic effects of associations: internal and external.[41] Putnam outlines internal effects as those attached to the mobilization (control over collective resources and political participation) and socialization (a sense of concern for public affairs and mutual respect and acceptance) of members of associations and external effects as those "related to the role of associations in the processes of articulation and aggregation of interest."[42] I extend an examination of external effects as well into the realm of substantive democracy by considering the outcome of the philanthropic or resource distribution aspects of associations (through giving circles). Each of the main questions to be addressed, as articulated above, is examined in more detail next.

The Civic Education and Participation of Members

What do giving circles, as new forms of philanthropy and voluntary association, mean for the civic education and participation of members? More specifically, how well do giving circles provide members with opportunities for democratic deliberation and participation and broaden their identification with the needs of others in their communities? Alexis de Tocqueville pointed out nearly two centuries ago that voluntary associations serve as a means for citizens to achieve the virtues necessary for democratic citizenship.[43] As "laboratories for democracy," voluntary associations are said to help citizens learn the civic virtues of trust, moderation, compromise, and reciprocity; learn the skills of democratic deliberation; check the power of government; improve the quality and equality of representation; and create opportunities to participate directly in governance.[44] Voluntary associations are often seen as a key to enhancing political participation in the wider community.[45]

Voluntary associations in the past have also served to link individuals' private interests to broader community interests. According to Putnam, voluntary associations are essential to the production and reproduction of social capital—the "features of social organization such as networks, norms, and social trust that facilitate coordination and cooperation for mutual benefit."[46] Especially important for our purposes here is the value of bonding and bridging social capital for democracy. As Putnam explains, some forms of social capital are inward looking and tend to reinforce exclusive identities and homogeneous groups. This is *bonding* social capital. Other social networks are outward looking and encompass people across diverse social cleavages; this is *bridging* social capital.[47] Bonding social capital is important to internal democracy because it enables members to get to know one another and hence make listening and trusting easier.[48] Bridging social capital is important for external or substantive democracy because of its value in transcending social differences, including identity (race, ethnicity, religious tradition, sexual preference, and national origin) and status (vertical arrangements of power, influence, wealth, and prestige) differences.[49]

Yet, as discussed further in chapter 2, since the mid-nineteenth century in the United States and continuing through the scientific charity and philanthropy movements of the early twentieth century to today, philanthropy and voluntary association have become more modernized—rationalized and professionalized—and marketized, which has in many ways meant *less* opportunity for democratic, face-to-face, local citizen participation and social capital building in the sense praised by de Tocqueville and others. The most recent manifestation of such modernization is the decline of traditional voluntary associations—such as Kiwanis, Lions, Rotary, and League of Women Voters—and the addition of a new wave of national and international, more marketlike and professional, voluntary associational launchings—such as the AARP, World Wildlife Fund, and Children's Defense Fund. According to Theda Skocpol, "Social movements of the 1960s and 1970s helped to trigger a reorganization of national civic life, in which professionally managed associations and institutions proliferated while cross-class membership associations lost ground."[50] These groups have narrower missions and either few or no members or thin memberships based on computer-directed mailings to individuals (skewed toward the upper end of the U.S. income distribution), who send checks and perhaps occasionally read a newsletter. Individualized contact and narrow, instrumental foci are the norm. Within these groups, there is no longer face-to-face contact with membership or a concern for citizenship; thus ordinary citizens are less likely to be mobilized at the local level. Members are joined by common symbols, common leaders, and perhaps common ideals, but not with one another.[51]

The new forms of organization and modes of participation represented by giving circles and other informal groups discussed above may run counter to these modernization trends. Chapter 5 in particular will examine the degree to which giving circles enhance the civic education and capacities of members to fully engage in community issues.

Meeting Social Needs and Solving Community Problems

Scholars are only beginning to explore the implications of the new forms of civic engagement and association described above for community problem solving, especially within the context of government retrenchment and privatization. What do giving circles, as philanthropic voluntary associations, mean for the broader capacity of voluntary action to meet social needs and solve community problems in an environment of governance beyond the state? Most of us assume that voluntarism is good for democracy. It can serve to provide a democratic political opportunity structure, encourage leadership, help individuals to understand and connect with communities, and provide a forum and training ground for citizenship. Yet "voluntary failure" (as Lester Salamon describes it) or "philanthropic failure" (as Peter Frumkin describes it) poses critical challenges to the presumed capacities of voluntarism to address society's needs and contribute to addressing community problems.[52] This is because voluntarism often leads to an inadequate distribution of resources, is fragmented and focused on the short-term, enables elites to maintain their status and power in society (and thus maintain an uneven distribution of resources), and creates asymmetric relationships among citizens—all of which are detrimental to substantive democracy and thus the ability of voluntarism to address community needs and problems.

For example, voluntarism cannot guarantee equity of support for a variety of institutions, causes, and citizens because both private giving and volunteering are inherently limited by choice and geography.[53] Because giving and volunteering are so decentralized and locally focused, they are not able to reallocate resources from affluent to distressed communities. Beyond issues of redistribution, it is clear from available data that the voluntary sector does not have the capacity to adequately provide needed social services.[54] Even in cases where certain charitable causes enjoy popularity among donors and where there are many organizations providing services—such as in the arena of emergency food relief—there are difficulties associated with meeting the needs of the poor and addressing deep-seated societal problems. Voluntarism is often parochial and episodic, and it has the vice of "inconstancy" because people usually give out of surplus and a doctrine of "love without ties."[55] Philanthropy in particular allows wealthy elites to cover up the control they have in society, which perpetu-ates their wealth and powerful positions.[56] Furthermore, embedded in the vol-untary system is the perception that people who need help are inferior and the help they receive is a gift in response to a deficit rather than an entitlement or earning. When the social world becomes divided into givers and receivers, "haves" and "have-nots," a conceit or moral superiority is encouraged among benefactors and a feeling of demeaning inferiority results among beneficiaries. Ultimately, this may serve to erode "the cultural prerequisites for a vigorous de-mocracy [because] we become a society of givers and receivers, rather than a commonwealth of fellow citizens."[57] These failures will be discussed more ex-tensively in chapter 1.

Can giving circles counter or ameliorate any or all of these voluntary and philanthropic failures and thus serve to create a more democratic voluntarism that adequately addresses social welfare needs and community problems? I ad-dress this question in chapter 5. I conclude that giving circles seem to democ-ratize voluntarism to varying degrees depending on their size, structure, and internal activities, but perhaps not to the extent necessary to adequately ad-dress these voluntary and philanthropic failures in the context of governance beyond the state. Giving circles do serve to enhance the civic education and participation of its members; however, the broader capacity of these groups to meet social needs and solve community problems is extremely limited and problematic in an environment of governance beyond the state. Revealing this tension between two aspects of democratic associationalism (internal democ-racy and substantive outcomes) enables us to raise and begin to answer a more general question about the role that philanthropy and voluntary association can or should play in democratic society.

The Research Project

The core of this book includes results from the first two phases of a multiphase research project on giving circles. The first phase involved an ex-ploratory study of the giving circle movement and gathered qualitative and quantitative data from interviews with giving circle leaders and members and philanthropic professionals, as well as other documentation and secondary data. To determine the interview sample, a database was created in 2005 that in-cluded 188 giving circles. These were categorized by membership fee, organiza-tional structure and size, and activities. From this, a representative sample was drawn to gain maximum information about giving circles' processes and im-pacts, and then leaders of several giving circles were interviewed. Several mem-bers in one case study giving circle were also part of the interview sample. In addition, the philanthropic professionals I interviewed were purposefully se-lected based on their reputation in working with giving circles or because they were referred, through snowball sampling, by other philanthropic professionals. News articles, websites, and other documents written about giving circles were found through Google, Lexus-Nexus, and other article database searches. Secondary data came from a survey conducted by the Forum of Regional Associations of Grantmakers.[58] The survey was sent to founders, members, or staff identified by the Forum through their contacts with community foundations across the country. It was a web-based survey, and individuals were asked to participate via email. Responses were obtained for 61 giving circles. The other major sources of secondary data came from published case studies. The second phase of the research project involved interviewing nonprofit professionals (primarily executive-level and development directors from nonprofit organizations) about their experience receiving funding from and working with giving circles. For more on the research methodology of both phases of the study, see the appendix.

Plan of the Book

The rest of the book is organized in the following manner. To understand voluntarism and its changing nature in the United States, it is important to understand the environment in which voluntarism exists and out of which giving circles have emerged. Chapter 1 provides a discussion of voluntarism's relationship to democracy and the political economy, conveying the potential democratic and antidemocratic effects of voluntarism. Chapter 2 outlines trends in the modernization and marketization of society broadly and philanthropy and voluntary associations particularly, with special attention given to the detrimental impacts of these trends on the democratic contributions of voluntarism. Chapter 3 discusses changes taking place within society and within voluntarism more specifically that may run counter to the negative aspects and modernization of voluntarism discussed in earlier chapters. These include a shift to a posttraditional society and the emergence of new forms of association and organization—different from traditional voluntary associations—that may bring about different democratic effects than traditional voluntary associations. The point made in this chapter is that changes in voluntarism and the emergence of giving circles is a reflection of larger societal transformations, and these societal shifts and changes in modes of organization and participation have significance for the democratic effects of voluntarism. The chapter includes a prescription for a democratic voluntarism given this context.

Based on a comprehensive study of giving circles across the United States (see the appendix for a discussion of the methodology), chapter 4 provides an overview of the giving circle landscape, including several case studies of various types of giving circles and an analysis of why people participate in giving circles and what makes them different from traditional voluntary associations and philanthropy. Chapter 5 looks closely at the potential democratic effects of giving circles, examining the degree to which they provide opportunities for meaningful democratic participation, broaden individuals' identification with the needs of others, and expand who benefits from voluntarism. The data in this chapter suggest that giving circles do democratize voluntarism to varying degrees depending on their size and structure and primary activities. However, if one looks deeper, it becomes apparent that each type of giving circle has its strengths and weaknesses regarding internal and external democratization effects.

Chapter 6 provides an analysis of the key research questions posed in the introduction about the meaning of giving circles, as forms of philanthropy and voluntary association, for the civic education and participation of members, and the broader capacity of voluntarism to meet social needs and solve community problems in an environment of governance beyond the state. In particular, it highlights the tensions and limits of voluntarism in the context of governance beyond the state and concludes with a discussion of implications for the role of voluntarism in democratic governance. I conclude that voluntarism's most important role in society may be nothing more or less than enabling people to be philanthropic: to liberate the "human aspiration to give" and "enable human beings to develop their full human potential."[59]

1 Democracy, Voluntary Association, and Philanthropy

This chapter provides a discussion of voluntarism's relationship to democracy and the political economy. It addresses the question: What are the potential democratic effects of voluntary associations and philanthropy? As a central concern of the book, I start this chapter by first defining the meaning of democracy. I then turn to a review of the literature on voluntary associations' and philanthropy's potential contributions to democracy and then a review of their potential threats to democracy. I conclude that voluntarism contributes much to democracy in its civic and social effects on members of voluntary groups and in the pluralistic nature of voluntary association and philanthropy; however, voluntarism also has many shortcomings if one is concerned with creating greater democratic outcomes in society.

Defining Democracy

There are numerous models of democracy, but the United States has been influenced largely by two: classical liberalism and classical republicanism. Of these, classical liberalism has been dominant. Emerging from the European Enlightenment of the eighteenth century, liberal thought has emphasized notions of freedom and the rational capability of the individual as "generator of social and political creations." Its emphasis on individualism has been described by Bellah and colleagues as America's "first language" of moral discourse. Liberalism is based on the belief that individuals are atomistic beings that first exist and then come together to form society; it is largely self-interest that drives individuals to form associations. Thus the role of the state in this context is not to develop citizens but merely to act as a neutral mediator of competing interests and rights and guarantor of some of these rights. Individuals pursue their private self-interests while government exists to balance these interests. Citizenship is for the most part a procedural responsibility to honor contractual relationships to others and the state while popular sovereignty is limited primarily to voting for governmental representatives.[1]

Although liberalism has been dominant throughout most of American history, a classical republican undercurrent has also existed that reemerges in importance at various times.[2] Classical republicanism is predicated on a set of values that stress simplicity, patriotism, integrity, valor, and a love of justice and liberty.[3] Self-government and community are at the heart of this philosophy. Unlike classical liberals, classical republicans believe in a high level of interaction among citizens and between citizens and government. This approach is based on a tradition of face-to-face problem solving, with an implicit belief that people can "rise above their particular interests to pursue a common good."[4] To do this, citizens must be able to deliberate on the issues of the day and come to some consensus on what is best for the community, as well as feel a sense of mutual responsibility for one another. The ability to do this depends not only on a virtuous citizenry, equally capable of participation, but also on the ability of citizens to understand each other and come to some notion of the common good.

Both of these models largely focus on procedural democracy; that is, democracy that emphasizes the equal right of citizens to participate in the economic and public life of a society. They do not directly address issues of *substantive* democracy or the extent to which inequities of wealth, power, and privilege are allowed to influence democratic outcomes. A third, more radical notion of democracy, much less influential in the United States historically (in comparison to most European countries), supports not only broader, more direct citizen participation in public decision making and deliberation, but also challenges power that is taken for granted and other imbalances. This view of democracy envisions a more egalitarian society in which "citizens of all backgrounds could take part on equal footing in the democratic process, with reasonable hope that public dialogue on issues of importance would yield a society that curbs excess wealth, redistributing some part of it to ordinary citizens in the form of improved education, health care, and other social benefits."[5] This notion of democracy is closely related to the "full democracy" described by Adams, Bowerman, Dolbeare, and Stivers: "Full democratic rule (a) ensures that all adults have a genuine opportunity to participate in public discussions of issues that affect the conditions of their lives and to exercise decisive judgment about public actions that may affect those conditions, and (b) achieves outcomes that are consistent with choices the people collectively make about the public conditions of their lives."[6]

This third notion of democracy is especially relevant to consider today as we witness growing disparities in wealth and life opportunities in the United States. Over the past two decades, economic disparities have reached proportions similar to that of the late nineteenth-century Gilded Age: an age well known for extravagant consumption by wealthy "robber barons," while immigrants and others languished in extreme poverty in urban slums. Then as now, there was a large gap in income and wealth between the rich and poor, with a small or shrinking middle class.[7] For example, in 1890, it was estimated that more than half of all wealth was held by just 1 percent of families in the United States. Today, it is estimated that the top 1 percent are 875 times wealthier than the bottom 40 percent of all families and that households in the top 5 percent of the wealth distribution hold more than half of total wealth in the nation.[8] With the growth of the new economy in the 1980s and 1990s, the gap appears to have widened further; only a small percentage of Americans have made substantial gains in personal wealth. According to a report in the *Chronicle of Phi-*

lanthropy, "from 1979 to 2005, the average income of the top 10 percent of earners more than doubled after taking inflation into account, according to a Congressional Budget Office study of after-tax income. In contrast, people in the bottom 20 percent saw their net take-home pay increase by an average of just 6 percent during those years."[9] As discussed below, this divide in income and wealth translates into disparities for some nonprofit organizations in fundraising because wealthy individuals tend to give to colleges, hospitals, and arts organizations and not to social service organizations.[10]

We have also seen a steady growth of social welfare problems in recent years. For example, in 2001, 41.2 million people in the United States (14.6 percent of the U.S. population), including 8.5 million children (people under 18 years of age), had no health insurance coverage. By 2004, this number rose to 45 million (15.6 percent of the U.S. population), and the percentage of people without health insurance continues to grow.[11] The official poverty rate in the United States has also increased, from a twenty-six-year low of 11.3 percent in 2000 to 12.7 percent in 2004. This means that 37 million people lived below official poverty thresholds in 2004, which is 5.4 million more than in 2000. The poverty rate for children increased from 16.2 percent to 17.6 percent over the same period.[12] As a result, according to a 2006 report published by the U.S. Conference of Mayors, the demand for emergency shelter and food in U.S. cities has increased substantially in the past decade but about one-quarter of requests for emergency food and shelter could not be met.[13] Social service nonprofit agencies across the country continue to report an increasing demand for such services.[14]

Some philanthropic scholars have put an optimistic spin on these social and economic inequities by emphasizing the potential for nonprofit organizations serving these populations to capture a massive "transfer of wealth" that is predicted to occur over the next several decades in the United States.[15] Fundraisers and philanthropic professionals all over the country have put their hopes in this prediction, though it seems to be offered without much thought as to the reasons why such disparities exist, their implications, or the true potential for voluntary contributions from this transfer of wealth to actually serve the most pressing needs in the community. An alternative perspective might posit that in a society where such wide disparities exist and so many are in need, it is difficult if not impossible for people to understand each other or have any notion of shared values or a common good. Economic and social inequalities eventually lead to inequalities in citizens' opportunities and capacities for participating as political equals in governance. "Democracy" in this context is embedded in a socioeconomic system that systematically grants privilege to wealthy and elite interests, likely causing some groups to feel unwelcome and to cease participating altogether.[16]

Keeping these issues in mind, what follows is an overview of the potential democratic and perhaps not-so-democratic effects of voluntary associations and philanthropy in society. It lays the foundation for an analysis of giving circles and their potential contributions to democracy to follow later in the book. It also goes some way in raising concerns about the potential for a "golden age of philanthropy"[17] to contribute to addressing some of the social problems outlined above.

Voluntarism's Benefits to Democracy

Voluntary associations and philanthropy have long been important symbols of what many see as America's collaborative but independent spirit. They have also played an important part in western political and social theory. Communitarian, liberal, and radical left thinkers have all promoted these institutions as important for good governance and for limiting, supporting, or extending the state.[18] Communitarian approaches emphasize the socially integrative functions of association.[19] Liberal approaches put emphasis on the freedom to associate, which is justified by a liberal commitment to the moral dignity and priority of the individual, and the ability of associations to enable the experience of pluralism, which is believed to contribute to a democratization of everyday life.[20] Thinkers on the left see associations as mechanisms for challenging the state and representing those often not heard in the typical policymaking process.[21] There are counterarguments to many of these beliefs discussed below.

The prevalent beliefs we have about the democratic effects of voluntary effort in the United States are largely attributed to Alexis de Tocqueville's observations, published in *Democracy in America,* of association and voluntarism that came from his tour of America in the early nineteenth century. During his visit, Tocqueville witnessed "the rise of formal, voluntary associations, organized by people in towns, counties, and states to meet an extraordinary array of social, educational, religious, and cultural needs."[22] He observed that "Americans of all ages, all conditions, and all dispositions" continually joined together in informal voluntary associations for mutual benefit.[23] Largely based on Tocqueville's analysis, Fung outlines at least six ways that associations are said to enhance democracy depending on the kind of association and the political context in which it operates. These are "through the intrinsic value of associative life, fostering civic virtues and teaching political skills, offering resistance to power and checking government, improving the quality and equality of representation, facilitating public deliberation, and creating opportunities for citizens and groups to participate directly in governance."[24]

Edwards and Foley also examine these contributions to democracy in the context of civil society. Though a contested term, civil society is defined here as "the space of uncoerced human association and also the set of relational networks—formed for the sake of family, faith, interest, and ideology—that fill this space."[25] Civil society is important for democracy because it is the "free space" in which democratic attitudes are cultivated and democratic behavior is conditioned.[26] The level of participation in voluntary associations is important then because they promote a high degree of interpersonal contact that is critical to building a vibrant civil society.[27]

Edwards and Foley outline three democratic roles played by civil society and in which voluntary associations are active: enabling the provision of services to the community that would not be available otherwise, holding the government and market accountable by representing or advocating for citizens, and enhancing the capacities of citizens to participate in governance.[28] In the first role, civil society institutions carry out a variety of public and quasi-public functions, including providing services to the community. Voluntary associations and their philanthropic supporters enable the provision of a broad array of activities and services that may not be provided otherwise. Service delivery by voluntary institutions has been a main focus and growth area in recent years for voluntary organizations due to government downsizing and privatization in the United States and elsewhere.

Civil society also "stresses the *representative or contestatory functions* of social organizations outside the state."[29] Here, civil society institutions can serve to hold the state accountable, ensure that multiple voices are heard in the policy process, and use associative action for economic, social, and political change. They also permit a range of values and points of view to be expressed within society. Encouraging such a pluralist environment preserves choices and enables individuals to act on their own ideas and values in relation to the common good. As Berry notes, nonprofit and voluntary associations "usually are the only organizations that work on behalf of the poor, those without health insurance, immigrants, the disabled, and most other marginalized constituencies."[30]

Finally, civil society includes an emphasis on socialization where "the associations of civil society are thought to play a major role . . . in building citizenship skills and attitudes crucial for motivating citizens to use these skills."[31] In this case, civil society institutions' "special strength is in providing a democratic political opportunity structure, encouraging indigenous leadership capabilities, shifting to an asset rather than a deficit-based understanding of communities, and providing a forum for citizenship."[32] Based in particular on Tocqueville's observations, voluntary associations are seen as a means for citizens to achieve the virtues necessary for democratic citizenship: trust, moderation, compromise, reciprocity, and skills of democratic discussion and organization.[33] Voluntary associations are said to link individuals' private interests to broader community interests, mediating between the private sphere of the individual and the public sphere of the state and larger society, and counteracting the processes of fragmentation and individualization within modern society.[34] Today, voluntary associations are often seen as key to enhancing political participation in the wider community.[35]

Greatly influenced by Tocqueville, Robert Putnam suggests that voluntary associations are significant contributors to the effectiveness and stability of democratic governance due to the internal effects on members who develop habits of cooperation, solidarity, and public spiritedness and external effects that include effective social collaboration and self-government. Putnam believes voluntary associations have the potential to strengthen citizenship that he claims is marked in a civic community by active participation in public affairs. Putnam claims members of associations display more political sophistication, social trust, and political participation than others and argues that since voluntary associations represent horizontal relations of reciprocity and cooperation, rather than vertical relations of authority and dependency, they are essential to the production and reproduction of social capital. Putnam defines social capital as the "features of social organization, such as trust, norms, and networks that can improve the efficiency of society by facilitating coordinated actions"[36]

Philanthropy is also said to share many of these democratic attributes. Frumkin outlines several aspects of philanthropy that might benefit democracy. Because "philanthropy allows private actors to act in public ways," it enables donors to use private funds to create social and political change, locates and supports important social innovations, meets the psychic and social needs of donors, and affirms pluralism as a civic value. In the first case, "philanthropy ultimately allows some individuals to act as their own private governments, whose power can be used to challenge that of the state and force it to reexamine its priorities and policies." One avenue for doing this is the ability of philanthropy to locate and support important social innovations. In this regard, philanthropic funds can also serve as a form of social venture capital used to promote new thinking and programs that can sidestep the bureaucracy of government and take greater risks than government. Frumkin also believes that philanthropy can serve to achieve a modest measure of economic equity by giving money to nonprofits that serve needy populations. This often takes a local form with small-scale redistribution and sharing. As noted below, there is a good deal of evidence against this claim. Furthermore, Frumkin notes that the expressive function of philanthropy helps to meet the psychic and social needs of donors, which support the self-actualization of donors by helping them translate their values into action. This allows individuals to find meaning and purpose in their lives and thereby take an active role in society. Finally, and very much in line with the democratic benefits of voluntary association noted above, Frumkin writes that "giving allows a multiplicity of ideas and programs to exist in the public domain, rather than a limited number of 'preferred' solutions."[37]

Overwhelmingly, the literature on voluntary association and philanthropy supports assertions about the important democratic benefits of these institutions. Yet institutional structures that so many claim can do so much for democracy should also raise a flag of caution. Less widely discussed in the literature is what some see as negative or antidemocratic aspects of voluntarism, and it is to these that we now turn.

Voluntarism's Threats to Democracy

Voluntary associations and philanthropy may serve as mechanisms for civic participation and pluralism, as Tocqueville and others have observed, but they may also serve as threats to democratic institutions. Warren argues that

Tocqueville worked with a relatively simple bipolar model of state-civil society relations and thus conceived of associational effects within this model. The problem is that this model did not consider that associations always work within fields of power relations. The Tocquevillian model "makes it difficult to conceive the (real) possibility that associational life might replicate, reinforce, and even enhance power relations among groups, even if they develop and reinforce egalitarian norms within associations."[38] This produces a limited conception of what counts as political and goes some way in explaining why the politics of voluntary association and philanthropy are rarely discussed in the literature or within voluntary organizations.[39]

Indeed, many kinds of associations do not seem at all good for democracy. There are many examples of "bad civil society" organizations or illiberal associations; that is, groups that advocate hate, fascism, or bigotry like those that gave birth to the Nazi movement during the Weimer Republic in Germany, the fascist movement in Italy, or the Ku Klux Klan in the United States.[40] Tamir argues:

> In the real world, it is unrealistic to expect that in a voluntary process, free from state intervention, associational life will foster tolerance, modesty, and reciprocity; strengthen liberal democratic beliefs and tendencies; restrain the rule of the majority; balance the activities of the state; give individuals a public voice; and stabilize democracy. A few associations may indeed fulfill all (or most) of these functions effectively, but many will fail to do so. . . . When allowed to associate, individuals quite often opt for illiberal, authoritarian, non-democratic options.[41]

Philanthropy also has its own share of antidemocratic effects. It can defuse grassroots opposition and rebellion by offering small amounts of aid and mask larger inequities because it is typically "divorced from the fact that it can only exist through profit, exploitation, and their result, alienation and poverty."[42] Roelofs argues that philanthropy and its institutions essentially serve as a protective layer for the vagaries of capitalism.[43] Taken together, voluntary associations and philanthropy can fail in democratic outcomes by maintaining social and economic divisions and inequality. This voluntary or philanthropic failure happens because voluntary institutions cannot sufficiently and evenly distribute resources, they are short term in focus and fragmented when it comes to addressing problems in the community, they enable the maintenance of elite control and wealth inequalities in society, and they create asymmetric relationships among citizens. These are discussed in more detail next.

Inadequately Distributes Resources

One of the reasons that Americans support voluntary organizations is their belief that this support largely benefits the poor and the most disadvantaged in society.[44] Certainly, the voluntary sector is a significant force in the United States. In 2004 there were more than 1.4 million public charities and foundations receiving over $1.4 trillion in revenue and holding $3 trillion in assets.[45] The Independent Sector estimated in 2001 that over 70 percent of American households give money to charities and that over 50 percent give their time. According to 2006 estimates from *Giving USA,* private charitable contributions from households, private foundations, and businesses amounted to $260.3 billion.[46]

But for whom and for what does the philanthropic sector actually serve? Although these institutions perform many necessary functions, they cannot guarantee equity of support for a variety of causes and constituencies because voluntarism is inherently limited by choice and geography. Philanthropic particularism (the way voluntary agencies and nonprofit organizations, their donors, and volunteers choose to focus on particular causes) and philanthropic disparity (the charitable differences among communities) invariably affect who benefits from voluntary efforts. Hodgkinson points out that "such particularism can . . . exacerbate the mismatch between society's needs and available resources. . . . The American Cancer Society and the American Heart Association, both dealing with major threats to our health, are the giant fundraisers. Yet the nation's fourth biggest killer, kidney disease, ranks at the bottom in health fundraising efforts."[47] In addition, because the voluntary sector is so decentralized and locally focused, it does not have the capacity to reallocate resources from affluent to distressed communities. This is a significant problem when one considers that about 90 percent of charitable contributions are raised and spent locally, affluent communities tend to be more generous than distressed communities in which there are wider variations in income and racial/ethnic populations, and there has been an increasing residential segregation of Americans by income over the past forty years.[48]

Empirically based research strongly suggests that philanthropic giving does not go to those most in need. Private charitable donations go primarily to religious organizations and private higher education rather than to areas like human services. In fact, Hodgkinson finds, since the 1970s, giving to higher education, the arts, and private foundations has increased as a percentage of total individual giving while giving to human services, health, and international aid has declined. Wolpert estimates that only about 10 percent of charitable contributions are targeted to the poor. More recently, a study sponsored by Google and conducted by the Center on Philanthropy at Indiana University found "that less than one-third of the money individuals gave to nonprofits in 2005 was focused on the needs of the economically disadvantaged. Of the $250 billion in donations, less than $78 billion explicitly targeted those in need." Similarly, a 2007 study by the Institute for Jewish and Community Research found that only 5 percent of the total dollars from mega-gifts (gifts of $1 million dollars or more) go to social service groups.[49]

These giving patterns reflect that people give to whom and to what they know and to causes with which they can identify and are physically or emotionally attached.[50] According to Schervish and Havens, "The more closely donors are associated with charitable causes, and the more intensely donors feel the beneficiaries of their giving share a fate with them, the greater is the amount of charitable giving."[51] Wealthy philanthropists—who provide the bulk of philanthropic dollars—tend to give the majority of their donations to organizations from which they or their family directly benefit such as the symphony, church, or their alma mater as well as to amenity services such as education, culture, and health.[52] This is true as well for private giving more generally. Overall, most donations go to support community churches and synagogues, YMCAs, museums, and parochial schools—"services that donors themselves use—and are not freely available to target the neediest and to sustain safety nets."[53] Philanthropy has appeared to become even more focused on amenities in the past twenty years. Diaz concludes that the types of organizations that benefit from private philanthropy are elite institutions that serve non-poor, non-Hispanic whites.[54] Certainly, the analysis of mega-gifts by Tobin and Weinburg shows this to be the case for wealthy donors who give 44 percent of total dollars to colleges and universities, followed by 16 percent to hospitals and other medical institutions and 12 percent to arts and cultural organizations. Only 5 percent went to social services.

Data also suggest that voluntary organizations that rely heavily on philanthropic donations are less likely to serve the poor. For example, Salamon found in a study of human service organizations that the majority of organizations studied did not provide services or advocacy for the poor. Of 1,474 agencies reporting on whether they served poor clients (family income below the official poverty line), only 27 percent indicated that most of their clients were poor. Another 20 percent indicated that they served some poor clients (between 21 and 50 percent of the total client base), suggesting that the remaining 53 percent had few poor clients (below 20 percent). Among those that did serve the poor, the bulk of their funding was from *government* sources as opposed to private giving.[55] Galaskiewicz and colleagues also found that nonprofit organizations in low-income neighborhoods had a high percentage of government funding and almost no philanthropic support.[56] Indeed, there is strong evidence that the voluntary sector has historically been reliant on government support and that private giving is significantly linked to government funding levels.[57] To wit, Wolpert found in a study done in the early 1990s that "places that are generous in their state and local government programs tend to be generous in their charitable contributions as well."[58]

Beyond issues of redistribution, it is clear from available data that voluntary institutions do not have the *capacity* to provide needed social services. If one analyzes the past thirty years, charitable giving in the United States continues to represent less than 2 percent of personal income and 2 percent of the U.S. Gross Domestic Product. In fact, Burke notes, "As measured by individual contributions as a percentage of after-tax (disposable) income, Americans became less generous despite great increases in standards of living, education, and the reach of liberally oriented mass media since the 1960s."[59] This is also despite a significant growth in personal wealth in recent decades where the number of households with a net worth of $1 million or more has grown from 3.5 million in 1994 to an estimated 8.3 million in 2000.[60] Among the super rich (defined as taxpayers with incomes of $1 million or more), using an index of 100 for 1980, giving declined to 29 on the index by 1994. In other words, this wealthy group gave at just a quarter of what it did in 1980, taking into account its increased wealth in constant dollars. At the same time, giving by the middle class, defined as those with between $35,000 and $50,000 in gross income, declined from an index of 100 in 1980 to 91 in 1994.[61] More recent data, from 2000 to 2005, shows that there was virtually no change in level of giving if measured in constant (inflation-adjusted) dollars, although the U.S. economy expanded by more than 12 percent and total personal income increased by more than 7 percent.[62]

Part of the reason for this decline or stagnation may be attributed to changes in tax policy. According to Hodgkinson, "Beginning with the Reagan tax cuts of 1981, Congress has generally acted over the past two decades to lower income tax rates, capital gains tax rates, and estate tax rates." With estate taxes, the amount of giving subject to taxation dropped from 70 to 55 percent; the exemption level was raised to $600,000 for a single person and to $1.2 million for a married couple (which has gradually been increased to $2 million over the past several years to offset inflation); and full estates may be passed on to the living spouse.[63] These changes may reduce the incentive to give at death by increasing the cost of such giving.[64] The U.S. Department of Treasury found that only 18 percent of those paying federal estate taxes (estates valued at $600,000 or more) reported charitable bequests in 2003. This represents only 7 percent of the total net worth of these estates.[65] According to a 2007 article in the *Christian Science Monitor*, "From 1998 to 2006, the estimated yearly number of people who left money to charity has dropped from 17,587 to 9,522, according to Internal Revenue Service data. Over that period, fewer estates became subject to federal tax as the threshold for taxable estates rose from $625,000 in 1998 to $2 million in 2006."[66]

Another reason for a decline in giving may be the growing economic inequality that has occurred over the past few decades. A growing gap between the rich and poor has significant implications for household giving. National surveys of giving and volunteering in the United States conducted by the Independent Sector show that financial worry is the most prevalent reason individuals cite for not giving. As Hodgkinson reports:

> In 1998, 67 percent of respondents reported worrying about money, a slight decrease from 74 percent in 1996. Among those individuals who reported having serious financial concerns, 55 percent reported contributing and 43 percent reported volunteering. By contrast, among the 30 percent who did not worry about money, 71 percent reported contributing and 54 percent reported volunteering.[67]

Ultimately, because many organizations seek donations and volunteers from higher-income families, increasing income inequality could erode efforts to expand giving and volunteering as fewer and fewer families are asked to participate.[68] Meanwhile, nonprofits that have donors squeezed by lost income feel the pain of lost fundraising revenue.[69]

Thus one result of the decline or stagnation in giving is that private giving to voluntary organizations as a share of total income has declined substantially. Wolpert writes that "as recently as the mid-1950s, charitable organizations raised 70 percent of their income from donations."[70] However, private contributions as a percentage of charitable organizations' total annual funds declined to 18 percent by 1992 and 12.5 percent of total revenues by 2004.[71]

Focus Is Short Term and Fragmented

Even in cases where certain charitable causes or voluntary organizations serving the poor enjoy popularity among donors, and where there are many organizations that provide services, there are still difficulties associated with meeting the needs of the poor and addressing deep-seated societal problems. The emergency food relief system is a good example. The current emergency food system in the United States, begun in the 1980s, consists of tens of thousands of emergency food programs serving nearly one-tenth of the American population.[72] Volunteers and donors from all walks of life and economic levels show their support for food banks and soup kitchens—from Boy Scout canned food drives to multimillion-dollar corporate food donation programs. Yet, even with such widespread support, there are many problems with the system:

- Donated food items are often given in amounts that are too small or too large and/or are given because they are not good enough for others to purchase. Additionally, it is often difficult to choose and serve the kinds of food that people will like.
- The nutritional value of donated items is often inadequate. A 1986 study of soup kitchen meals in the state of New York found that over half the soup kitchens studied did not provide at least one-third of the Recommended Dietary Allowances for an adult.
- Many programs are inaccessible. There is a lack of convergence between need and supply, and so there are gaps in coverage. Additionally, many of those who need help the most do not have reliable transportation to obtain food.[73]

Although each emergency food organization may be extremely efficient, the system as a whole is highly inefficient and inadequate because of these and other problems. As noted above, most charitable organizations cannot easily transfer their resources from one community (of affluence) to another (less affluent community).[74] Ultimately, the voluntary sector is a fragmented service system with considerable confusion and lack of quality for needy groups.[75]

The problems associated with emergency food relief are like those found with many other voluntary organizations that depend on private donations and volunteering. This is because the inherent character of voluntarism is fragmented, inconsistent, and has a tendency toward short-term problem solving rather than addressing underlying social problems. Voluntarism is often parochial, episodic, and "too dependent upon the moral imagination of its affluent members." It has the vice of "inconstancy" because donors and volunteers usually give out of surplus and a doctrine of "love without ties"—they want to give without getting entangled in the ongoing toils of the receiver.[76] Even when volunteers desire a more intimate charitable relationship with beneficiaries, such as "adopting" a family in need, "intense interpersonal relating" largely serves to heighten "volunteers' sense of their separation from some of their fellow citizens" as Lichterman found in his ethnographic study of church group volunteers.[77] Giving and volunteering are often viewed as individualistic, heroic efforts, based on individual choice; there is typically little incentive or even ability for individuals to look at more comprehensive efforts for fundamental, long-term change.[78]

Because of these inherent difficulties, voluntarism frequently serves merely as a Band-Aid for deep structural problems. Poppendieck shows in the case of emergency food relief that many serving in this industry are so busy building bigger, stronger, and better food programs, they lose sight of the reasons why people need such services in the first place.[79] This sentiment is not new among scholars and philosophers. Henry David Thoreau attacked the hypocrisy of philanthropists "who relieve misery just enough to perpetuate the system producing that misery" and John Stuart Mill argued that "it is the great error of reformers and philanthropists in our time to nibble at the consequences of unjust power, instead of redressing the injustice itself."[80] In the early days of the American Republic, James Madison was well aware of the "mischief of faction" or problem of fragmentation caused by a heavy reliance on voluntarism. He knew that associations could not maintain equality of condition, only equality of opportunity, and that there was a need for a high level of civic consciousness among citizens if democracy was to succeed in this environment.[81]

Poppendieck suggests the general popularity of giving and volunteering can perhaps best be explained by their function as a moral safety valve to relieve the discomfort people feel when they are confronted with privation and suffering amid general comfort and abundance. In this context, voluntarism serves to mitigate guilt while economic and political systems maintain poverty and inequality. Poppendieck believes emergency food programs serve as an *illusion* of effective community action, lulling the public into complacency: canned food drives give people a warm, fuzzy feeling but do not cause them to think about why people continue to be in need. Voluntary action, as in the case with emergency food, convinces politicians and the public that the immediate problem is under control and that it is the appropriate response to poverty and economic inequality. With the outward appearance that no one will starve, emergency food makes it easier for society to shed its responsibility for the poor. Poppendieck writes, "By harnessing a wealth of volunteer effort and donations, it makes private programs appear cheaper and more cost-effective than their public counterparts, thus reinforcing an ideology of voluntarism that obscures the fundamental destruction of rights." This represents a larger trend in American public policy, prevalent since the 1980s, to shift from rights to gifts.[82]

Maintains Elite Control and Representation

As early as 1828, Rev. William Ellery Channing wrote about the hazards posed to democracy by voluntary associations because they accumulate power in a few hands:

> In a large institution, a few men rule, a few do everything; and if the institution happens to be directed to objects about which conflict and controversy exist, a few are able to excite in the mass strong and bitter passions, and by these to obtain an immense ascendancy. . . . They are a kind of irregular government created within our Constitutional government. Let them be watched closely.[83]

Tocqueville himself warned that private associations could form something like a separate nation within a nation. He and others saw that such intermediary bodies often formed around special interests that not only diminished the sovereignty of the state but also favored propertied minorities with the resources to devote to their establishment and perpetuation.[84] Rousseau wanted to outlaw secondary associations altogether in *The Social Contract* because he thought they were incompatible with the common good.[85]

Indeed, voluntary organizations today are typically governed by private, self-perpetuating boards, which can "divert decision making in the arts, culture, education, health, and welfare from public representatives to a private power elite," providing the philanthropic elite with a vehicle to make public decisions with little accountability to, or scrutiny by, the general public and elected officials.[86] In contrast to deliberation and action, through democratic processes, individual donors can use wealth to project their own values, commitments and beliefs into the public sphere without the need for collaborative decision making. Donors can act as legislatures and executive branches, authorizing themselves to work in the public interest. As Frumkin notes, "When donors act as seemingly miniature, undemocratic, and personal governments, tensions may surface around issues of class, race, and politics because the deliberative and consultative aspects of democracy have been bypassed."[87]

In this regard, Nevarez presents at least three ways in which voluntarism has helped the traditional urban business community promote its political agenda and maintain its elite status.[88] First, civic nonprofit boards of directors provide networking and deal-making opportunities that complement other corporate interlocks; second, business leaders socially construct a sense of "we feeling" by offering financial gifts, management advice, and opportunities for collaboration with charitable organizations, which in turn can positively influence third parties such as residents and decision makers; third, philanthropy allows businesses to influence the political climate by shaping the agenda of resource-dependent charitable organizations and neglecting controversial groups and causes that criticize business. Because local businesses and political leaders work to enhance the exchange value of their community, they engage in voluntarism that will enhance the marketability of their community as well as maintain their positions of power within the community.[89] The current popularity of corporate philanthropy or corporate social responsibility may be a relatively new version of such efforts by wealthy business elites to maintain a good public image and thus enhance profits.

Philanthropic foundations have also long been criticized in the United States for their undemocratic nature and use of assets to bring about change in their own elite interests. In 1915, the federally appointed Walsh Commission attacked foundations as bastions of corporate capitalism and as subversive to American democracy. Basil Manly, research director of the Walsh Commission, charged:

> As regards the "foundations" created for unlimited general purposes and endowed with enormous resources, their ultimate possibilities are so grave a menace, not only as regards their own activities and influence but also the benumbing effect which they have on private citizens and public bodies, that if they could be clearly differentiated from other forms of voluntary altruistic effort, it would be desirable to recommend their abolition.[90]

Of course, foundations were not abolished with the Walsh commission but were also not free from subsequent attacks.

Foundations became the objects of criticism again during the McCarthy years after World War II "when foundations were criticized for what were viewed as 'suspect' liberal ideologies."[91] The Select Committee to Investigate Foundations and Comparable Organizations, established in April 1952 and led by Congressman E. Eugene Cox, accused powerful foundations of giving money to support anti-American, pro-communist causes. René Wormser, counsel to the committee, wrote in reference to philanthropic foundations:

> An "elite" has thus emerged, in control of gigantic financial resources operating outside of our democratic processes, which is willing and able to shape the future of this Nation and of mankind in the image of its own values and concepts. An unparalleled amount of power is concentrated increasingly in the hands of an interlocking and self-perpetuating group. Unlike the power of corporate management, it is unchecked by the people; unlike the power of Churches, it is unchecked by any firmly established canons of value.[92]

More recently, scholars influenced by Antonio Gramsci have criticized philanthropic foundations for using their resources to create a "hegemonic class" of intellectuals who support their commitment to industrial capitalism.[93] Arnove argues that foundations have a corrosive influence on a democratic society because "they represent relatively unregulated and unaccountable concentrations of power and wealth which buy talent, promote causes, and, in effect, establish an agenda of what merits society's attention. They serve as 'cooling out' agencies, delaying and preventing more radical, structural change."[94] In this regard, Jenkins and others have shown empirically the ways in which foundations can co-opt or channel the structure and focus of social movements away from radical and civic building activities.[95] For example, most foundations engage in philanthropic exclusion and/or marginalization of popular social movements for social change. They do this by denying funding opportunities to specifically targeted social movements or according movement organizations a highly limited and peripheral status in comparison with other grantees. Many foundations also engage in philanthropic exclusion and/or marginalization of select organizations for social change within normally funded popular movements, encouraging and supporting more politically centrist organizations and campaigns within movements. Finally, foundations engage in philanthropic colonization of previously radical organizations and/or movements for social change by giving money with stipulations and restrictions that limit autonomy of the movement, providing short-term rather than multiyear grants that allow for planning and program development, demanding immediate returns on foundation investments, and issuing project-specific funding as opposed to general support grants.

Creates an "Us vs. Them" Ethic

In the context of voluntary associations, freedom to associate also implies freedom to exclude and discriminate, "which can have antidemocratic effects if an association controls significant resources."[96] Likewise, embedded in the system of voluntary giving is a social world divided into givers and receivers, "haves" and "have-nots." This system depends upon the perception that people who need help are inferior and the help they receive is a gift in response to a deficit rather than an entitlement or earning. For example, images of emergency food clients used to attract donors are often of patient sufferers, humbly waiting for help; the homeless are forced to remain supplicants and objects of charity if they want to receive help.[97] If the poor or homeless organize and make demands, they lose appeal as a charitable cause. This "inhibits direct, aggressive action by poor people on their own behalf, which is essential to the initiation of political reform."[98] Psychologically, beneficiaries are put in a position that is demeaning and destructive to the human spirit because asking for help can be perceived as an admission of inadequacy.[99]

A society relying too exclusively on voluntary giving can easily fall into moral traps because it creates the fiction of a self-sufficient giver, where donors can become too overbearing and too demeaning, too insensitive to long-range negative side effects of interventions, and too oriented to their own glory.[100] Certainly, this seemed to be the outcome of several early charitable "Christian" movements in the United States, like those to "save" American Indians and the urban poor or British efforts to "civilize" the "heathen poor" of Africa and India.[101] A system of voluntary giving, then, can encourage a conceit or moral superiority among benefactors and a feeling of demeaning inferiority among beneficiaries. This "us vs. them" dichotomy can eventually lead to extreme and dangerous behavior. Wagner notes, "The rhetoric of virtue has always coexisted with a deep-seated streak of violent repression in America: the physical and cultural genocide against American Indians, the enslavement of Africans, and the conquering of foreign lands."[102] Such social control appears to continue yet today in efforts by philanthropists to bring about "good governance" in developing countries.[103] Ultimately, philanthropy may serve to erode "the cultural prerequisites for a vigorous democracy [because] we become a society of givers and receivers, rather than a commonwealth of fellow citizens."[104]

Jane Addams, one of the founders of the settlement house movement during the Progressive Era in the United States, criticized the principle of philanthropy or voluntarism because of these problems. Fischer writes, "For Addams, philanthropy, defined in terms of voluntarism, is conceptually tied to an obsolete view of ethics—one that is no longer appropriate to the current stage of social and industrial development." She called this obsolete view "individual ethics." According to Addams, individual ethics supports the belief that poverty is the fault of the poor and wealth is indicative of individual effort and success. For Addams, this was not plausible in an urban and industrialized society and could only cause harm and perpetuate injustice because one's obligation in an individual ethic is not to society at large. In addition, the relationship between benefactor and beneficiary is hierarchical and not based on equality.[105]

Conclusion

This chapter provides a discussion of voluntarism's relationship to democracy. It shows that voluntarism seems to contribute much to democracy in its civic and social effects on members of voluntary groups and in the pluralistic nature of voluntary association and philanthropy. However, it also shows that voluntarism is no panacea for creating democratic outcomes. Indeed, philosophers of associationalism such as Warren and Rosenblum have concluded that voluntary associations do not in and of themselves create democratic outcomes; rather, it is the freedom of association that is integral to free human life and thus to creating a democratic society.[106] It is the pluralistic nature of this freedom to associate that is significant. It follows logically that because the point of many kinds of association is precisely their freedom and spontaneity, state intervention cannot help but damage their effects.[107] Efforts to control the direction of philanthropy as well can threaten the idea of a vital and independent civil society.[108] As Warren notes, "Even if it were possible to encourage through law or incentives those groups that produce democratic effects, these strategies would endanger goods that are valuable in their own rights, the identity and character-forming goods that are irreducibly a part of the freedom of association."[109]

A dilemma arises, then, for understanding the democratic effects of voluntarism in the context of governance beyond the state, in which there are increasing calls for more reliance on voluntarism to address community needs. Can voluntarism's democratic contributions somehow be enhanced without state intervention while at the same time minimizing voluntarism's antidemocratic effects? Examining giving circles from this viewpoint may help us to begin to address this question and the larger issue about the role of voluntarism in a democracy. The next chapter outlines trends in the modernization (and marketization) of society broadly and philanthropy and voluntary association particularly, paying special attention to the detrimental impacts of these trends on the democratic contributions of voluntarism.

2 The Modernization and Marketization of Voluntarism

Over the past century or more, we have witnessed the ongoing erosion of voluntarism's ability to enhance civic engagement or other democratic contributions because voluntary organizations and philanthropy, embedded in the larger context of modernization, have become increasingly professionalized, rationalized/bureaucratized, and marketized in their operations and approaches. Thus, even as there are greater calls to rely on voluntarism in an era of government retrenchment and privatization, the democratic effects of voluntarism are being worn away.

Modernization and Its Effects

There has been revived attention to community and civic engagement, largely due to evidence that traditional community and civic participation have deteriorated over the past several decades.[1] What Robert Putnam calls social capital—features of social organization such as networks, norms, and social trust that facilitate coordination and cooperation for mutual benefit—as well as civic engagement are apparently in decline. Putnam shows, for example, that turnout in national elections, attendance at public meetings, and attendance at political rallies has fallen, while churches, labor unions, parent-teacher associations, and fraternal and traditional voluntary organizations have experienced dwindling memberships. The reasons for these trends, Putnam suggests, are pressures of time and money, including the pressures on two-career families; suburbanization, commuting, and sprawl; the technological transformation of leisure (television and computers specifically); and generational changes.[2] Overall, Putnam and others argue that we are generally experiencing an eroding sense of community and civic engagement in American society today.[3] While Putnam may be correct in some respects, what we seem to be witnessing is less of a *decline* in a sense of community and civic engagement and more of a change in *how* people are engaging and participating in modern society (for more on this, see chapter 3). Loss of community and declining civic engagement may be due to larger changes related to modern societal structures and deeply engrained ways of thinking, which transpired much earlier in the United States than the more recent trends identified by Putnam. These structures (such as big government and corporate bureaucracies and commercialization) and ways of thinking (such as professional and technical-rational approaches to making sense of the world)—instruments of modernity—emerged during the Enlightenment of the eighteenth century and gained dominance during the industrial age.

The concept of modernity is organized around "mechanical metaphors, deterministic logic, critical reason, individualism and humanist ideals, a search for universal truths and values, attempts to construct unifying and comprehensive schemes of knowledge, and optimistic beliefs in progress and the movement of history toward a state of human emancipation."[4] When one thinks of modernity, it is of science and innovation, "instrumentality, emotionlessness, accumulation, skepticism, individual consciousness, standardization, and objectification," as well as expert knowledge, the lifeblood of professionalism.[5] The modernist view of human nature, emphasizing individual reason based on Descartes' "Cogito ergo sum" (I think, therefore I am), conceives of individuals as self-directed rather than inclined to sociability. One of the implications of this is that community and common property are replaced by a "society of strangers" enjoying private pleasures.[6] Thus modernity has served to create an environment where the self is defined not as part of the community but in opposition to "the other" and others.

Emerging from the modernist context, and still dominant in society today, is the rational-bureaucratic model of organization. This model is built on the machine metaphor of organizations that draws an analogy between the instrumental relationship among the parts of a mechanical device and the relationship among positions in an organization. These parts and positions are designed to complete the job—whatever it may be—as efficiently as possible.[7] Weber's theory of bureaucracy has had great influence on this model. He identified six central elements in a bureaucracy: (1) clearly defined division of labor and authority, (2) hierarchical structure of offices, (3) written guidelines prescribing performance criteria, (4) recruitment to offices based on specialization and expertise, (5) officeholding as a career or vocation, and (6) duties and authority attached to positions, not persons.[8] Embedded in the model of bureaucracy are the central principles of formalization, instrumentalism, and rational-legal authority. Formalization refers to the degree to which rules, procedures, regulations, and task assignments exist in written form. They are designed to direct and regulate organizational behavior after one has been slotted into a formal position. The concept of instrumentalism conveys the notion that the organization is like a tool or machine designed to achieve a particular purpose. Rational-legal authority is based on the formal position of the authority figure within the organization, as opposed to authority commanded on the basis of tradition or charisma. This is coupled with the belief by subordinates that structural arrangements represent the best means to achieve organizational objectives.[9]

In reaction to these structures of modernity, Weber contended that the modern forces of rationalization have stifled affective human relations. Emile Durkheim also argued that the rise of instrumental social relations and the division of labor in modern bureaucratic organizations created disintegration, normlessness, and anomie, which have ultimately resulted in "a life devoid of reflection" for individuals caught up in these systems.[10] Mancur Olson also shows that as organizations become more formally structured around principles of rationality and bureaucracy to meet environmental demands, they become more exclusive and less participatory and democratic; formalization closes out opportunities for community participation while hierarchy reduces the number of people who can make legitimate claims to participate in decision making.[11]

Some believe the public sphere is in a state of crisis because of the effects of modernity. Habermas describes the public sphere as "a space of institutions and practices between the private interests of everyday life in civil society and the realm of state power."[12] In its ideal form, the public sphere is "made up of private people gathered together as a public and articulating the needs of society with the state."[13] Thus the public sphere consists of social spaces where individuals gather to discuss their common public affairs and to organize against arbitrary and oppressive forms of social and public power. Voluntary associations can certainly fall into this category. However, Habermas argues that the public sphere has increasingly become colonized by the systems of modernity such as state capitalism, the culture industries, and big business, which penetrate the lifeworld in which people reside and shape the way they think about collective values. As a result, economic and governmental institutions have come to dominate the public sphere, while citizens are "content to become primarily consumers of goods, services, political administration, and spectacle . . . dedicating themselves more to passive consumption and private concerns than to issues of the common good and democratic participation."[14]

Habermas's observations capture not only the negative impacts of large modern bureaucracies on the public sphere but also the problematic tension between the market and democracy. As Anderson notes, the market is essentially antisocial, based on self-interest rather than disinterest or the public good. Thus shared values and democratic collective effort cannot be realized through market transactions.[15] Yet the discourse of the market seems to increasingly pervade all aspects of society today. As one indication of this, consumerism is increasingly recognized as a key form of political action in an environment where public spaces are either disappearing or increasingly made "safe for shopping."[16] The voluntary spirit as well is increasingly co-opted by the market through cause-related marketing and celebrity philanthropy.[17]

As noted in the previous chapter, voluntary associations are often looked to as an important remedy for many of the negative effects of modernity mentioned above. Voluntary associations are said to link individuals' private interests to broader community interests, mediate between the private sphere of the individual and the public sphere of the state, and counteract the processes of fragmentation and individualization within modern society.[18] Much like Tocqueville's assertions in *Democracy in America,* Habermas sees voluntary association as potentially playing a significant role in allowing the public sphere to emerge as uncoerced, nonmarketized spaces for deliberation, civic action, and engagement. For these reasons, voluntary associations and philanthropy are often promoted as ways to encourage greater community building and civic participation and thus reason enough to encourage and support their formation by the U.S. government, allowing these institutions tax exemption and special organizational status. However, the degree to which voluntary associations and philanthropic institutions today truly link individuals' private interests to broader community interests and counteract the processes of fragmentation and individualization within modern society is in question within the context of modernity. The rationalization, professionalization, and marketization of the voluntary sector over the last century or more has run counter to these democratic effects. For example, the demise of traditional voluntary associations and the rise of professional advocacy and tertiary organizations (or checkbook charities, as some have described them) have meant less opportunity for individuals to come together in a face-to-face setting and do anything more than read a newsletter or write a check to their charitable cause of choice. In addition, voluntary action itself has increasingly been co-opted by a market ideology that individualizes collective problems and their solutions.

The Rationalization and Professionalization of Voluntarism

The history of voluntarism in the United States truly began with the people who inhabited America long before European settlers arrived.[19] Giving and voluntary association were, and continue to be, integral aspects of American Indian culture. In this context, however, "giving" means something different than the conventional sense of charity as almsgiving in European culture. For American Indians, wealth is measured not in net worth but as a combination of spiritual qualities, material goods, and behavior; giving is seen as a system of sharing, with no encumbrances of a moral hierarchy that places the giver above the recipient. Exchange of goods and services is seen as essential to social relationships and leads to forms of generosity such as "neighboring back and forth" and "barn raising."[20]

Building on these roots, and other Western European values based in religion and economics, voluntarism in colonial America emphasized the cooperative or collaborative association of individuals. Well into the eighteenth century, charitable giving was construed to be "a charitable attitude or feeling toward others that prompted benevolent behavior."[21] It was the practice and prerogative of the many, rather than the privilege of the few and citizens were essentially duty bound to share their wealth with their communities.[22] It was near the end of this colonial period that Tocqueville made his observations about associations in America. According to Gross, the institutions Tocqueville depicted in *Democracy in America* played little part in colonial society. Rather, Tocqueville was witness to a new phenomenon that was remaking life in the wake of the American Revolution: "the rise of formal, voluntary associations, organized by people in towns, counties, and states to meet an extraordinary array of social, educational, religious, and cultural needs."[23] Tocqueville captured the decisive moment when an older tradition of charity and grassroots voluntary action was giving way to a new, modernist mode of voluntarism.

A major turning point for this transition was the Dartmouth College case of 1819, which pitted the trustees of the Christian-based Dartmouth College against the (classical) republican New Hampshire state legislature, which was attempting to take over the college. It was primarily a conflict over the teaching of the young and more generally over a vision of American society. McGarvie writes: "Republicans sought to teach practical knowledge and a humanistic morality fitting the young for business, politics, and citizenship. Their opponents objected to the loss of deference to God, the threat to social order, and the degradation of public morals that such a humanistic curriculum promised."[24] The Supreme Court decided in favor of the college trustees, leading to the creation of formal legal structures for religious and voluntary organizations and the separation of government institutions from private charitable corporations. More than this, the case encouraged a move from a colonial model of giving— where community involvement reflected informal personal relationships— toward a modern society premised on contract and formal philanthropic institutional structures.[25]

As life in early America became less communal and relied more on the rational dictates of law, social organization adopted a more systematic approach where organized voluntary and philanthropic institutions were created to solve social problems that were not addressed adequately by individual charitable acts. It was as early as the 1840s that "national associations rationalized the business of benevolence. They kept watch over huge sums of money through sophisticated cost-accounting; they replaced inefficient volunteers with paid agents recruited and trained for the job, and supervised them through a network of regional offices; and they relied on regular memos and reports to communicate with employees and on national magazines to publicize the cause to the public."[26] Many of these national associations eventually became federated, with local groups taking shape within broader movements and trans-local organizational frameworks.[27]

One such movement to emerge in the mid-nineteenth century, at the height of the industrial era, was the "scientific charity" movement. The stated aim of this movement was to promote cooperation and higher standards of efficiency among relief-dispensing voluntary societies. The movement occurred at a time when urbanization and industrialization intensified problems of social control and economic deprivation, while public policy turned to the elimination of outdoor assistance to the needy and the institutionalization of the poor. Within such an environment, charity organizations became the leading architects of welfare bureaucracy and its professionalization. These organizations operated through professional staff and trained volunteers who collected large amounts of data to develop "laws" of charity and reform and made "friendly visits" to monitor the poor. Professional staff were said to be needed because the environmental demands of the day "seemed to call for more efficient organiza-tion, more highly developed technical skills, and greater monetary support than agencies controlled by volunteers could command."[28]

During this time, institutionalized philanthropy also emerged on a national level to create a more scientific method of giving. This manifested itself in the creation of foundations and federated giving programs. By the end of the nineteenth century, philanthropic giants such as Ford, Rockefeller, Carnegie, and Kellogg—all self-made men—created large foundations to distribute their funds in a more scientific, orderly, and systematic manner. "Scientific philan-thropy" became a popular model within these foundations. The focus of such giving was on creating knowledge and then finding solutions to societal prob-lems. It was seen as "wholesale" rather than "retail" giving, seeking to address causes and cures rather than treating victims.[29] Likewise, the federated giv-ing or community chest movement was established in 1913 in Cleveland with the focus of making fundraising more efficient while expanding the number of contributors to the city's charities. This movement was also founded in re-sponse to donors' lack of information: the funds relieved donors of the com-plicated task of dividing up their gifts among charities by performing auditing and monitoring functions that assured donors their money supported "repu-table" organizations.[30] Federated giving programs operated by collecting and distributing funds through a broad base of support, with the goal of rational-izing giving habits to insure the stable income needed for skilled personnel, ad-ministration, and coordination within charities.[31] Today's United Way came out of this movement.

It should be noted that there was an attempt during this time to retain a sense of a more traditional, community-based charitable impulse. The settle-ment house movement was part of a larger response by Progressives, Populists, and other reformers to deal with what they saw as challenges to the tenets of de-mocracy caused by industrialization, immigration, and other problems of the city.[32] Jane Addams, founder of one of the first settlement houses in the United States (Hull House in Chicago) and a leader of the American settlement house movement, saw the work of the settlement house as "democracy in action."[33] A core aspect of the settlement movement was its emphasis on building commu-nity and "binding" the social classes in a common purpose. It did this primarily by bringing the "affluent and the poor in contact with one another by attracting idealistic, college-aged, upper middle-class youths to settle in poor neighbor-hoods or, at least, to volunteer some time."[34] By bringing people together and through its programming, settlements became a space for civic engagement, a space for the public sphere to emerge. Lectures, civic interest groups, and civic discourse were all important elements of this.

Even though the settlement house movement made important contributions to society and our understanding of voluntary action, much of voluntarism as we know and practice it today has followed the model set out by the scien-tific charity and philanthropy movements, while other less "scientific," ratio-nal, and bureaucratic forms of charity have to some degree disappeared (but may be reemerging as the giving circle movement seems to indicate). For example, Trolander shows that in the decades after the New Deal, the settlement house approach was lost in the mix of changing neighborhoods and the rise of the professional social worker, among other reasons.[35] Today, with the drive to increase the importance of voluntary associations for delivery of social welfare services in the United States, we have seen even greater pressure put upon voluntary organizations and philanthropy to become more rationalized and professionalized.

Over the past few decades, the modernization of the voluntary field has been motivated by a drive by major foundations in the United States, especially the Ford Foundation, to create a national professional philanthropic infrastructure to respond to societal needs. In the 1980s, major foundations supported new graduate-level academic programs to train nonprofit professionals and funded philanthropic research entities such as the Aspen Institute's Nonprofit Sector Research Fund, the Association for Research on Nonprofit and Voluntary Action (ARNOVA), and the International Society for Third Sector Research (ISTR).[36] Simultaneously, there has been a growing professionalization of fundraising led by large universities, where trained technicians have replaced traditional alumni staffs. Major hospitals and cultural institutions nationwide have followed suit.[37] Voluntary organizations, in particular larger organizations, have increasingly emphasized the use of fundraising methods such as grant writing, workplace solicitation, telemarketing, direct mail campaigns, telephone solicitation, donor-advised funds, and e-philanthropy, rather than more personal methods of solicitation, to try to keep pace with the imperative to grow.

Retrenchment and shifts in government support have also put increasing pressure on voluntary institutions not only to address a growing number of social problems in the United States but also to maintain accountability to the public in addressing these problems. Workers in these nonprofit, voluntary organizations essentially become "street level bureaucrats" with a more diluted line of authority. The response by voluntary institutions to these pressures has been to focus more on demonstrating efficiency and short-term effectiveness, which in turn has demanded greater emphasis on a professional orientation in operations. As will be discussed next, voluntary institutions have also adopted more marketlike approaches to raising funds and increasing efficiency to meet demand for their services.

The Marketization of Voluntarism

In recent decades, voluntary organizations and philanthropists have increasingly adopted the approaches and values of the private market, leading to what Salamon calls the "marketization" of the field.[38] Environmental constraints and influences have compelled voluntary organizations to adopt the methods and values of the market in several areas. Major public policy changes over the past few decades have played a significant role in nonprofit organizations' reliance on the generation of commercial revenue as well as increased emphasis on performance-based contract competition for government funding. Donors have also taken on a more entrepreneurial way of giving while the staff of many voluntary organizations have embraced social entrepreneurship as a model for organizational management.

Due to federal and state budget cuts and changing government policies, escalating needs in the community, and growth in the number of organizations to meet these needs, voluntary organizations have become increasingly reliant on commercial income such as fees for services, product sales, and other profit-making ventures to operate.[39] Although some of these activities have long been utilized by voluntary organizations, their use has increased substantially since the 1970s.[40] According to Salamon, commercial income accounted for "52 percent of the growth of the nonprofit sector during the 1982–92 period."[41] Kerlin has found more recently that from 1982 to 2002, commercial revenue for nonprofit organizations has increased as a percentage of total nonprofit revenue and at a greater rate than private contributions and government grants.[42] More general data indicate that of the total annual revenue for voluntary organizations in 1997, 38 percent came from private payments in the form of dues and fees for services. This is compared with 20 percent of revenue from private contributions and 31 percent from government sources.[43]

As a result of public policy initiatives during the past few decades, influenced by the reinventing government and new public management movements in the United States, sweeping changes have also occurred in the structure of government outsourcing to voluntary organizations.[44] There has been a shift away from using grants to using contracts and vouchers, with increased emphasis on competition and performance measurement for the delivery of social services. The contract approach incorporates the language of the market (i.e., risk sharing, pay-for-performance, and bonuses) and methods of the market, shifting risk to providers who only get paid for successfully completed assignments on a fixed-rate basis.[45] With this shift, government agencies have also become more open to outsourcing work to for-profit organizations instead of taking the traditional approach to contracting in social services: a noncompetitive, quasi-grant arrangement, primarily involving charitable organizations.[46] In today's environment, government agencies no longer award contracts to providers "because of what they are but what they can do" and how efficiently they can do it.[47] These combined changes—government utilizing the competitive performance contract approach and no longer giving voluntary organizations preferential treatment in outsourcing—provide for-profit organizations with an edge in the bidding process because they generally have more capital to assume greater risk and greater information technology capacity to meet contract requirements.[48]

Philanthropists are also increasingly pushing for more marketlike behavior among voluntary organizations. According to Foster and Bradach, "Many philanthropic foundations and other funders have been zealously urging nonprofits to become financially self-sufficient and have aggressively promoted earned income as a means to 'sustainability.'"[49] Such donors scrutinize charitable causes like potential business investments. They desire a way of giving that is "consistent with their own results-oriented values and their own patterns of behavior."[50] Some of these donors like to practice "venture philanthropy," or "the application of venture capital principles and practices to achieve social change. . . . [These donors] want a ROI (return on investment), a SROI (social return on investment), FROI (financial return on investment), or EROI (emotional return on investment)."[51] This new style of giving is most visible in the numerous venture funds created in recent years. For example, the Roberts Enterprise Development Fund: "develops and implements innovative approaches to critical social issues based on its experience *investing* in a *portfolio* of nonprofit-run social purpose *enterprises* in the San Francisco Bay Area."[52]

Voluntary organization professionals are also embracing market values and methods through what has come to be called "social entrepreneurship." Social entrepreneurs are described as nonprofit organization executives who pay attention to market forces without losing sight of their organizations' underlying missions, and who seek to use the language and skills of the business world to advance the material well-being of their members/clients.[53] They are driven by two strong forces, according to Reis and Clohesy: "first, the nature of the desired social change often benefits from an innovative, entrepreneurial or enterprise-based solution. Second, the sustainability of the organization and its services requires diversification of its funding streams, often including the creation of earned income streams or a partnership with a for-profit."[54]

As a result of this entrepreneurial attitude, as well as in reaction to funding constraints, voluntary organizations are entering into various new relationships with for-profit organizations. For example, instead of making a donation to the Boys and Girls Clubs of America, a few years ago Coca Cola Company negotiated a $60 million "marketing contract" with them.[55] Similarly, the American Cancer Society agreed in 1996 to "endorse" NicoDerm CQ nicotine patches, Nicorette nicotine gum, and Florida orange juice for several million-dollar grants.[56] This trend in "cause-related marketing" has grown in recent years.[57] In addition, some organizations are creating for-profit enterprises to supplement their operating expenses, like starting bakeries, restaurants, or bicycle repair shops. Some organizations, especially in the health care industry, have gone so far as to convert to outright for-profit status.[58]

Implications for Civic Engagement and Democracy

The Effects of Modernization

The modernization of voluntarism has no doubt increased the capacity of voluntary institutions to provide services; however, it has also led to a greater emphasis on rational bureaucratic organizational structures, professionalism, and efficiency at the expense of individual impulse, neighborliness, and community engagement. There are many examples upon which to draw in this regard. For instance, though creating many venerable institutions and improving the quality of life in several areas, foundations and federated giving programs have also served as a buffer between philanthropists and the beneficiaries of their giving. From Gross's point of view, these "philanthropic institutions reduced charity to a token act. . . . An individual could contribute funds to a house of industry for the poor or to a refuge of unwed mothers, secure that he or she would never come into contact with any of the inmates."[59] Federated giving programs in particular were, as Lubove writes, "the ultimate in bureaucratization, in the shift from cause to function. An anonymous public supported an anonymous machinery to serve anonymous clients."[60]

Modern voluntary institutions have also served to escalate the "bureaucratization of private charity" by hardening the distinction between volunteer and professional and redefining citizen-volunteers into fundraisers.[61] In the first case, many modern voluntary institutions are structured to support the notion that institutional leadership and client care are prerogatives of the trained and the skilled—the professional—rather than the volunteer, who has largely become quite subordinate to the professional within voluntary agencies. As Lichterman finds based on his ethnographic research, many of us "take for granted today a specialized, task-oriented, time-limited 'volunteer' role, the duties of which are defined by social service professionals."[62] Thus today, when agencies use volunteers, it is through careful screening, training, indoctrination, and supervision, using volunteers for certain tasks without compromising organizational efficiency and administrative integrity. Lichterman calls this "plug-in style volunteering," in which volunteers need to "get things done," often under the direction of a professional who defines the tasks for them; there is little or no room for garnering an understanding of voluntary effort in the context of larger political or policy issues.[63] He also finds that this style of volunteering does not build meaningful relationships, strengthen "we-ness," or otherwise build up social capacity in the ways that Tocqueville imagined such civic activity might engender. Plug-in style voluntarism and an emphasis on professionalism to address community problems have subsequently led to the negation of spontaneous or sentimental charity and, according to Lubove, "the substitution of the social agency for the benevolent individual as the repository of philanthropic wisdom."[64]

Thus volunteerism is now viewed less as a duty of the citizen in a democratic society and more as "a privilege granted by philanthropic agencies to those who accepted [sic] their discipline."[65] Volunteers and donors have moved from a role of civic stewardship to one of money giver, with this giving often described as an "investment" requiring much thought and care. In other words, intelligence, not caprice or emotion, has become the standard for governing altruism. Federated giving programs have long fed into this philosophy with promises to eliminate waste and increase the effectiveness of individual gifts because they serve to "approve" what they believe to be the most efficient, worthy, and necessary organizations in the community. This has ultimately served to restrain grassroots efforts within communities because federations serve to heighten the financial difficulties of smaller, innovative, or dissident organizations "by leaving them outside of the bounds of respectability."[66] Milofsky describes the ways in which neighborhood organizations in urban communities, many of which are committed to participatory democracy, are driven to develop bureaucratic, organizational hierarchies to gain support from more hierarchically organized donor organizations such as federated giving programs; this also reduces their ability to enhance citizen participation.[67]

The relatively impersonal fundraising techniques used by federated giving programs and other voluntary organizations more recently continue to have negative impacts on direct participation in voluntary institutions today. Fundraising mechanisms such as grant writing, workplace solicitation, telemarketing, direct mail, telephone solicitation, and the like have generated more income for charitable causes and organizations from diverse groups of people.[68] But these new techniques have also created "little stake in the organization or social connectedness for the individual."[69] These fundraising approaches serve to tighten the link between wealth and voluntarism, rather than making voluntary action attainable for all citizens. As an example of this, Milofsky shows that the process of obtaining funding through grants has become so complex and difficult that organizations can no longer rely on volunteers to appeal to many funders: "the growth of this sort of funding militates against the amateur leadership which is the essence of community self-help" because amateurs are unlikely to know the lay of land in this funding world.[70]

Similarly, at least partly as a consequence of the effects of modernization, there has been a growing decline in traditional voluntary association memberships in the United States. Large federated voluntary associations such as Kiwanis, Rotary, and the League of Women Voters used to involve considerable popular participation, mobilizing people from different occupational and class backgrounds into the same or parallel groups.[71] Local associational affiliates of these federated associations also used to offer many leadership opportunities to average (middle-class) members; even the nonelite could move up ladders of organizational leadership into state and national positions.[72] As Skocpol argues, voluntary membership federations "inculcated the core values underpinning republican citizenship . . . basic values of charity, community, and good citizenship."[73] However, today most of these traditional associations are slowly dying out, barely surviving with shrunken networks and dwindling, aging memberships and thus diminishing the importance of traditional voluntary associations as mobilizing agents for citizenship.[74] Based on an analysis of data from the European Values Survey and the Danish Study of Citizenship, which found no relation between belonging to a voluntary association and political interest or participation in political discussions, Gundelach and Torpe conclude that "in the present individualized society the voluntary associations do not seem to play the roles which were identified by Tocqueville and others more than 100 years ago."[75] It appears that these groups are being replaced by various types of organizations and associations such as professionally run advocacy organizations or very informal, loosely networked associations. It is not clear whether these alternative associations can make the same kind of demo-cratic contributions we typically attribute to voluntarism, an issue we can begin to address through an analysis of giving circles.

The Effects of Marketization

Voluntary organizations receive several benefits from the marketiza-tion trends discussed above, including creating more reliable resource streams, greater efficiency and innovation, better targeting of services, increased legiti-macy, and greater accountability.[76] However, these achievements may also be at the expense of voluntarism's role in enhancing democracy. Some believe, as indicated in chapter 1, that voluntary organizations are important in and of themselves because they protect "a sphere of private action through which indi-viduals can take the initiative, express their individuality, and exercise freedom of expression and action."[77] That is, voluntary institutions can contribute to creating the public sphere and thus face special societal expectations where "how the organization goes about setting and attaining specific goals becomes as important as the goals themselves."[78] Yet, according to Alexander and Weiner, a marketlike model that stresses the values of strategy development, risk tak-ing, and competitive positioning seems to be incompatible with a voluntary model that should stress the values of community participation, due process, and stewardship.[79] With increased involvement in for-profit social enterprises, voluntary organizations may have a difficult time balancing the preservation of their organizational mission with meeting their financial bottom lines. Sev-eral studies have found this to be the case. In a survey of twenty-five commer-cial "venturers," Adams and Perlmutter found that twenty-two identified con-flicts between the venture's goals and the organization's goals and mission.[80] Haycock also found in a survey of ten small charitable agencies utilizing com-mercial ventures that the two with the greatest commercial successes experi-enced a shift away from their stated missions.[81] Likewise, Alexander, Nank, and Stivers found in a study of social service agencies that market-oriented orga-nizations shifted their focus from public goods such as research, teaching, ad-vocacy, and serving the poor, to meeting individual client demands.[82] More re-cently, Dart found in a single-case study of a voluntary organization in Canada, known for its strong mission focus and businesslike approach in its programs, that "other forms of valued service provisions and the enactment of other im-portant pro-social values were diminished because of the need to focus on revenue-producing, mission-focused services."[83] Cooney similarly found in an ethnographic study of a social purpose enterprise that the organization faced a tension between meeting business contract demands and meeting their mission of educating and training welfare-to-work clients.[84] Voluntary institutions can also play an important role in mobilizing public attention to social problems and needs, serving as conduits for free expression and social change in society.[85] However, market-based government contract-ing has had a detrimental impact on such advocacy efforts. For example, when voluntary organizations "are consumed by the challenges of becoming competitive providers," they have less time and energy for providing public goods such as education and advocacy.[86] Indeed, regardless of resource and time constraints, some organizational executives have reduced advocacy efforts because they "are unsure if they could keep their contracts if they became critics of government or private sector contractors."[87] The values of social entrepreneurs may also encourage voluntary organizations to eliminate unprofitable activities such as education and advocacy. On its website, the National Center for Social Entrepreneurs has promoted the strategy of "cutting programs no longer needed or valued by the market" and generating "significant increases in earned income by finding new payer sources, identifying new markets, developing new programs, or changing pricing policies." It has also promoted partnerships with businesses as a potential revenue source. Yet businesses generally do not have policies that seek to create social change or alter the status quo; rather, they want to tie their business or product to noncontroversial causes that add to their investment potential and bottom line.[88] As a result, growing partnerships between voluntary organizations and businesses may serve to keep voluntary organizations from addressing the underlying social issues that led to the creation of their organizations in the first place.

Putnam has described how voluntary organizations create and sustain social capital. Though all types of organizations may contribute in some way to social capital, Putnam and others believe voluntary organizations "may be more capable than government or market organizations of generating social norms of trust, cooperation, and mutual support due to their noncoercive character and appeals to charitable and social motives."[89] Yet one of the main reasons given for voluntary organizations to become more marketlike and take on marketlike approaches to revenue generation has been to break down these social bonds and dependencies. Zimmerman and Dart note that the use of commercial strategies for revenue generation started as a need for a "quick fix" in the face of government cutbacks in Canada, but then came a growing belief in commercialization as *the way* for voluntary organizations to gain freedom from the restraints of government grants and the whims of the electorate and donors.[90] There is now a drive for nonprofits in Canada, the United States, and elsewhere to be operationally autonomous, free to "formulate and pursue [a] self-determined agenda without undue external pressures, wherever the pressures come from."[91]

Marketization activities seem to have a negative effect on voluntary organizations' ability to create social capital and enhance civic engagement in at least two major areas. First, voluntary organizations have less need to build strong relationships with traditional key stakeholders or constituencies. In the past, the long-term survival of a voluntary organization depended largely on its capacity to sustain relationships with core constituencies, such as private donors, members, community volunteers, and other community organizations, thereby creating a network of social trust around the organization. These social networks were essential for mobilizing collective action and for addressing social problems.[92] However, when voluntary organizations rely on commercial revenue and entrepreneurial strategies, there is less need to build networks among constituencies, thus discouraging civic participation.[93] Estelle James notes that voluntary organizations undertaking commercial ventures weaken their appeal to donors because people think their donations are not needed by an organization that is commercially successful.[94] Or, as Zimmerman and Dart note, people think they give to the organization by purchasing a product: "If prospective donors see the commercial exchange as a gift, then the total dollars available for charitable works could decrease with the cannibalization of donations for exchanges."[95] In this context, stakeholders who were once donors or members become consumers or clients and the focus of the organization shifts from creating networks of trust to creating opportunities for selling more products or services to individuals. Likewise, the emphasis on competition within the government contracting process threatens interorganizational networks because voluntary organizations are increasingly forced to compete with each other as well as with for-profit organizations.[96] Contract competition's increased focus on professional competency areas also devalues the work of volunteers.[97]

Second, marketized voluntary organizations may not have or provide the extra support or resources for a voluntary organization to spend on building social capital. In expressing his concern with voluntary nonprofit organizations' competition with for-profit providers for government contracts, Ryan suggests citizen engagement is endangered "when a nonprofit seeks to become a more competitive provider. In most cases, nonprofits are not being funded to strengthen society but to provide social services. As the market pressures them to become more competent at jobs like project management and more attentive to the strategic demands of their industry, how committed can they remain to this civic dimension?"[98] Alexander, Nank, and Stivers also note that the focus and influence of government and business to do more with less "inevitably forces priorities to be set in terms of the bottom line rather than in terms of building social capital."[99] As an example of this, Backman and Smith describe an arts organization that eliminated its volunteer program because it was not considered to be "cost-effective."[100] Another example is the trend for voluntary organizations to replace community volunteers with entrepreneurial business representatives on their boards of directors.[101]

Conclusion

This chapter has outlined trends in the modernization of society broadly and philanthropy and voluntary association particularly, with special attention given to the detrimental impacts of modernization and marketization on the democratic contributions of voluntarism. The growing reliance on voluntarism to govern beyond the state will only exacerbate the erosion of these democratic contributions because, as increasingly important actors in providing for social welfare needs, there is also growing concern about how to ensure that voluntary organizations maintain accountability to government, citizens, and clients. Much like earlier administrative reforms in the United States, the most popular means for ensuring this accountability has been for government agencies to use legal and bureaucratic control mechanisms, such as outcomes based assessments, auditing, and provider self-reports to try to achieve such accountability.[102] Yet these very mechanisms to ensure accountability can also serve to co-opt or subvert organizational missions or displace organizational goals.[103]

We find ourselves, then, in a situation where there are calls for voluntarism to play a more central role in society, but the very reasons we want to be more dependent on them instead of government—their contributions to civic engagement, democracy, and grassroots community and citizen participation—are being eroded. What is the potential to get beyond this conundrum? Perhaps societal changes manifesting themselves more recently—including the emergence of giving circles—may provide some answers. We turn next to a discussion of these recent societal changes in society and community engagement and begin to focus on the emergence of giving circles and their potential to democratize voluntarism.

3 The Democratization and New Shape of Voluntarism

We are witnessing today society's transformation from modern to postmodern and from traditional to posttraditional. The emergence of giving circles and other "new" modes of organizing and associating are indicative of these societal trends and may offer a remedy to the problems of a modernized and marketized voluntarism. They may also revive the democratic effects of voluntarism discussed by Tocqueville and others. Alternatively, their apparently more fragmented and porous nature may mean that the antidemocratic aspects of voluntarism are exacerbated. This chapter discusses changing societal trends and the potential for new modes of organizing and associating to democratize voluntarism.

A Model for Democratizing Voluntarism

Before examining current social trends and their influence on voluntarism, we should define what a democratic voluntary structure might look like. The nature of the social and political environment in the United States seems to necessitate reliance on voluntary institutions to some degree. Americans have always had a certain fear or dislike of excessive state power, and it is clear from the past that the market cannot be depended on to adequately address citizens' needs.[1] This explains the sustained reliance on voluntarism in the United States and provides a good reason, especially within the context of governance beyond the state, to understand how it can be organized to enhance democracy.

Few have sought to create a normative definition of democratic voluntarism. There are many definitions and models of democracy, but these often do not take into account the nature of modernized and marketized voluntarism.[2] There are also writings that mention voluntarism's democratization, but these are narrowly defined and do not ground their definitions in democratic theory or adequately consider the negative aspects and modernization of voluntarism. For example, most people who write on this subject associate the "democratization of philanthropy" merely with more choices and opportunities for people to give.[3] To associate the democratization of voluntarism only with increasing the number of people who participate in voluntary action does not account for the threats to democracy inherent in voluntarism (see chapter 1) or to the eroded state of its democratic effects caused by modernization and marketization (see chapter 2).

Given this, the democratization of voluntarism must include a broader view of democracy and account for voluntarism's shortcomings and shifts within modernity. The keys to this include expanding voluntary participation not only to counter the effects of modernization but also to combat elite hegemony, asymmetric relationships among citizens, and unequal voluntary outcomes; broadening the identification that individuals have with the needs of others to counter asymmetric relationships and bring about more equitable outcomes; and expanding who benefits from voluntarism to increase the redistribution of resources and nullify the fragmentation and short-term focus of traditional voluntarism. In summary, a democratic voluntarism would provide opportunities for meaningful democratic participation, broaden individuals' identification with the needs of others, and expand who benefits from voluntarism.

Providing Opportunities for Meaningful Democratic Participation

One aspect of democratizing voluntarism should include getting more people of diverse backgrounds to participate in giving and volunteering; making this participation meaningful in the sense of emphasizing relationships and engaging individuals *routinely* in civic relationships over time that build social capacity; and providing equal opportunities for members to participate in agenda setting, deliberation, and decision making.

Who tends to give and volunteer today? The perception we have is that donors are typically older, male, and white. To be sure, research has shown that giving is frequently higher for those nearing age 65 than for those between 25 and 44.[4] However, people between 35 and 44 are more likely to volunteer in an organization than people 65 and older or between 16 and 24.[5] There has also been an assumption that men are more likely than women to give; however, recent research suggests that women, especially wealthy women, give a larger percentage of their income than men and are more likely to volunteer.[6] Michael Anft and Harvy Lipman find that "married couples and single women—especially single mothers—are far more generous than single men (whether they are parents or not). High-income men living on their own (those earning $50,000 or more annually) typically donate only about 2 percent of their discretionary income to charity, about one-fifth of what single mothers with similar incomes give." Paul K. Minsk shows that "among Caucasians, African Americans, and Latinos across all income levels, Caucasians have the highest average of giving at $1,218 per household, followed by African Americans at $1,094 per household, and $528 per Latino household." But Anft and Lipman find that black households "give 25 percent more of their discretionary income to charity than do whites. For instance, blacks who make between $30,000 and $50,000 give an average of $528 annually, compared with $462 donated by whites in the same income range." Likewise, individuals of Asian and Latino/Hispanic descent give and volunteer a good deal, but much of it is directed informally to family, kin, and social circles and so typically it is not reported for tax purposes or included in calculations of organized volunteer efforts.[7]

Thus providing more people of diverse backgrounds with more choices and opportunities to give and volunteer assumes that diverse groups are not already doing so, and it does not adequately address the point that increasing the opportunities for voluntarism may only exacerbate some of its antidemocratic effects, such as its fragmentation and asymmetry in the charitable relationship. It also does not account for inequities in the distribution of wealth that still privilege whites and men, enabling them to have more money to give away.[8] While it is important from a pluralist democratic perspective to provide people with more choices, we must go beyond this simple equation of "more giving equals more democracy" if we are to attempt to democratize voluntarism in its full sense. We must also consider the quality of this participation.

Meaningful democratic participation, then, should also involve the degree to which members (and those affected by a decision) have equal opportunities to participate in setting the agenda, deliberating, and making decisions. Harry Eckstein argues that if society has vigorous associational life but associations themselves are highly undemocratic, democracy will not be stable.[9] John Gastil suggests that for a group to be democratic, it must be inclusive. That is, those significantly affected by the decisions of the group ought to have full membership and a voice in its governance. As Gastil writes, a democratic group "must distribute its power among the membership. Every member of a small democratic group must ultimately have equal power with regard to group policies."[10] Democratic deliberation involves allowing participants to discuss all sides of an issue. This includes articulating opinions, persuading others, voting on preferences, and expressing dissent. Gutmann further suggests that the more economically, ethnically, and religiously heterogeneous the membership, the greater an organization's capacity to cultivate public discourse and deliberation that is conducive to democratic citizenship.[11]

Finally, participation should be meaningful in the sense that it engages individuals routinely in civic relationships over time and builds social capacity. Paul Lichterman identifies three features of Tocqueville's view of civic groups that might support this: First, Tocqueville emphasized the "meaningful relationships that people develop and transform in the course of interaction in civic groups. Through 'the reciprocal action of men one upon another,' people's imaginations would grow bigger. Through that process, civic relationships would take on new definitions and purposes." Second, Tocqueville saw in civic groups the importance of instituted action; that is, civic groups can engage individuals "*routinely* in civic relationships over time, not merely sporadically." Finally, these civic relationships could cultivate what Lichterman calls social capacity: "people's ability to work together organizing public relationships rather than ceding those relationships entirely to market exchange or administrative fiats of the state."[12]

This aspect of democratizing voluntarism assumes that citizen participation is necessary for a strong and full democracy and that voluntarism can be seen as part of a broader program for fostering social cohesion and civic participation.[13] Opportunities for democratic participation are important to voluntarism as well. One of the most consistent predictors of charitable giving among individuals is participation in community groups and organizations, and members of voluntary organizations are twice as likely as nonmembers to give.[14]

Broadening Individuals' Identification with the Needs of Others

A second aspect of democratizing voluntarism can be defined in relation to voluntarism's role in linking citizens to one another across social and economic differences. This draws from Tocqueville's emphasis on the importance of cultivating meaningful relationships through voluntary associations, but extends our understanding of these relationships to connections with individuals beyond the group. Tocqueville argued "that civic groups potentially would encourage relationships with people of diverse stations, outside as well as inside the group."[15] In *Bowling Alone*, Robert Putnam describes the importance of social capital for building these relationships.[16] He writes that some forms of social capital look inward and tend to reinforce exclusive identities and homogeneous groups; this is *bonding* social capital. Other social networks look outward and encompass people across diverse social cleavages; this is *bridging* social capital.[17] Bonding social capital is important for democracy because it enables members to get to know one another more easily and hence makes listening and trusting easier.[18] Bridging social capital is more likely to consist of less intimate, or even "weak," ties, and it focuses on relationships that span different groups, linking these groups as a means of strengthening the larger society.[19] It is important for democracy because it points to the value of transcending social differences, including identity (race, ethnicity, religious tradition, sexual preference, and national origin) and status (vertical arrangements of power, influence, wealth, and prestige).[20]

Bridging social capital is similar to Jane Addams's philosophy of "social ethics." Her idea was based on the belief that the relations of economic classes were interdependent and reciprocal. For this reason, social ethical action should be done through people working together cooperatively, rather than through individual action. According to Marilyn Fischer, Addams's social ethics had to do with understanding the value of human life and the interconnected nature of society and emotions. It acknowledged the unique value of each person and supported the notion that all people should be able to develop their potential richly and fully. To move from an individual ethics to a social ethics, Addams believed, one must immerse oneself in the direct experience of life as lived by people of all backgrounds. She saw democracy as a matter of enacting social ethics in all aspects of life and saw her work at Hull House "as quite simply exhibiting the duties of democratic citizenship."[21]

Linking social groups—or building commonalities—and generating awareness of others is important for enhancing democracy and of great practical relevance for voluntarism. Schervish and his colleagues have found that philanthropic commitment depends on individuals' networks of social connection and the type and degree of empathetic identification they have with the needs of others. In other words, generating broader generosity among individuals, so that they give to others outside of their normal frame of reference, depends on expanding their identification with other "human beings in wider fields of space and time."[22]

Expanding Who Benefits

A third aspect of democratizing voluntarism should relate to the democratic outcomes of voluntarism, especially those related to resource distribution. This aspect of democratization connects with theoretical views of substantive and radical democracy (see chapter 1). Achieving a full democracy depends not only on procedural fairness but also on fairness in outcomes, by minimizing wide disparities so that people are able to understand each other and come to some notion of the common good. Expanding who benefits can be defined as expanding what types of groups and organizations typically receive resources in general from donors and volunteers (as compared with the typical recipients of voluntary support) and expanding the issues and areas to which donors and volunteers provide support beyond the direct benefit of themselves and their families.

First, a more democratic outcome would lead to an expansion of what types of groups and organizations typically receive resources from donors and volunteers. This can be broken down in several ways. A more equitable outcome could mean more support for smaller grassroots organizations rather than the larger charitable institutions receiving the majority of private funding today. Although representing 80 percent of charitable institutions, smaller organizations—those with budgets under $2 million—typically receive the least amount of private funding. The largest charitable gifts—those of $1 million or more—tend to go to the wealthiest organizations.[23] Funding smaller organizations may indicate a donor's desire for a more equitable distribution of funds and support for smaller grassroots initiatives important to democratic self-governance.

In addition, a more equitable outcome may mean funding overlooked issues or organizations to a greater degree. If one looks at the distribution of private charitable giving (see Figure 3.1), one can see that only a relatively small percentage goes to human service organizations (10 percent), although presumably these do the most to aid the poor and needy in the United States.[24] Tobin and Weinberg also show that the largest share of mega-gifts ($1 million or more) go to colleges and universities (44 percent), hospitals and other medical institutions (16 percent), and arts and cultural organizations (12 percent) rather than to social service groups (5 percent). Religious organizations capture the largest portion of private giving (32.8 percent).[25]

If one examines giving by individuals or households, an even larger percentage is given for religious purposes (60 percent, or $92 billion in 2002).[26] Although part of this funding gets funneled through to help the poor, a large portion stays in the religious organization to benefit church members. Saxon-

Types of recipients of contributions, 2006
Total = $295.02 billion

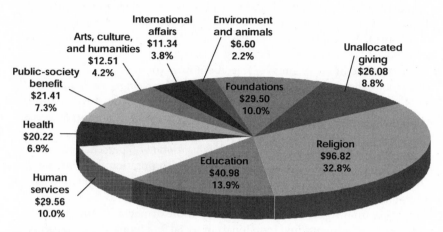

Figure 3.1. Recipients of private contributions in 2006.

Harold, Wiener, McCormack, and Weber found in a 1996 survey that of the $9.6 billion given to churches by their members, 66 percent was distributed within the denomination, 23 percent went to organizations outside the denomination, and only 11 percent was given in direct assistance to individuals.[27]

The data in Figure 3.1 show private giving by individuals, foundations, and corporations. The patterns of grants made by foundations and federated giving programs are different than private charitable giving as a whole, which is heavily dominated by individual contributions (donations by individuals represent about 85 percent of private giving). In 2006, larger foundations gave 14 percent of grant funds to human services, 23 percent to education, 23 percent to health organizations, and little more than 2 percent to religious groups.[28] Most United Way grants go to well established health and human service agencies rather than to small or grassroots groups.[29] Based on this data, we might conclude that institutions, rather than individuals, are more likely to address social welfare issues. However, even these institutions seem to give only a quarter or less of their resources to these areas and tend to support larger, rather than smaller, charities.

There are also data to indicate that organizations serving women and minorities receive a very small percentage of private contributions. For example, in 2005, only 1.9, 1.3, and 0.3 percent of foundation giving was designated for African Americans, Hispanics, and Asian/Pacific Islanders, respectively (a decline from 1998). This is true even though ethnic groups compose nearly a third of the U.S. population, and poverty rates are much higher for these groups than for whites. According to the U.S. Census Bureau, the official poverty rate for whites in 2006 was 8.2 percent compared with 24.3 percent for blacks, 20.6 percent for Hispanics, and 10.3 percent for Asian and Pacific Islanders. Only 6.4 percent of private foundation funding in the United States was designated for women and girls in 2005. (This does not include unspecified funds that already reach women and girls.) This gender bias persists despite the fact that women, especially single women with children, have lower incomes than men and are far more likely to be living in poverty.[30]

There is less information available about how volunteer hours are distributed among the areas noted above. According to the *Nonprofit Almanac*, of the 109.4 million American adults who volunteered in 1998, most worked in the areas of informal volunteering (helping friends and family or providing assistance on an ad hoc basis to organizations: 20.3 percent), religion (25.8 percent), youth development (15.4 percent), education (17.5 percent), and human services (12.7 percent).[31] Recent data from the Corporation for National and Community Service show that in 2006 people volunteered mainly in the areas of religion (35.3 percent), educational or youth services (27 percent), or social and community service (13.1 percent).[32] More democratic outcomes in this area might include engaging individuals in social and human services, areas in which they might not otherwise give or volunteer.

The second aspect of creating more democratic outcomes is expanding the issues and areas to which donors give so that they reflect giving that is beyond the donor's or donor's family's direct benefit. As discussed in chapter 1, donors typically give to whom and to what they know and to organizations from which they or their families directly benefit, such as their alma mater, religious institution, amenity services, and so on.[33] Given this, it is no surprise, then, that mega-gifts mostly go to educational, medical, or arts institutions.[34] More equitable outcomes would be achieved if individuals gave to and volunteered at organizations serving lower-income and needy clients and organizations that work in areas beyond the typical frame of reference of most donors and volunteers.

Posttraditional Society

With a model of democratic voluntarism in mind, we can now turn to an examination of changes in society that may encourage the democratization of voluntarism. Partly in reaction to the effects of modernity, we are undergoing a shift in how individuals think about the world and live their lives within it. Some have described this as a shift from the modern to the postmodern, which involves a rejection of modernity's unifying, totalizing, and universal schemes in favor of new emphases on difference, plurality, fragmentation, and complexity; renouncement of modernity's closed structures, fixed meaning, and rigid order in favor of play, indeterminacy, incompleteness, uncertainty, ambiguity, contingency, and chaos; abandonment of modernity's unmediated objectivity and truth, in favor of perspectivism, antifoundationalism, hermeneutics, intertextuality, simulation, and relativism; and a new emphasis on deconstructing boundaries within and among different disciplines.[35]

This change has also been described as a shift from traditional to posttraditional. According to Thomas Catlaw, "'What has been' no longer provides the moral and normative content for 'what should be done' in any general way." That is, posttraditional philosophers and increasingly individuals in society see the world from a social constructivist perspective. They challenge the "myth of the given," believing knowledge and tradition are socially constructed human choices. Therefore, writes Paul Heelas, individuals believe they have the power to construct their own lives, which means "a shift of authority from 'without to within.'" As Gundelach and Torpe note, "Traditional structures of authority are no longer regarded as valid sources of norms." For this reason, a posttraditional society is an individualized society because with a crisis in traditional authority, individuals are increasingly required to construct their own lives. According to Ulrich Beck, "for the sake of human survival, individuals are compelled to make themselves the centre of their own life plans and conduct."[36]

A posttraditional society, then, is also a "risk society" in that individuals are forced to rely on themselves rather than on larger societal institutions for survival. This is especially true within the context of "the dissolution of the traditional parameters of industrial society," such as the dissolution of the welfare state over the past several decades in the United States and elsewhere.[37] The danger is that individualized authority or autonomy can easily fall into anomie—a "glorious, but terrifying isolation."[38] This condition "produces a radical inward turning as individuals become increasingly worried and concerned about their own futures and social positions and less concerned with collective and institutional . . . ends."[39] This creates a situation in which there is greater opportunity for the exploitation of individuals while it appears less likely that collective issues can be addressed.[40]

In posttraditional society, societal institutions, such as the welfare state and traditional voluntary associations, are giving way to governance networks and informal modes of association. Social relations have changed from being close to loose, permanent to provisional, and thorough to superficial. We have less need for and obligations to our immediate neighbors or kin and thus more choice about when and with whom we will have social relations. As Robert Wuthnow points out, today "community is less often simply the place one lives and more often an empathetic bond that links diverse people together."[41] Because of the transitory solidarities and risk linked with a posttraditional society, individuals must associate with one another in a more fragmented and selfish fashion.[42]

The New Voluntarism

In posttraditional society there has been a shift from bureaucratically structured, membership-based traditional voluntary organizations to value-based, nondemocratically structured professional advocacy organizations (such as the AARP, National Wildlife Federation, and Greenpeace) and to an expanding field of informal, self-organized, and decentralized initiatives. The first, according to Leslie Hustinx and Frans Lammertyn, "are highly centralized and market-oriented, with a structural tendency to reduce the membership role to a type of 'vicarious commitment' by which individuals 'contract out the participation task to organizations.'" The latter consist of few institutional links transcending the local level, no clear center of authority, and limited, project-oriented objectives. In both, people join on the basis of shared interests; volunteer activities, if available, are chosen depending on their concrete and practical nature.[43] These associations develop to respond to specific needs and definite objectives.[44]

In relation to democratizing voluntarism defined above, the clear shortcoming of political advocacy organizations is that many appear to discourage active members. Individualized contact and narrow, instrumental foci are the norm.[45] Membership is increasingly defined merely as financial support for the organization.[46] This exacerbates the impacts of modernization on voluntary institutions and the problems of fragmentation and elite control inherent in voluntarism. Within these groups, there is little or no face-to-face contact with membership, and thus ordinary individuals are less likely to be mobilized at the local level. Member ties are through common symbols, common leaders, and perhaps common ideals, but not with one another.[47] Putnam argues that these organizations do little to prepare citizens for their role in democratic society.[48] On the surface, informal associations appear to do a much better job in this area; they seem to be much more like the associations so admired by Tocqueville.

These "new" informal associations include a growing number of small, self-help or support groups, network associations, and minipublics. Examples of small, self-help, and support groups include Bible study groups, therapy groups (such as Alcoholics Anonymous), book discussion groups, study circles, money clubs, and some types of giving circles.[49] Wuthnow found several years ago that at least 40 percent of the American adult population claimed to be involved in "a small group that meets regularly and provides caring and support for those who participate in it."[50] Gundelach and Torpe and Wuthnow have also identified the emergence of what they call "network associations": loose, informal, and personal forms of association that typically form around specific short-term projects.[51] Individuals who participate in these associations do not necessarily see themselves as members and certainly not as "members for life," as in more traditional associations. Bang and Sørensen describe individuals participating in network associations as "Everyday Makers": people who are highly engaged in community and politics by navigating an environment of loose connections through association.[52] Everyday Makers' community engagement is directed toward concrete problem solving in everyday life more so than on the performance of large bureaucratic organizations such as government or traditional voluntary associations.

Archon Fung also describes what he calls "minipublics": modest projects to convene relatively small groups of citizens in self-consciously organized public deliberations. As Fung notes, "Sometimes they resemble town meetings, and sometimes they function as purposeful associations." He describes three types of minipublics that have emerged recently in the United States: The *educative forum* "aims to create nearly ideal conditions for citizens to form, articulate, and refine opinions about particular public issues through conversations with one another." Examples include the deliberative polls invented by James Fishkin, the Kettering Foundation's National Issues Forums, and study circles supported by the Topsfield Foundation. The *participatory advisory panel* aims "not only to improve the quality of opinion, but also to align public policies with considered preferences" by linking deliberative outcomes to political decision makers, and then "to transmit preferences after they have been appropriately articulated" by citizens. Examples include Oregon Health Decisions, where town meetings were convened all over the state to discuss public medical priorities, and the Citizen Summit priority and budget-setting process in Washington, D.C. The *participatory problem-solving collaboration* "envisions a continuous and symbiotic relationship between the state and public sphere aimed at solving particular collective problems such as environmental degradation, failing schools, or unsafe streets." Examples include grassroots ecosystem management collaboratives and neighborhood involvement in school administration and policing in Chicago.[53]

The emergence of these new forms of association show that the so-called decline in civic participation proclaimed by Putnam seems to be in reality less of a *decline* and more of a *change* in how people participate in a community.[54] Indeed, in the years just prior to Putnam's analysis in *Bowling Alone*, the number of volunteers was increasing, although the Independent Sector found that "41 percent of volunteers contributed time sporadically and considered it a one-time activity."[55] To be sure, such episodic volunteering is as old as volunteering itself, but it seems to be growing in importance today as a way for individuals to "give back" in the midst of their hectic lives, in their own way, and within the parameters of their own needs and interests.[56] As Macduff notes, this shift in the behavior of volunteers has occurred "because the individual in the 21st Century is left to cobble together his or her own biography. . . . [Episodic] volunteering comes about because the individual in the postmodern era is a 'reflection' of the change in institutional conditions."[57]

Not all of today's donors and volunteers seek to be episodic volunteers. Some want *more* engagement in their giving and volunteering, but they also want more control and strategic effect with their giving and volunteering. These "new and emerging donors" want to control where and how their gift is spent, fund issues rather than institutions, and often emphasize impact and accountability with their funding. They also typically mistrust large, bureaucratic institutions.[58] Reis and Clohesy point out that these donors "want to solve defined problems in a specific way. They do not want to simply earmark money for 'some vaguely benevolent purpose.'"[59] In many ways, the philanthropic style of these donors harkens back to the previous century's scientific philanthropy movement with its emphasis on control and the importance of information and impact.[60] Yet the hands-on, engaged, and collaborative style of these donors indicates a shift away from modern philanthropy. In the case of both types of donors—episodic and engaged donors—their style of giving and volunteering is a reflection of posttraditional society. They want more control over their giving and volunteering in a way that is meaningful to them.

The Democratic Effects of Informal Associations

What does the literature say about the democratic effects of these newer informal associations? Wuthnow believes that they have "emerged as a serious effort to combat forces of fragmentation and anonymity in our society."[61] They attract people who want to combat the breakdown of traditional support structures, such as neighborhoods and family. However, they also attract people who are fed up with large-scale institutions. People want to be part of a community, but in their own way and outside of traditional structures. For this reason, these groups seem to have mixed effects on the democratic attitudes and behavior of those who participate in them. For example, they promulgate a different kind of community than that espoused by Putnam and other Tocquevillians: that of deep commitment and extensive participation and civic engagement. These groups do not require great social or personal sacrifice. Instead, they provide a kind of social interaction that busy, rootless people can grasp without making significant adjustments in their lifestyles.[62] The connections within the group may be purely instrumental and not mature into deeper friendships or social relations that build trust within and across groups. Lichterman writes of his ethnographic study that "volunteering in a loosely connected network gave me and other volunteers practice creating brief interpersonal—sometimes very impersonal—relationships. It did not teach us how to create more enduring bridges."[63] Some also worry about the homogeneity and self-interestedness of many of these groups. Their homogeneity can clarify social identities but also *reinforce* exclusion.[64] Their self-interestedness, especially in self-help groups, may merely provide occasions for individuals to focus on themselves in the presence of others.[65]

Yet Wuthnow also finds in the case of small and self-help groups that, although they may focus on members' addictions or personal needs, their role in overcoming these addictions or meeting personal needs may empower members to lead more productive lives in the wider world and become more engaged in their communities. People who are overcome by their own problems tend to be too afraid of what may happen to risk helping others. They may fear failing or being rejected. They may feel their time, and even their money, must be safeguarded. Being in a group can give them greater confidence in themselves and in the future. Thus self-help groups may enhance the community by freeing individuals from their own insecurities so that they can reach out more charitably to other people. Indeed, Wuthnow's research shows that small and self-help groups do extend their help to others outside their immediate circle. In a survey of members, nearly two in three said they had "worked with the group to help other people in need outside of the group." Almost as many claimed to have donated money to charitable organizations other than their church or synagogue because of their group, and half said they got involved in volunteer work in the community because of the group.[66]

Informal associations may also contribute to democratic capacity building. Wuthnow points out that individuals in these groups are "becoming knowledgeable about their communities, taking an active interest in social and political issues, gaining greater confidence in their own abilities, acquiring social and civic skills, and learning how to be patient and trust others to do their part."[67] Others note that these groups can represent a "healthy development in democratic societies by establishing intersecting webs of allegiance" and small-scale socialization "that is key to the development of democratic citizens."[68] Fung points out that minipublics encourage and enhance deliberation that is tied to public policymaking.[69]

Informal associations' effects on democratic outcomes seem less promising. Based on Wuthnow's study of small groups, many tend to discourage debate or criticism of others' opinions, explicitly ruling out discussions of social and political issues. Because of this, they tend to extend trends that are already under way, without setting forth visions of a better world that could radically transform the way things are.[70] One result is that action within these informal associations may be much less effective in dealing with many large-scale collective problems, as Wuthnow found in his examination of loose connections.[71] Likewise, Lichterman found limitations to voluntarism in addressing the problem of poverty in the context of welfare reform. The busy, mobile individual participants in the network of volunteers he studied "could choose their niche, assuming that someone else was figuring out the bigger picture," but it was not clear that anyone was figuring out the bigger picture.[72]

Thus, the literature indicates that in a procedural democratic sense, informal associations seem to do much to enhance the democratic effects of voluntarism. Their democratic effects on substantive outcomes are much less certain. An examination of giving circles in the following chapters will provide a way to further examine empirically the effects of informal association in a posttraditional environment.

Conclusion

This chapter examines changes taking place within society and within voluntarism that seem to run counter to the negative aspects and modernization of voluntarism discussed in earlier chapters. It shows that we seem to be in the midst of a social transformation to a posttraditional society in which individuals seek out engagement in their community, but in new ways. These changes are reflected in the emergence of new forms of informal association. Giving circles are examples of these. The degree to which they might democratize voluntarism indicates the degree to which informal voluntary associations more generally may democratize voluntarism.

In upcoming chapters, I examine the potential giving circles have—as reflections of larger shifts in society and ways that people want to engage in community—to democratize voluntarism in such a way that problems in society are adequately addressed while members learn the mores and ways of democratic governance. Do giving circles provide opportunities for meaningful democratic participation? This will be examined by studying different types of giving circles and the processes and activities that go on in them, as well as examining who participates in giving circles and the level and quality of this participation. Do giving circles broaden members' identification with the needs of others? This will be examined by studying the degree to which giving circles build bonding and bridging relationships among members and between members and others in need as well as the degree to which giving circles expose members to issues and areas outside their typical frame of reference. Finally, do giving circles expand who benefits from voluntarism? This will be examined by looking at what types of organizations, areas, and people are supported— through time and money—by giving circles and their members as well as the degree to which funding might be targeted to community problems.

4 The Giving Circle Landscape

Giving circles have been described as a cross between a book club and an investment group.[1] They entail individuals pooling their resources to support charitable organizations, individuals in need, and individuals doing good works. Giving circles also include social, educational, and engagement components that seem to connect participants to each other and to their communities in different ways than traditional voluntary associations and philanthropy. It is impossible to say how many giving circles exist because of their grassroots nature. Since the Forum of Regional Associations of Grantmakers began to track these groups in 2004, the number of giving circles identified has more than doubled to well over 500 groups. There is strong indication that many more exist and many more continue to be created. Most giving circles are relatively new, having started in the last five to ten years.

Giving circles are located in at least forty-four states and the District of Columbia. They have also been identified in Canada, Japan, South Africa, Australia, and Great Britain. In 2005, of the giving circles for which data were available, nearly $32 million had been given away by these groups (for all years giving circles had been in operation) and nearly 8,000 individuals participated in giving circles. More recent research by Jessica Bearman and the Forum of Regional Associations of Grantmakers estimates that giving circles have given more than $68 million over the course of their existence and have engaged at least 11,721 people.[2]

The information provided in this and later chapters is based on an analysis of 188 giving circles, the total population of giving circles I was able to identify in 2005; a study of giving circle funding recipients conducted in 2006; and data from reports and studies done by others over the past several years. The data were gathered through interviews, document analysis, and secondary survey research. See the appendix for a full discussion of the studies' methodology.

The Dimensions of Giving Circles

Giving circles are difficult to define. They come in many shapes, sizes, and foci. As one philanthropic professional interviewed for this study said, what makes giving circles exciting is "that there is no one mold or model. It is very much based on the people who start them and who is at the table."[3] Nonetheless, it is possible to describe at least five major dimensions of giving circles. Generally, they pool and give away resources, educate members about philanthropy and issues in the community, include a social dimension, engage members, and maintain their independence.

Pool and Collectively Give Away Resources

One of the main functions of giving circles is to enable individuals to pool their resources and then collectively give them away. The common perception is that members contribute equal amounts, but data suggest that in many cases, the amount of money paid into the giving circle by each member may not be equal across the membership or, in some cases, may come from outside of the membership. Of the giving circles for which data were available at the time of the study (152 groups), 40 percent required no fee or a very loosely suggested minimum fee, leaving the contribution and its amount up to the individual participant. For example, members of the New River Valley Change Network in Blacksburg, Virginia, set a goal of $100 per year per member, but no one keeps track of how much money each person puts in the collection bowl at each meeting. Several giving circles (about 12 percent) had multiple giving levels where, for example, a member could join at the $1,500 or $5,000 level or was free to give more than the expected minimum. Multiple giving levels is often used as a tool to attract more diverse individuals to participate in the giving circle. Rutnik and Bearman believe that stratified membership levels can raise issues of power, influence, and privilege in the groups. But the data from this study suggest the level of contribution generally does not seem to influence the level of decision-making power within the group.[4] The reason for this may be because the amount given by each member often is kept anonymous. Finally, several giving circles raise money from outside of their membership. For example, most Bread for the Journey affiliates conduct fundraising events and send out newsletters asking others to contribute to a pooled fund. Members of the Omaha Venture Group, a young leaders fund, solicit funds from other local foundations and donors to match members' contributions.

All giving circles give away money, and some, like Womenade and Bread for the Journey, provide in-kind gifts like diapers, furniture, or used vehicles to individuals in need. A few giving circles like Social Venture Partners (SVP), the Giving Circle of Hope, and the Women's Giving Alliance also connect members to volunteer opportunities with nonprofit organizations. There is variation as to where, to whom, and how giving circles provide funds. This will be discussed in more detail in chapter 5, but generally giving circles give to nonprofit organizations, individuals doing good work (who are not affiliated with a particular organization), and individuals in need. If funding nonprofits, giving circles generally are interested in small grassroots organizations because they want to make a big impact with their funding. For this reason, giving circles also tend to fund fewer organizations for (relatively) larger amounts of money. Giving circles seem to be split in funding capacity building and day-to-day operations or programs and projects. Many giving circles, especially more formally structured ones, are interested in knowing what happens with their gift. They want to see where the money goes and what the outcomes were. SVP in particular requires funding recipients to show measurable outcomes in order to obtain and renew funding for multiyear grants. Alternatively, many less formal giving circles seek to create as nonbureaucratic a process as possible for grant making, trusting that people working at nonprofit organizations know what they need. Some tend to give money directly to people they see or hear about who are doing good work in the community. For example, one Bread for the Journey group, after reading about a high school student who fixed up old computers and then gave them to a local youth group home, met with the student and then wrote him a check for a few hundred dollars so he could continue his work. Many Womenade groups give money and other in-kind support directly to individuals in need.

Educate Members

Another key aspect of most giving circles is their educational component—specifically, informal and formal education about philanthropy and issues in the community. Education about philanthropy takes place informally through the running of the circle and giving away money—that is, tracking donors, learning about the grant-making process, going on site visits, and so on—and more formally through educational sessions such as workshops, seminars, and presentations by guest speakers. All types of giving circles participate to varying degrees in the former, but it is mainly the larger, more formal giving circles that feature a comprehensive educational program on issues of philanthropy. Education about issues in the community also takes place on an informal and formal basis. Informally, members of all types of giving circles, to varying degrees, learn about issues in the community through group discussions, independent research, or site visits and visiting with nonprofit staff or individuals doing good work. Some giving circles also have very formal educational programming on issue topics. For example, Community Capital Alliance in Minneapolis/St. Paul, a giving circle made up of young professionals, has four educational forums each year featuring guest speakers and panelists, from policy specialists to nonprofit professionals to gang members. Such formal educational sessions mostly take place in the larger, more formally organized circles.

Provide Social Opportunities

Whenever a group of people comes together to do anything, there is social interaction; giving circles are no exception. However, in some giving circles, the social aspect is a primary focus. For example, the Everychild Foundation in Pacific Palisades, California, creates opportunities throughout the year where members can network and socialize. As they state on their website: "A strong goal of the Foundation is to build a *community* of women who enjoy working together."[5] There are similar opportunities in larger, more formal giving circles, such as those trying to attract young professionals. Indeed a member of a young leader group I interviewed lamented that "the social piece tends to be a little bit more popular than the educational pieces."[6] Members of smaller, informal giving circles repeatedly brought up the social aspect of the giving circle as an important element of their experience. In some cases, especially among women's circles, the driving force of the group is its "social with a purpose" aspect. The reason for this was summed up in a news article on giving circles: "In the end, that's the real power of giving circles: a rare chance for busy women to enjoy each other's company while doing good."[7]

Engage Members

There is almost always a strong voluntary engagement aspect to giving circles as well. Even in cases where there is some staff support, giving circles are largely volunteer-driven. Especially among the less formal groups, volunteers conduct all aspects of the giving circle's administration. Members are also engaged in the grant-making process. With a few giving circles there is also direct volunteer engagement with nonprofit agencies. For example, SVP members can choose to work directly with grantees on various management and technology projects. Often the more formally structured and larger giving circles tend to encourage these types of volunteer opportunities for members.

Maintain Independence

Finally, there is an element of independence associated with giving circles. This is somewhat complicated to describe because it depends upon understanding the traditional or modern philanthropic environment, discussed in chapter 2, which places institutional fundraising—the demand side of voluntarism—at the center of philanthropic efforts. What is unique about giving circles is that they are typically not tied to any one charity, and it is the members, rather than nonprofit or philanthropic professionals or experts, who decide where funds should be distributed. The focus is on the supply side of voluntarism.[8] To clarify this a bit further, consider the practice among many nonprofit organizations to create what are called "donor circles." These are groupings of donors based on their level of giving to the organization. For example, any donor who gives $1,000 or more is placed in the "Gold Circle" and receives special benefits from the nonprofit organization like newsletters, invitations to events, and so on. These donors *do not* have a say in how this money is distributed. Giving circles are *not* donor circles. Giving circles are about something other than giving a certain amount of money to one particular charity and they *do* involve members deciding together where to give resources away. Ultimately, this is a new way of thinking about philanthropy that goes beyond particularistic, institutional fundraising to a "promoting philanthropy" paradigm.[9] There are blurred boundaries and exceptions to this, of course. A few giving circles are associated with university foundations. Their members remain independent in that they still decide where the money is given, but they are limited to giving the money within the university.[10] It is not clear that these groups should indeed count as giving circles except that they are largely donor led and share some of the other aspects of giving circles discussed above.

Types of Giving Circles

The discussion above provides some generalizations about the characteristics of giving circles, with some indication of differences among them. Next, I present a more clearly differentiated typology of giving circles based on data gathered for the giving circles identified in the study's database. I identify here three "ideal" types of giving circles: small groups, loose networks, and formal organizations (see table 4.1 for defining characteristics of each type based on the population of 188 giving circles identified in 2005). I also provide more details and examples of each type below through an analysis of several case studies. Certainly, a giving circle can be a blending or mixture of these three types, but in most cases where enough data were available, it was possible to place giving circles easily into one of these discrete types. In addition, though there is variation within each type, these three types provide an extremely descriptive explanation of the universe of giving circles that will aid in understanding their various democratic effects, discussed in the next chapter.

Small Groups

Small groups typically consist of small groups of people (twenty-five or fewer) who pool funds and then decide together where to give these away. The amount of funds pooled by each member tends to be in equal amounts ranging from $50 to $5,000, though there are several small groups (at least eleven were identified) where the amount paid into the fund is left to the discretion of the individual. Because the group is small enough, leadership is often shared and all are able to participate in the decision-making process. About half of small group giving circles for which data were available used a consensus decision-making process, and about 30 percent used some kind of voting procedure. The two major foci of small group giving circles seem to be social and educational activities; there is less emphasis on volunteering or substantial engagement with funding recipients. The social aspect is emphasized through informal group interaction and discussions. The educational aspect is also informal in nature, taking place through conducting the grant-making process, site visits, meetings with nonprofit staff, and information sharing among group members. Finally, about 70 percent of small groups identified and for which data were available seem to be affiliated with some type of organization or host that typically acts as a fiscal agent or in some cases provides staff and other support. Next I present a more in-depth look at two small group giving circles.

Table 4.1 Three "ideal" types of giving circles, 2005

Type	Small groups 41 identified (22% of all GCs)	Loose networks 49 identified (26% of all GCs)	Formal organizations 86 identified (46% of all GCs)
Number of members	5–25, average 13	2–140, number fluctuates	5–500, average 84
Gender	Half women-only; half mixed	Mostly women	Mostly mixed
Member fee per year	$50 to $5,000 or discretionary	$25 to $35, discretionary	$250 to $5,700
Organizational structure	Shared leadership, closed membership	Informal network, people come in and out with core group leading	Formal, committees, focus on growth
Grant decision making	All participate, consensus and vote	Board or lead group, consensus	Committee (in some, members ratify), consensus and/or vote
Major activities	Social and educational (mostly informal)	Social and fundraising (mostly informal)	Educational and volunteer engagement (mostly formal)
Affiliations	Community foundation or other organization serves as fiscal agent, sometimes provides staff support	National affiliation to headquarters or part of independent movement	Community foundation or other organization; several become independent 501(c)(3), many with staff support
Examples	— AsiaNextGen — New Mountain Climbers — Shared Giving	— Bread for the Journey — Party with Purpose — Womenade	— Everychild Foundation — Latino Giving Circle of Chicago — Omaha Venture Group — Social Venture Partners Seattle

Case Study: Shared Giving

Interviews with eight members in 2004 and analysis of other documentation provide in-depth data for an examination of this small group giving circle. Shared Giving, located in Durham, North Carolina, has sixteen members who all belong to the Eno River Unitarian Universalist Fellowship (ERUUF). The idea for Shared Giving began in 2000 when Marilyn and Don Hartman were doing their taxes and realized that they were giving away a lot of money, but in small amounts and sometimes to organizations they knew very little about. Marilyn described it this way:

> We were pleased with the total we had given, but we didn't feel satisfied and wondered if these small contributions were really making a difference. We wondered what people were actually getting for that $25. And if we mailed it, say, to New York, we never really saw what the money did.[11]

They had the idea to create a "reverse investment club" and went searching for potential models, finally coming across the concept of a giving circle on the Giving New England website. They announced the forming of the group in the Fellowship's bulletin and asked a few friends to participate. The group began meeting officially in late 2001. The members are mainly activists in the church and community and primarily middle-aged and white, reflecting the makeup of ERUUF. Many of the members work for (or are retired from) universities and are well informed and comfortable financially. Each of the group's members gives at least $500 a year, making at least a three-year commitment, though some give more than the minimum. The amount given is kept confidential by the group's treasurer. ERUUF acts as Shared Giving's fiscal agent.

The group took a good deal of time—five or six meetings—to decide on a focus for their funding. As one member put it:

> The hardest part about forming a giving circle is agreeing on what you're doing, and that can take a year if you've got big-mouthed people in your group with lots of opinions. Everybody wants to have their say. I think with any group, once you create a mission statement, your work is half done. But it takes forever.[12]

The group decided to focus their giving on social justice issues, giving to small locally based organizations. The group did *not* spend a lot of time discussing the decision-making structure or processes of group agenda setting, however. They just naturally followed the Unitarian principles of "joining in a constant search for the truth and to honor everybody else's opinion."[13] At every meeting, somebody volunteers to run the meeting, which means getting the room assignment, soliciting agenda items, creating the agenda, and running the meeting. The group also decided early in the process to limit the number of members.

The group does not have rules as such about deciding what to fund. One member described the group as operating in a "stealthy fashion." There is no proposal process. Rather, they seek out organizations and projects. As one member described it: "We come to meetings and we talk about what we've seen and we've done. Sometimes a group of us will go and do a site visit."[14] By 2004, about half of the members had made recommendations to the group and participated in site visits. Members bring ideas to the meetings, there is discussion, and the group tries to reach consensus. Then a vote is taken: each person has one vote regardless of the amount of money put into the group. Members are either enthusiastic about a project or not. Sometimes no money is given at all, or the amount given is debated. Sometimes they leave the meeting without deciding on anything except to gather more information.

Regarding funding, several members commented on the difficulty of finding the "best" organizations that have a real need for their help. As one member described it:

> Most of the time it is not that we have had a lot of competing priorities. Most of the time it is hard to find things to give to that seem to satisfy everybody in the group and appear to meet the mission.[15]

Yet, according to several members, where the money goes is not nearly as important as the *discussions* about where to give the money. As one member stated: "I mean the reality of our meetings is that I go just for the meetings. We eat most of the time, and then talk and laugh and do a little business, and that's it."[16] The social aspect and discussions in the group are, perhaps, the most important part of the process. According to another member:

> The things that have impressed me about it, though, just through the social aspect and the discussion that we have, is really getting to hear the diversity of opinions that people have about what matters or what is important about a given initiative.[17]

The group gave its first grant in early 2002, and over the next two years they have given grants of between $1,000 and $5,000, usually for specific programs or projects: a family violence prevention center, a community center that provides tutoring for Hispanic children and their parents, a Hispanic community organization providing after-school programming, an organization that helps seniors with medical prescription costs and management, and a daycare program for people with mental illnesses. The type of organizations funded was summed up by one member this way: "We certainly are attracted to the ones that seem to be well organized. The ones who know what they are asking for, understand what we're about, and are willing and able to let us know afterwards how it went." But the group does not always find out how things went, and a few members felt that some of the funds given were not necessarily used as they were intended. Several members complained about one organization in particular that did not even acknowledge receipt of their gift. However, as one member said, because of the giving circle, "I usually feel better about the sense that either they did what they said or if they didn't that the executive director may have made some other decision that was intelligent and defensible and that we would have said, 'Oh, sure, of course you did it that way.'"[18]

Case Study: AsiaNextGen

Information about this small group was gathered through an analysis of various published documents, news articles, and websites. AsiaNextGen is a "group of young professional Asian Americans seeking to address community needs and to engage in high impact philanthropy by coming together and strategically funding issues of common interest." It started in 2004 with five friends, all young Asian American professionals, who donated $4,000 each to the fund. Today, there are still five core members, but the group is making efforts to attract new members, who are asked to make a minimum tax-deductible commitment of $1,000 per year for two years. Its mission is to educate and empower both grant recipients and members through compassion for Asian Americans in need. Members believe that this can only be achieved through the direct involvement of time and skills and money. The goals of the group, then, are to impact social change, leverage monetary contributions, infuse expertise and skills with financial and intellectual capital, and educate and grow a new generation of philanthropists. The group is interested in giving to what it describes as small grassroots nonprofits in the areas of health and nutrition, medical issues, research, and the elderly. Funding decisions and education about community issues are informed by guest speakers or workshops about philanthropy and issue areas, site visits to nonprofit organizations, group discussion, and connections to philanthropic networks.[19]

AsiaNextGen's first financial gift was given in 2006 to the Child Center of New York's Asian Outreach Program. This is a New York State licensed mental health agency whose mission is to relieve the suffering of troubled Asian children and families. AsiaNextGen awarded the organization $20,000, allowing it to hire two part-time psychiatric social workers. In 2007, the group awarded $25,000 to the Sino-American Community Center in support of Project CARE, Chinese Americans Restoring Elders, which hopes to reduce and prevent elder abuse in New York City's Chinese American community.[20]

The idea for AsiaNextGen "grew out of a networking event of young professionals in New York City who gathered at a reception sponsored by the Asian American Federation of New York (AAFNY) to introduce them to the concept of philanthropy," and the group continues to be hosted by AAFNY.[21] Founding member Michelle Tong, also director of donor relations for AAFNY, notes: "We were talking about our jobs, where we came from, what opportunity our parents gave us so we can do something in this country, how proud we are. We all felt that since we were born here, educated and grew up here, and possess a western independent mind, we would like to give something back to the community."[22] With the fragmented nature of Asian ethnic backgrounds in the United States and Asian people's traditional focus on supporting family and kin, AsiaNextGen is truly a unique enterprise.[23] Members like Gary Lee, a Wall Street analyst, and Michelle Tong, "believe they are pioneers of a more vocal, hands-on Asian-American philanthropy," writes Nina Bernstein. As noted in her January 2007 *New York Times* article:

> "The majority of the Asian ethnic groups, they don't want to draw attention to themselves," said Ms. Tong, who joked that she absorbed outspokenness with the lox and bagels she ate growing up in Bergen County, N.J. "Once they've achieved a certain level, some of them tend to distance themselves from where they come from. They want to show that they've made it. They want to blend in with the mainstream. They don't go back to Chinatown."[24]

This group *is* focused on giving back to Chinatown and other areas that help the Asian community in New York.

Loose Networks

Loose networks are giving circles that are typically structured around a core group of people who do the ongoing organizing, planning, and grant making for the group while individuals, who may or may not consider themselves to be members, are loosely affiliated with the group. Thus individuals outside of the core group tend to participate intermittently, usually attending special events like potluck dinners or social gatherings. Individual participants can make funding recommendations to the core group but typically do not make funding decisions. There is no or very little staff support for these types of groups; rather, everything tends to be done by volunteers. In addition, very few of these groups (only four were identified at the time of the study) are affiliated with an organization or host. Rather, members praise these groups for their flexibility, independence, and organic, nonbureaucratic nature. There is typically no minimum fee to participate in loose networks, and any amount given is left to the discretion of the individual, who gives money as part of an event or activity. The amount that is given tends to be small: $25 to $35 dollars an event. Loose networks are especially attractive to women. Among the loose networks for which information was available, nearly all members (85 percent) were female-only groups. Many of the women who participate in these groups see it as an opportunity to fit "doing good" into their busy lives. The case studies below provide examples of two loose network giving circles.

Case Study: Womenade

This case study was compiled through data from an interview and examination of several news articles about Womenade. At least thirty-eight Womenade groups have been identified across the United States, and for the most part, these groups are not affiliated with one another. The movement started in Washington, D.C., when Dr. Amy Kossoff and her friends decided to hold a potluck dinner and ask attendees to donate $35 to a fund that would enable Dr. Kossoff to continue to give financial assistance to her clients for prescriptions, utility bills, and rent. Dr. Kossoff did much of her work in homeless shelters and public clinics and regularly provided assistance to her clients out of her own pocket. The women called the group Womenade and held their first potluck in March 2001.[25] Nearly 100 women attended, raising $3,000. In August 2002, *Real Simple* magazine did a story on Washington Womenade, including a section on "How to Start a Womenade," and the idea seemed to take off from there.[26] Not only were Womenade groups created across the country but this article also gave Marsha Wallace the idea to create Dining for Women, which is now a national network of more than 177 groups across the country in which women meet for dinner on a monthly basis and pool the funds they would have spent eating out to support international grassroots programs helping women around the world.

A group of women in a midsized midwestern city saw the *Real Simple* article and started their own Womenade in September 2002. One of the key persons was a stay-at-home mom whose family had just moved into a new suburban neighborhood. As she put it:

> We had just moved into this house, and I was sitting around, believe it or not, feeling sorry for myself because we had left a neighborhood where there were kids everywhere, and we moved here, and it was like nobody even noticed that we entered the planet.[27]

She read the *Real Simple* article and thought immediately, "I can do this!" She got her friends together, asked them to invite their friends, and now there are well over 140 names on their email distribution list.

The group has a five-member board that plans events and makes decisions on how to spend the money. Participation in the group, beyond the board, is sporadic. Some women only come to an event once. Others come to every event. Some invite others to attend, some do not. Events typically draw sixty to eighty people, and there are at least four functions per year: three potluck dinners and a home vendors' shopping bazaar/fundraiser. Occasionally the group will invite speakers (mostly nonprofit staff) to the potluck dinners as well as report on how money was spent. Money is collected and deposited into an organization checking account. The group is incorporated as a nonprofit with the state but does not have tax-exempt status at the federal level. Because most members donate $75 or less in a year, they can write the donation off their taxes without a receipt and without the group going through the hassle and expense of becoming a 501(c)(3).

Because the members were not connected directly to needy clients like Dr. Kossoff in Washington, D.C., finding people in need was one of the most difficult aspects of organizing the group. The board had a hard time at first convincing local nonprofit organizations to help connect Womenade to people in need because the nonprofit organizations did not understand that Womenade wanted to *give* money rather than get something from the organization. The founder/member interviewed explained her initial contact with a church that serves people in a disadvantaged part of the city:

> So I called the priest, and he said, well, why don't you talk to the secretary, because he thought I was trying to sell him something. So I called back and talked to the secretary, and she does think I am trying to ask her for money in some way. But what I am trying to do is ask to *give* the money. She jokes about it today, saying, you know, nobody ever calls here asking to give us money. Everybody calls here asking *for* money.[28]

Through this organization and others, as well as through member recommendations, the group has paid utility bills and provided Thanksgiving dinners, grocery gift cards, furniture, Christmas gifts, snacks for vacation Bible school, and Easter baskets. They rely on nonprofit organizations to screen the individuals in need and contact Womenade on behalf of individuals. A member of the group will then deliver a gift card or check (to be given to the power company, for example) directly to the individual in need.

The leaders of this Womenade believe an important aspect of the group is empowering women. The founder talked about feeling empowered herself when she helped to start the group and about the ways the group can help empower other women. Speaking of her experience with the group:

> It's just the greatest feeling thinking, "We did this." Without anybody telling us what to do, we did this. We thought we could do it, and we did. So it is very, very satisfying in that way.[29]

Women in the group range from stay-at-home mothers to working professionals, between 30 and 60 years old: they are a "great range of people, great diverse crowd," as the founder of Womenade describes it. Most are white, and many are new to the giving side of voluntarism. The women of this Womenade and elsewhere tend to see the structure of the group as an easy thing to be a part of; where busy women, who do not have much time to volunteer, can still do something that "makes a difference" in the community.

Case Study: Bread for the Journey

This case study was compiled using data from interviews with one Bread for the Journey (BFJ) staff member and one affiliate member and analysis of documentation about BFJ. BFJ International is a nonprofit organization with about twenty chapters across the United States. The chapters are loosely connected to the international headquarters in Mill Valley, California. The international office has a group letter of exemption from the U.S. Internal Revenue Service, and the chapters also have their own tax identification number, incorporate in their own state, have their own checking account, and create their own boards of directors. The chapters typically consist of a small group of people—"people who know and love each other," as a BFJ staff member stated it—who then ask their friends, family, and others to donate money to them to give away. The people in BFJ chapters seem to come from various backgrounds and are at different points in their life: some working, some retired, some with children. They are usually not wealthy people with large sums of money to give away, and they have not had much experience with philanthropy before getting involved with BFJ. People attracted to the group have their own idea about what they want to do, and they like the independence of not having others telling them how to do it. As the BFJ staff member put it:

> Members get to create what they want, and they want to have that freedom, I think, to be able to come and go as they please. There is no overhead with Bread for the Journey, and there are no monthly bills they have to meet, so there is no reason to keep the wheel turning. If life ebbs and it's time to not be together for a couple of months because there are other things more pressing, well, then they don't have to answer to anybody to do that.[30]

Doing something simple, small, direct, and with care is at the foundation of the BFJ philosophy. It is based on the belief that "our healing as individuals is made full and complete through attending to the healing of others, and that each one of us stands in kinship with those who experience economic, emotional, social, or physical suffering." BFJ International was founded by Reverend Wayne Muller, a therapist who has published several self-help books on spirituality, prayer, and living a meaningful life. He came up with the BFJ model after friends and acquaintances began giving him money to give away. BFJ describes its model of giving as "relationship-centered" or "grassroots neighborhood philanthropy" and follows several principles: give grants mindfully; support relationships, not proposals; assess strengths, not needs; keep it simple; cultivate true wealth; and trust people. Following these principles, BFJ chapters have very simple, nonbureaucratic grant-making processes that enable them to "catch the wave of readiness that arises out of people's lives."[31]

One BFJ chapter began in California in 2000 when four friends (two couples) ran across Wayne Muller's work. The board, made up of the two couples, meets once a month to eat lunch, visit, and conduct business. They raise money by sending out a newsletter twice a year to about 100 people they know. One member describes their organization as "low key"; they do not have the desire to get big and do a lot of fundraisers. They have very little overhead except for stamps and stationery (and the money it cost them to apply for tax exemption). Their grant-making process is also simple and typically follows a consensus model. As the member interviewed described it: "If we find somebody good to grant, we go and meet them and talk to them, and if we think that it's a really good idea, we just write a check right there."[32]

The group tends to fund individuals with a good idea rather than organizations, giving away about $3,000 each year. As with other BFJ chapters, they are also asked to make a 5 percent donation to the BFJ International office. The members find people to fund through newspaper articles or through recommendations from their donors. Hearing and responding to stories is an important part of their grant-making process, which is also true for other BFJ chapters. The BFJ staff member described it this way:

> When people come to us and say they want a little bit of money, we don't want a written grant proposal. We don't even have grant guidelines. We ask them to come to a meeting, and we sit in somebody's living room with tea and cookies and conversation, to hear the story of what they are doing.[33]

Formal Organizations

Formal organizations are larger and more formal in their structure and decision-making processes compared with the other two types of giving circles. They look very much like a traditional membership organization structure with a board or lead group, committees, and often professional staff support. These groups also tend to focus on growing the organization as much as possible. Thus the membership size of formal organizations tends to be relatively large: on average eighty-four members per group, based on the data available in 2005. The total membership of formal organizations represents a high percentage of the membership for all types of giving circles. The cost to participate in formal organizations also tends to be on the higher side compared with small groups and loose networks: the modal amount is $5,000 to $5,700. Most formal organizations are mixed gender in their membership.

The grant-making process in formal organizations typically follows a format in which committees or investment teams make grant decisions directly or make recommendations to the membership, who then vote on grant awards. Within the committees themselves, there is often much discussion and consensus building. Outside of the committees, member votes, if taken, are often a formality. The two major activities of formal organizations are education and engagement. All of the formal organizations for which data were available have some kind of formal educational programming in addition to grant making and other informal educational opportunities. These include guest speakers and panel sessions, workshops, and other activities that provide education about philanthropy and community issues. There is also a strong emphasis on direct engagement with nonprofit organizations. About half of the formal organizations for which information was available provided opportunities for members to volunteer with nonprofit organizations, particularly with funding recipients. In most cases, members volunteer their expertise at the administrative level rather than through direct service.

There are several types of formal organizations, including the Social Venture Partner (SVP) model, the young leader and other affiliated funds model, and other independent 501(c)(3) organizations. SVP is structured to follow a venture philanthropy model, applying venture capitalist principles to their philanthropy. Its major goals are often to educate members about philanthropy and community issues while creating long-term, engaged, and supportive relationships with funding recipients. There are at least 25 SVP-type giving circles in the United States, Canada, and Japan. A more in-depth analysis of SVP is presented below. Young leader funds are giving circles organized to attract young professionals, often created with or by a community foundation. They feature social and educational events and opportunities to build future philanthropic leaders in the community. At the time of the study completed in 2005, there were at least thirteen young leader funds located all over the country, and several more have emerged since then. More information about one young leader fund, the Omaha Venture Group, is discussed below. Other affiliated funds include a diverse group of giving circles geared to attract various populations (such as women, Jews, African Americans, Latinos, Asian/Pacific Islanders, gays and lesbians, and so on), often created with or by a community foundation, charity, or women's fund/foundation. It is estimated that about half of the formal organizations identified are affiliated funds. A closer look at one affiliated fund, the Women's Giving Alliance, is presented below. Finally, there are a few formal organizations that are independent 501(c)(3) organizations.

These organizations seem to operate much like any other nonprofit organization or charity except that they implement the characteristics of the giving circle model.

Case Study: Social Venture Partners Seattle

This case study is based on data from an interview with a staff member, organizational documents, and other case studies written about Social Venture Partners (SVP) Seattle. SVP has probably been the best known and most studied giving circle model to date. There are at least twenty SVP affiliates across the United States and abroad, inspired by the first SVP, started in Seattle in 1997 when Paul Brainerd, the founder of Aldus Software and "father" of PageMaker, was looking for the "what next" after his successes in the high-tech world. He started the group with a few friends "to bring both money and motivated young technologists, venture capitalists and business people together to help nonprofits with programs for low-income families and children."[34] That is, he hoped to enable those with "new wealth," and often little experience with philanthropy, to help their communities. SVP was founded, then, with the dual objectives of "educating its member about philanthropy and helping various nonprofits with both money and expertise."[35]

The unique twist to SVP as a giving circle is that it was meant to follow a more hands-on "venture capital" model, attempting to use the tools of making money to give away money. The venture philanthropy model of grant making is described as "setting clear performance standards, creating close, long-term relationships with nonprofits, providing technical assistance and strategic advice, and developing a plan for the next stage of financing."[36] In reality, SVP started off with funding organizations for the short term and drawing little upon the venture philanthropy perspective. SVP board member Julie Weed describes the difficult balancing act of following a venture model and engaging SVP members:

> You want to give organizations multiyear grants because you don't want them to spend their time writing proposals rather than doing the work. But for the Partners there is considerable education in choosing the grantees and learning about new issues. If you have this monkey on your back of existing grants that you have to fund in the coming years, then the Partners, especially people who have just joined, have less choice.[37]

SVP's grant making generally has evolved more toward the venture model as it has matured as an organization.

SVP Seattle focuses on four grant-making areas: K–12 education, the environment, early childhood development, and parenting. Typically the group runs alternating cycles for two of these areas each year, making two to four grants in each area. The grant-making cycle is a six-month process in which two groups of approximately ten to fourteen partners serve. Any partner can serve on a grants committee, but they are required to make a commitment to be fully invested in the entire process. If they are not, they might be asked to leave the committee. The grant-making process starts with issue-area education using guest speakers, panels, and so on. SVP Seattle has a small staff that helps with this process, developing the reading materials and websites that they give to committee members to help them get up to speed on the issue. The "process is structured with the bias of partner education in mind," according to one SVP Seattle staff member.[38] Next, a call goes out to nonprofit organizations based in the greater Seattle area, asking them to submit a letter of inquiry. The committee works through the letters of inquiry using an evaluation tool created by SVP Seattle, shortening the list to six to eight organizations, then asks them for a more extensive application. The committee also visits these organizations.

The process for site visits and proposal review from this point is quite demanding. Typically, three or four people from the committee will go on a site visit, preparing questions for the nonprofit staff in advance. Immediately after the visit, the group will go out to coffee and " debrief on what they learned from the site visit, whether or not they have additional follow-up questions, and then they identify a lead person to do the followup where needed."[39] The team develops a three- or four-page summary for each of the proposals, which are then circulated to everyone on the committee. About a week after summaries are due and everybody has a chance to read them, the committee convenes. At that meeting, each team that went on a site visit does a presentation to highlight what they learned. There is time for discussion within the committee, and then they take a confidential vote. In its first year, SVP Seattle awarded $300,000 to seven nonprofits involved in education and children's issues. By 2008, SVP Seattle "granted in excess of $10 million to advance promising nonprofits."[40]

Having formed around a venture philanthropy philosophy, SVP is structured not just to give grants but also to help funding recipients with capacity building issues through partners' volunteer efforts. Thus each SVP Seattle funding recipient has assigned to it a team of ten to twelve partners who provide volunteer services. As the staff member described it:

> What we are looking for from a grant-making perspective is different than your typical grant maker. We have the intent of supporting nonprofits that are achieving programmatic outcomes in the areas that we care about, but we are also looking for groups that can benefit from the nonmonetary support that SVP provides. So we are looking for organizations that are at a specific stage in their development and where we can add value from a nonfinancial side of the situation. So it is really a blend of both.[41]

Volunteer work tends to be more infrastructure management-oriented rather than direct service volunteer work.

SVP Seattle currently has a membership of about 420, and each member makes a commitment of $5,700. SVP Seattle members are mostly in their thirties and forties, professionals with earned (rather than inherited) wealth, both men and women, and mostly white. As the SVP staff member describes the members:

> We have people that join SVP, and this is their first step into the world of philanthropy, so they have zero experience with nonprofits or grant making. They've never seen grant guidelines, never seen a letter of inquiry, have no idea what a proposal includes, or have no idea what a strong proposal would look like. Then you have people on the other end of the continuum who may have been running their family foundation for a while or who have served on a local United Way committee or who have been on the review board for their corporation, some kind of exposure, so you really get a range.[42]

According to a study done by Blueprint in 2003, "three-quarters of the Partners interviewed were not connected to organized philanthropy before joining SVP. Most were not involved in significant volunteering with local nonprofits when they joined."[43] One member, who joined SVP when it formed, said that "after practicing years of 'random philanthropy' by writing checks to various community groups, he was ready to really learn about the process and get engaged with the nonprofits he was supporting."[44]

Case Study: Omaha Venture Group

This case study is based on an interview with one member of Omaha Venture Group, documentation, and participant observation. The Omaha Venture Group (OVG) is a young leader fund that was started in Omaha, Nebraska, in 2002 by a young philanthropist in the Omaha area who was active with her family's foundation and her own foundation. She fits the profile of a "new and emerging donor" (described in chapter 3) in that she is very hands-on and engaged in her giving, likes to seek out funding opportunities, collaborates strategically with other funders, and is most attracted to funding small grassroots organizations. She modeled OVG after the Chicago Young Leaders Fund, gearing it toward attracting young professionals to invest $400 per year ($300 to grant making and $100 to administration) to fund grassroots nonprofit organizations. Members can also join at the $100 level as an affiliate member but then cannot participate in grant-making activities. Money given by participants is matched by outside donors and foundations, and there has also been some staff support for the group through the founder's family foundation and the local community foundation. OVG typically has approximately thirty to forty grant-making members participate each year who range in age from 25 to 45. They come from professional backgrounds in the business, nonprofit, and government sectors; and most are white.

As with other formal organizations, OVG has a tightly structured process for making decisions. Each year, after an initial orientation meeting, grant-making members break up into three "interest groups." In the first year, the interest group areas were arts and culture, youth and education, and neighborhood development. Each group creates a process for finding funding opportunities. For example, during the first year the arts and culture group sent out a request for proposals, picked the top proposals, and conducted site visits before interest group members voted on their top choices to forward to the entire membership. Alternatively, the neighborhood development group sought out neighborhood associations, visited with them, and then worked with the associations to create proposals to present to the entire membership. All of this work leads up to "funding day," when each interest group tries to make a case to the membership to support their recommendations. A member describes the funding day (described as the "big meeting") this way: "I think what you find in these meetings, in the big meetings, you see a real ownership, you see a real selling going on. You see also questioning going on about do these really fit in our guidelines? Some really good dialogue."[45]

At the end of the day, members fill out ballots, suggesting funding amounts for each recommended funding recipient. This process can get extremely complicated at the end when, inevitably, members want to give away more money than is available. This problem was addressed in the first year by creating an ad hoc committee (made up of the founder and others she selected) to decide how to distribute funds. This last-minute, ad hoc decision making caused some consternation within one interest group who felt they did not receive fair representation on the committee.

Beyond grant making, OVG conducts various social and educational events. Educational events in the first year included a bus tour of poverty-stricken areas of Omaha and a grant-making 101 workshop. These events were not as well attended as the social gathering at a local downtown pub, the grant-making meeting, or the event at which grants were presented to nonprofit and community funding recipients (the event took place the first year at a new Latino museum in an ethnically diverse area of town). Interest group members also gain insights about community issues through site visits, proposals, and other research done during the grant-making process. These new insights sometimes lead to new relationships between OVG members and the organizations funded by the group. According to the member interviewed, another OVG member's exposure to a nonprofit organization called Youth Emergency Services "was through OVG. She ended up building a relationship and ended up being asked to be on the board. I know there are a couple of other situations that exist like that, too, which is neat."

Case Study: Women's Giving Alliance

This case study is based on an interview with a member of the Women's Giving Alliance as well as supplemental data from other documents and news articles. The Women's Giving Alliance is one example of an affiliated formal organization. It is a donor-advised fund of the Community Foundation in Jacksonville, Florida, which was begun in 2001 when five women who had been very active with the Community Foundation's board of trustees "wanted to try to find a way to get women more involved in philanthropy and more active in making decisions about where their assets might go."[46]

The group has about 160 members who range in age from their late twenties to mid-eighties. Most are white and come from affluent parts of the community, although there are some members for whom the $2,500 membership fee is a stretch. Over 80 percent of the members did not have a donor-advised fund or any other contact with the Community Foundation before participating in the giving circle. Unlike many other giving circles, the $2,500 is broken down into four parts. The first $1,000 is used as a mini donor-advised fund where a member can recommend up to three organizations—any nonprofit organizations—to fund through the Community Foundation. Another $1,000 goes to a pooled grant fund, where a grants committee makes grants to organizations that affect women and girls in the community. Of the remainder, $400 goes into an endowment to benefit women and girls, and $100 is used for administration. Even with this administrative fee, the Community Foundation underwrites the majority of the costs of administering the giving circle, including providing staff support.

The funding focus of the group generally is to give to organizations and issues that benefit women and girls. But in order to decide the specific area of funding within this context, at the beginning of each year members are asked to rank issues through a ballot. The results from this vote guide the work of the grant-making committee. In 2004, rather than an issues ballot, the group used results from a research report on the status of women and girls to guide grant making. The grants committee typically has thirty-five members. Anyone can be on the committee and be part of the process as long as there is no conflict of interest. The process is highly structured and strategic. According to the member of the group interviewed for the study:

> It's a very traditional process. They have teams that do the site visits that come back and present their findings. They ask questions. They bring the organizations in to answer questions. They look at the overall benefit based on what the goals of the Alliance are and what the issues are in our community, and that is how they make decisions.

The grants committee is responsible for making grant decisions, which are sent to the membership for ratification. Unlike most giving circles, the Community Foundation board asks to ratify grant decisions. The Women's Giving Alliance also features comprehensive educational programming about philanthropy.

Why People Join Giving Circles

People join and continue to participate in giving circles for a variety of reasons. One of the most often cited is the chance to become more engaged in the giving process, to be doing more than just writing a check, and to interact directly with nonprofit organizations. This reason was cited especially by those in formal organization giving circles, such as Social Venture Partners, where

Table 4.2 Why people participate in giving circles

- To become more involved in the giving process
- To have fun
- To be part of a larger group and leverage individual contributions to make more of an impact
- To give back to the community
- To learn about community organizations and philanthropy in an anonymous, safe place
- To find a simple and nonbureaucratic alterative to the time commitment of traditional volunteering
- To seek individual empowerment
- To connect with others; to be social while doing good and/or to network with peers in the same industry
- To promote philanthropy
- To find a new focus after a life transition
- To fulfill a quest to be more spiritual and generous

volunteering with agencies is an important part of the venture philanthropy relationship. Yet even for other types of giving circles, the hands-on process of reviewing proposals and going on site visits created the more engaged philanthropy that several members desired. Members liked the greater control they seemed to gain over their giving.[47] Alternatively, several others said they participated in a giving circle because of the *minimal* time commitment involved. These were individuals, overwhelmingly women, who participate in giving circles where giving money is seen in many ways as an *alternative* to volunteering. As one magazine article about giving circles noted, for example: "It's an effective environment for women raising families to make a difference without removing them weekly or daily from their work and home obligations."[48]

Another frequently cited reason for participating in a giving circle was the fun or social aspect. Though true for all types of giving circles, this seemed to be the case in particular for those participating in less formal loose network giving circles. The giving circle is a chance to be social "while doing good." Women also brought up the attraction that giving circles hold as a tool for individual empowerment. The giving circle is seen as a way for a group to control how things go. For example, "I could do that" was a thought that many individuals had when they read about Womenade in *Real Simple* magazine and then started their own chapter of Womenade or Dining for Women.

The opportunity to be part of a group and leverage the amount of money an individual is able to give is another important reason members participate in a giving circle. Philanthropic staff mentioned that being in such a group makes members feel like they are part of a bigger movement fairly quickly, while magnifying their individual contribution. In the case of a giving circle like Silicon Valley Social Venture Fund, a member can contribute $5,000 but influence $700,000 in grants.[49] Cited as many times as leveraging individual donations was the chance to give back and make more of an impact in the community through the giving circle. Individuals participate as well because they want to learn more about nonprofit organizations, issues in the community, or becoming better philanthropists. For many, they are also attracted to the safety and anonymity the giving circle provides. As one philanthropic professional put it:

> You know, for many folks, if they've had their heads down either building a company or becoming a partner in a law firm, they've only done scattered and unfocused philanthropy, and if the nonprofit community found out that they were looking for an opportunity to get engaged, they would have 200 nonprofits sending them letters and emails trying to get them on their board and as a donor.[50]

Thus the giving circle provides a safe place to ask questions and learn the "ins and outs" of grant making.

Others see the giving circle as a tool for networking and connecting to their peers in their industry or line of work. Individuals also support and participate in giving circles because they want to promote an ethic of philanthropic behavior in others, whether it be with other women, their children, or their peers. For some, the opportunity to participate in a giving circle came at a time when they were looking for something new after a life transition such as a new baby, career change, or sudden increase in wealth. Finally, some expressed the importance of the spiritual aspect of participating in the giving circle. This is indicated by one giving circle member, who said:

> I've been trying for years to figure out how to be or what it would feel like to be a more generous person and challenging myself in different ways. Of course, that's not just with money, but all kinds of ways, and this seemed like a good opportunity to put that spiritual discipline into practice for me.[51]

Giving Circles Compared with Other Philanthropic Tools

As noted above, a group can be considered a giving circle if (for the most part) their resources are pooled and collectively given away, members are educated about philanthropy and issues in the community, there is a social dimension, members are engaged in running the giving circle and/or volunteering with nonprofit organizations, and the members decide on their own, independent of any charitable institution, where to give their resources. Every giving circle has varying degrees of each aspect, but some focus more on social or educational aspects, others on volunteering. Some consist of pooled money from members only, while other giving circles look to outsiders to provide support that is pooled to give away. Some are more independent than others. If one were to look at each aspect of these key components of giving circles independently, they would hardly seem like unique or new contributions to voluntarism (one can see similarities in the women's clubs of the late nineteenth century and the Kiwanis or Rotary clubs of today). However, as discussed in earlier chapters, the environment in which giving circles have emerged and in which they operate, and the combination of all five aspects do seem new for today's voluntary environment. What is also new is the underlying express purpose for creating giving circles: to give away resources for community betterment. Earlier institutions such as women's clubs and Rotaries often did not start or sustain such a focus; the philanthropic aspect either emerged later or was secondary to the main intent of the group.[52]

Overall, compared with other modern voluntary and philanthropic institutions, giving circle members and philanthropic professionals see giving circles as "something different." For example, they see it as a more engaged, personal process than individual check writing. As one member of a small group giving circle stated, "You know when you write a check to something, you have no clue where it is going, what it is going for, maybe the people involved. This much more personalizes some of these organizations."[53]

Giving circles also seem to be different from private foundations in several ways. First, the amount of money it takes to create a foundation is much greater than what it takes for an individual to participate in a giving circle. Even $5,000 or $10,000 to participate in some giving circles is small compared with the amount needed to start a foundation (at least $250,000 to $500,000). Members and other sources also note that the application process for funding is typically much more engaged through the giving circle. Rather than just sending out a request for proposals and waiting for a response, giving circle members often take a more hands-on approach to seeking out and working with potential funding recipients. Finally, educating giving circle members about the grant-making process and community issues is an ongoing project of most giving circles—directly or indirectly—whereas in many foundations, there are program officers who already understand the grant-making process and know the issues; there is no need to treat people doing the grant making as "fresh learners" every year, as one SVP Seattle staff member stated.[54] Some giving circles, like SVP, are also looking for ways to contribute nonfinancial value to the grantee, which is unusual for most foundations.

Nonprofit professionals working in organizations that have received support from giving circles also see giving circles as new fundraising territory to be navigated. On the one hand, they believe that giving circles have many benefits that are different from other philanthropic vehicles: they can be easier to work with and bring a multidimensionality or "value-added" element to the funding relationship. On the other hand, the funding relationship with giving circles can be more complicated than with traditional funding sources because of their structure and member-driven nature.

Particularly with more informal types of giving circles (small groups and loose networks), many nonprofit professionals interviewed mentioned how easy it was to get funding from the giving circle. Interviewees noted that the process was informal and flexible, there was little bureaucracy, and they were given few or no forms to fill out. One executive director described her experience this way:

> People were happy to give away money. Like I said, it was just so effortless. I didn't have to write a grant. I didn't have to sign in blue ink. I didn't have to show a copy of my 501(c) 3. It wasn't any of that like checking "Are you legit? Are you for real? What are you doing with the money?" It's like the people understood that their money went to a good cause and whether it went toward buying books or paying a trainer or helping to pay for my health insurance, or whatever, it wasn't that sort of "I need a receipt with exactly where this money went." It was that sort of feeling, which was pleasant for me.[55]

This was not necessarily the case in funding relationships with more formal organizations such as SVP, where the funding process is typically much more involved and intensive. However, SVP's focus on capacity building, multiyear funding, and assistance from volunteers and staff can serve to balance the intensive time commitment involved.

The other major benefit noted by several nonprofit professionals was the multidimensionality or value-added element that giving circles can bring to the relationship, in addition to financial support. Giving circles do give substantial amounts of money, but they also can bring to the funding recipient the introduction of giving circle members with contacts to others in the community, new volunteers, a seal of approval, and other capacity-building resources. Bringing this multidimensionality to the relationship is important because giving circles largely seem to fund only for the short term. Especially in the case of funding from small group and loose network giving circles, funding recipients may receive a onetime gift (as opposed to multiyear gifts, which are more often the case from formal organizations). In this context, one executive director described giving circles as practicing "flavor of the month" giving, similar to the money she receives through special events.[56] Another executive director described the funding from the giving circle as a "bonus." Funding recipients said they generally could not depend on giving circles for continual or long-term support (although there were a couple of interviewees who said that they had long-term relationships with some loose network giving circles). For this reason, the value-added element that giving circles can bring to bear on funding relationships can be very important.

Several nonprofit professionals interviewed, particularly those who seemed to be quite positive about their experience with giving circles, noted the importance of what seemed like a more personal dimension to their relationships with giving circle members compared with other funders. Such personal relationships can cause members of the giving circle to have a more nuanced understanding of the issues addressed by the organization and bring a partnership mentality to the relationship. However, this can also make the funding relationship more complicated from a fundraising point of view because it can be very time-consuming and more difficult to navigate. One reason for this is what some see as the lack of transparency in their relationship with the giving circle, partly because giving circle members themselves are trying to figure out what they are doing and partly because this kind of relationship is new for the nonprofit. According to an executive director funded by two formal organizations:

> Usually you're talking to a private foundation, a corporate foundation, or an individual, and it's pretty clear what their goal is. Their goal is to give away money according to certain criteria or values or something. And then we get it, and our job is to spend it on what we said we would and then report back that that's what we did. And I think that is how those relationships are supposed to work. I don't think anybody is scratching their heads and saying, "Gee, what happens next?" Everyone understands it. And I think with these giving circles it's a little less clear to us exactly what we're supposed to do, so I think there's some ambiguity.[57]

Another example of the new complexity involved with giving circle funding is the more complicated nature of cultivating relationships with individual members in the group. Over half of those interviewed brought up how difficult or impossible it was to connect with individual members in the giving circle—either by design or by default. Some giving circles actively discourage funding recipients from following up with or cultivating their members for individual gifts by not sharing the member mailing list or not allowing funding recipients opportunities to interact with giving circle members. Others noted that they were not explicitly told they could not cultivate individual members, but they got the impression that it was just not acceptable. For example, when asked if her organization had tried to cultivate relationships with individual members within the giving circle from which they received funding, one executive director said:

> No, we haven't. It's almost the rule of thumb around United Way in our region. We can't have campaigns when they're having a campaign. So I guess we just made an assumption, and we haven't gone directly to the giving circle people.[58]

This seems to counteract the value-added element that giving circles can bring with their funding as mentioned above and can make for a frustrating experience for the nonprofit professional. According to one executive director describing her struggle with this issue:

> They have an approach that makes it seem like, "Oh, my God, this is going to change your whole life." You know, it just doesn't, because the challenge for nonprofits especially at this stage is to cultivate individual donors, and they have access to so many. And when you want to send anything to anyone you've ever met there, you have to call and ask. They will not give you contact information. You have to get approval. So they resist. So you have to go and say, "But she's come to three of our things. Could you ask her if she would let us put her on our mailing list?" And it takes a lot of time, which is fine. They're protecting their donors. But the point is that if you have an organization in which you have somebody who's been on a committee that's reviewed your organization, and they've come to three of your things via the giving circle, you should automatically be getting contact information.[59]

Regardless of the new benefits and difficulties posed by giving circles, nonprofit professionals interviewed overwhelmingly said that fundraising from giving circles, like fundraising from individuals, corporations, or foundations, is still about showing that their organization can make a difference. It is also still very much about relationship building, although this relationship may be harder than other types of fundraising to sustain.

Conclusion

This chapter has described the general landscape of giving circles, including their key characteristics—they pool funds and give away resources, educate about philanthropy and issues in the community, include a social dimension, engage members, and maintain independence—as well as their unique qualities and appeal to members. Three major types of giving circles were presented—small groups, loose networks, and formal organizations—and in-depth case studies of these ideal-types were provided. These represent the shape of the giving circle universe and provide a framework for discussing their democratic impacts in the next chapters. While giving circles seem to share many similarities with other traditional voluntary associations, they also represent a new way of associating in a changing voluntary and societal context. The next chapter examines the democratic effects of giving circles.

5   The Democratic Effects of Giving Circles

This chapter examines the democratic effects of giving circles and the degree to which they might serve to ameliorate antidemocratic aspects of voluntarism and run counter to the negative effects of modernization on voluntarism. More precisely, this chapter examines the degree to which giving circles might serve to democratize voluntarism: provide opportunities for democratic participation, broaden individuals' identification with the needs of others, and expand who benefits from voluntarism.

Providing Opportunities for Meaningful Democratic Participation

One aspect of democratizing voluntarism, as presented in chapter 3, may be voluntarism's ability to provide opportunities for a more diverse group of individuals to democratically participate in their communities and provide or enhance the tools and capacities for individuals to participate in civic life. Do giving circles provide opportunities for meaningful democratic participation? Specifically, what types of people are participating in giving circles? Do they come from diverse backgrounds? Are they new to voluntarism? Or, if not new, has participation increased or deepened their level of participation? Is this participation meaningful? Meaningful in this case means providing members with equal opportunities to participate in decision making and agenda setting; providing members with opportunities for deliberation; and helping members to form, enhance, and support their capacities for civic engagement. Opportunities for diverse and meaningful democratic participation in giving circles are analyzed next by examining member characteristics, members' participation in deliberation and decision making, and the degree to which members' capacities as citizens are enhanced.

The Characteristics of Members

Analyzing the characteristics of members is important for several reasons. According to Gastil, a democratic group is one that is inclusive, and as Gutmann notes, the more economically, ethnically, and religiously heterogeneous the membership of an association, the greater may be its capacity to cultivate public discourse and deliberation that is conducive to democratic citizenship.[1] In addition, democratizing voluntarism has been defined by many as

Table 5.1 Characteristics of giving circle members, 2005

Membership	Total number (% of N)	N (% of 188)
Age range	58 groups (84%) had members under 40; 25 groups (36%) were multigenerational	69 (37%)
Gender	82 groups (44%) were women-only	163 (87%)
Racial/ethnic/religious affiliation	44 groups (61%) were all or mostly Caucasian 6 groups (8%) were Jewish 6 groups (8%) were African American 1 group (1%) each Asian American, Latino, Hmong 12 groups (17%) had mixed membership with 15% or more nonwhite members	72 (38%)

more choices and opportunities in giving for more people, not just the wealthy or traditional donors.[2] The data from interviews and other documentation suggest that people from diverse walks of life do participate in giving circles; however, the largest percentage of giving circle members seem to be in their thirties and forties, predominantly female, and white.

Table 5.1 provides a summary of giving circle member characteristics based on the database I compiled in 2005 (see the appendix for more information). Age-related characteristics were available for 69 giving circles (37 percent of the 188 giving circles in the database at that time).[3] Of these 69, at least 58 (84 percent) included members who were younger than 40, although 25 giving circles included members of all ages. Younger adults participating in giving at this more engaged level is unusual. Research has shown that giving is typically higher for those nearing age 65 than for those in the age range of 25 to 44.[4] Rather, it is more typical for younger adults to give time instead of money.[5]

Based on this age-related data, it appears that giving circles are substantially made up of individuals somewhat new to the giving side of voluntarism, and this is one indication that giving circles are expanding who participates. Indeed, several members of the giving circles interviewed said that though they had volunteered their time for many years, giving money was relatively new for them. One said, "I was involved, definitely, always been a volunteer person, but I see myself more financially committed in this group."[6] Some of these "new" philanthropists said they had been too busy working and/or building businesses to participate in philanthropic activities before now; the opportunity to participate in a giving circle coincided with a time in their life when they either could finally spend the time to pursue their philanthropic interests and/or they were just gaining enough resources to give them away. Others seemed to be new to the giving side of voluntarism only in the sense of connecting to *organized* or formal philanthropy; that is, they have always given, but it had been in a more informal way or in a way that they did not think of as philanthropy. One philanthropic professional described the general membership of giving circles this way:

> I see that the makeup is certainly those usual suspect philanthropists, but there are many people who might be nonprofit professionals and likely have been philanthropists their whole lives but would never have called themselves such, and there's younger people who would never have considered themselves philanthropists but who now might.[7]

Women are the other major group of individuals participating in giving circles. At least 82 (44 percent) of the giving circles for which data were available in the 2005 database (163) were made up of only women. Many of the other giving circles also had a large female presence. There were also some identifiable differences in gender makeup across the three types of giving circles. In small groups, women-only giving circles and giving circles with both men and women were almost equally split: 20 women-only groups (50 percent) and 18 groups with men and woman (45 percent). Among loose networks, over 85 percent of groups were women-only. In formal organizations, the distribution was approximately one-third (36 percent) women-only and two-thirds (62 percent) mixed gender membership. Only two giving circles were found that contained only men. So, although women make up a large portion of giving circle membership in all types of giving circles, it is the loose network structure that is most predominantly female.

This trend in membership is also unique in relation to traditional philanthropy, or at least our perception of traditional philanthropy. While women (61 percent) tend to volunteer more than men (49 percent), there has long been an assumption that men are more likely to give than women.[8] However, recent research suggests that women, particularly wealthy women, give a larger percentage of their income than men.[9] The assumption that women give less may be based on myths about women's giving that keep fundraisers from asking women to give at the same level as men and take women's philanthropy seriously. It may also be due to the fact that women in the past have had less control over their finances and still earn only seventy cents to the dollar earned by men. Women also do not tend to think of themselves as philanthropists, and when they do give money, women tend to have a style of giving that is different from men and that fundraisers do not always understand.[10] So giving circles may be expanding who participates in voluntarism or at least expanding the amounts and ways that women give and providing some legitimacy to the potential for women's giving.

Although many of the philanthropic professionals interviewed for this study commented on what they saw as diversity *within* giving circles, giving circle members seem to be very similar to one another within their groups, often sharing certain characteristics such as gender, race, ethnic, or religious identities. I was able to gather limited data in this area, available for only 72 (38 percent of 188) of all giving circles in the 2005 database. Among these, 44 (61 percent) were made up of all or mostly (over 85 percent) white members. Other studies on young leader funds and small group giving circles also found that members were predominantly white.[11] At the time of the study completed in 2005, there were only 15 giving circles clearly identified as racially, ethnically or religiously based: 6 giving circles made up of black members, 6 with Jewish members, 2 with Asian-American/Pacific Islander members, and 1 with Latino/Hispanic members. Only 12 giving circles had what could be described as a mixed membership, in which 15 percent or more included nonwhite members.

It is difficult to determine clear differences regarding race/ethnicity among the three types of giving circles because of the limited data available. Nonetheless, a few conclusions might be drawn. Formal organizations and small groups seem to be similar in that, among giving circles for which information was available, over two-thirds were primarily made up of white members and less than a third had mixed memberships. Alternatively, 90 percent of loose networks were mostly white. It is interesting to note that among the 72 giving circles for which I had this data in 2005, nearly all of the identified racial, ethnic or religious identity-based giving circles were formal organizations. There were no loose networks in this group and only one small group of African Americans at the time of the study. Since 2005, however, the number of racially-, ethnically- and religiously-based giving circles has increased a good deal. The Forum of Regional Associations of Grantmakers' current database of giving circles identifies at least 34 of these types of giving circles: 11 African American; 9 Jewish; 8 Asian-American/Pacific Islander; 3 Latino/Hispanic; and 3 gay, lesbian, bisexual, transgender groups. All of these groups appear to be either small group (about 13) or formal organization (about 17) giving circles, and it appears that these groups, because of their organization around identity, continue to be limited in diversity *within* their groups. Current data from the Forum's database suggest that only about 30 (18 percent) of the giving circles for which data are available (165) have a mixed membership; that is, with 15 percent or more of members from diverse (nonwhite) racial or ethnic groups.[12] It is difficult to say that giving circles are expanding the participation of these groups. However, what giving circles may be doing, as with younger individuals discussed above (indeed, many of these individuals are also younger professionals), is expanding the participation of these groups into *organized* philanthropy.

Based on 2005 data, giving circle members also appear to generally *not* be the mega-wealthy, although the mega-wealthy do participate. Rather, members are perhaps more accurately described as middle and upper middle class. Hartman's study of small group giving circles also found this to be the case.[13] Members seem to be practicing or retired professionals—lawyers, high-tech entrepreneurs, and so on—and several giving circles include stay-at-home mothers and housewives. To some degree, the socioeconomic status of the members can be determined based on the membership fee of the giving circles. Obviously, giving circles that require a contribution of $1,000, $2,500, $5,000, or more each year have members who can afford such a sum. Nearly 40 percent of giving circles identified in 2005 required a minimum investment of $1,000 to join the group. On the other hand, loose networks, which ask for much smaller contributions ($25 to $35 per event), may include members with more modest means. The young leader funds and some small groups seem to have buy-in amounts that are a stretch, but affordable, for a young professional ($250 to $500). Additionally, there are several examples of small groups and formal organizations where members come from various levels financially: mega-wealthy with their own foundations mixed in with working professionals and stay-at-home moms. For example, the New River Valley Change Network includes graduate students, faculty members, grade school teachers, a retired lawyer, and a nonprofit professional. There are also a handful of giving circles that have varying and very low membership levels with the intention of attracting people from lower socioeconomic circumstances. Finally, it should be noted that there is a large contingency of nonprofit professionals participating in giving circles as full members. From a democratization perspective, this level of inclusiveness is important. These members, at least to some degree, provide a voice for nonprofit funding recipients in the group. There appeared to be no giving circles in which nonprofit funding recipients, their clients, or individuals in need were members; however, many giving circles do invite nonprofit professionals to speak at their meetings or otherwise seek guidance from nonprofit professionals on funding issues.

In sum, most of the giving circles for which data were available appear to be limited in diversity within the group, but fairly diverse across groups, attracting people not normally involved in organized philanthropy at a substantial level. Several of those interviewed and documentation about giving circles used the term *like-minded* to describe giving circle memberships. This seems to be quite accurate. The homogeneity of these groups is not surprising when one considers that the main recruitment tool for giving circles seems to be word-of-mouth and member referrals. This is typical of most voluntary associations.[14]

Participation in Deliberation and Decision Making

Tocqueville and others have looked to participation in voluntary associations as a way for citizens to practice governance and to achieve the virtues necessary for democratic citizenship. Democratic deliberation, according to Gastil, means that the group makes decisions through a deliberative process that involves speaking opportunities for each member and due consideration of members' opinions. Democratic deliberation should also include opportunities for members to set the agenda of the discussion, articulate opinions, persuade, vote on preferences, and express a dissenting point of view. Members must be able to comprehend and give due consideration to what is being said by others in the group. These are essential elements of a democratic group.[15]

The data suggest that in nearly all giving circles, members have some influence on the agenda of the group. This is important in the context of democratizing voluntarism because a democratic group "must distribute its power among the membership. Every member of a small democratic group must ultimately have equal power with regard to group policies."[16] In other words, members should have influence over what is discussed and a voice in the final decisions of the group. The data from interviews and documentation suggest that in all types of giving circles, members can make suggestions about organizational issues and potential funding recipients, but in the case of formal organizations and loose networks, members serving on the board or in committees can have much more influence.

With small groups, everyone tends to take part in the agenda-setting process, related to both organizational structure and funding. This tends to be an informal process where members discuss organizational and funding issues and potential funding recipients during the meetings. Members sometimes share leadership duties, as is done in Shared Giving, where a different person is in charge of setting the agenda and running each meeting. Funding nominations are typically raised in an ad hoc fashion by any member at meetings or, as in the case of at least two small group giving circles, members put names of organizations in a hat and one name is pulled out at each meeting. In one of these giving circles, the Red Heart Society, the person who nominates the organization is responsible for organizing the next meeting and inviting a representative from the organization to speak to the group.

In the case of formal organizations or loose networks, any member can make suggestions about funding areas or organizations to a board, lead group, or committee. This can be a formal process (such as filling out a survey or application, or encouraging a nonprofit organization to fill out an application, as is more typical of formal organizations) or sometimes it is ad hoc, as when a leader will ask members to make suggestions or recommendations (more typical with loose networks). For example, in the Quality of Life Giving Circle, a formal organization, members work directly with nonprofit organizations of their choosing to fill out an application for funding, which then goes to a committee for discussion. Alternatively, the organizer of the Womenade in Omaha, Nebraska, occasionally emails members and asks them for funding recommendations, and then the board decides.[17] However, within formal organizations and loose networks, members seem to have less influence on the agenda when it comes to the organizational structure itself unless they participate on the board, lead group, or relevant committee. Nonetheless, in most of these giving circles, anyone is eligible to serve on the board or committees.

Opportunities for deliberation and participation in decision making seem to depend largely on the type of giving circle. In small groups, everyone can participate. Of the twenty-four small group giving circles for which data were available in 2005, twelve did this through consensus, seven through a voting procedure, two by pulling names out of a hat, and one in which an individual could decide whether or not to give money to the featured organization at each meeting. The deliberation and decision-making process is often informed by a site visit, guest speakers, or research conducted by members. Through the decision-making process, then, most small group giving circle members take part in some amount of deliberation—about issues and organizations—and this is frequently the aspect of the meeting that they like best. These discussions often include a good deal of "give and take" and questioning, which one small group member said had "really just opened up my own thinking to looking at things differently."[18]

With formal organizations, the deliberation and decision-making process typically takes place in a committee. Of the fifty-nine formal organizations for which data were available in 2005, in forty-four a committee made the final funding decision and in twelve, a committee made funding recommendations to the members, who then voted. Committees are usually kept small, fifteen members or so, and in most cases it appears that the committee is open to any member who can devote the time and would like to participate. However, the time commitment in some groups can be substantial. For example, with SVP, there are rigorous expectations for attending meetings, going on site visits, and becoming informed about the issues and the funding applicants, a process that spans several months. A study of SVP Seattle published in 2003 found that only 30 percent of the members had served on a grant committee.[19]

The process of deliberation and decision making in formal organizations can also be quite complex. For example, several young leader funds follow a model in which an "investment team" (committee) conducts site visits, deliberates, and then forwards their top two or three recommendations to the membership. With the Omaha Venture Group, the investment teams make presentations to the membership, followed by discussion, and then there is a vote of the entire membership. Community Capital Alliance follows a similar process, but as one member said in an interview, they have run into some difficulties because the final distribution of funding does not always seem fair to group members. As with other young leader funds, there is often conflict and competition during the selection process.[20] Nonetheless, those interviewed saw a general commitment to the democratic process and trusted that others were acting in the best interest of the group. These are also essential elements of a democratic group.[21] Indeed, in some formal organizations, the vote of the membership is merely a rubber stamp because, with the intense amount of work that has gone into choosing the recommendations, members entrust the committee to make the decision.

A substantial amount of deliberation occurs within these grant committees. This is how one young leader fund member described it:

> During our little discussion, we in youth and education get together in a potluck, sit down, and hash out who went on this visit, what did you think about it, where do you think the money should go. To be honest, they get kind of intense. I guess that's the whole object of it, for people to really sell it.[22]

An SVP Delaware member also described the discussion that takes place in their group's grant committees:

The process that they used to get to the end result was a wonderful process; it really made me believe so much in this model. It was about a three-hour discussion, and it was very thoughtful and carefully articulated. And the reasons that they came to for not funding or not having this one particular organization move forward into the next round were good reasons.[23]

If the membership votes on the proposals, more deliberation often occurs when members ask questions as they determine how they will vote for various proposals. This type of deliberative practice is increasingly rare within voluntary organizations today but of great importance to creating the conditions conducive for democratic voluntarism and a democratic society.[24]

Within loose networks, the decision making rests almost solely with the board or lead group, and funding decisions are often made in a "spur-of-the-moment" fashion, although some deliberation does take place among the board members. In one Bread for the Journey affiliate, for example, the board meets with a person doing good work, hears the story of what they are doing, asks questions, and then talks among themselves until reaching consensus about whether to fund the person or not. Sometimes it is even quicker and less formal than that. This is how a Bread for the Journey member described their process:

Usually we do it right that day. We walk away or we look at each other and we just know that this is it. There was a high school kid who was getting old computers and erasing everything and getting parts and putting them together in his garage and giving them to foster homes for children who didn't have computers. We went to lunch with him, and we were just taken with this kid. He was so passionate about this. We took about fifteen minutes to decide how much we wanted to give him, and then we drove back to his house and wrote a check.[25]

With many Womenade groups, funding is given in response to an urgent need, and so it is often one person from the group who makes the funding decision. Because of these quick responses, there is not a great deal of deliberation. There is, however, considerable social talk at meetings and events that includes discussion of the individuals who are helped by the group's gifts.

Building the Capacities of Citizens

Capacity building for individuals means gaining the tools and skills necessary to participate in civic life. Tocqueville saw participation in voluntary associations as a way for citizens to practice governance and to achieve the virtues necessary for democratic citizenship. He saw in these groups the importance of instituted action; that is, they can engage individuals "*routinely* in civic relationships over time, not merely sporadically," and these civic relationships can cultivate what Lichterman calls social capacity: "people's ability to work together organizing public relationships rather than ceding those relationships entirely to market exchange or administrative fiats of the state."[26] Verba, Schlozman, and Brady have shown that members of voluntary groups, such as churches, can develop skills relevant for political action through their participation in such groups, and this may lead to being more politically active.[27] Yet, as discussed in chapter 2, these capacity building outcomes may be eroding with the modernization of voluntarism. Giving circles and similar informal associations may counteract the effects of modernization. In virtually all giving circles studied, there seemed to be some amount of member capacity building taking place.

One way capacity building takes place is through the educational process, a very important aspect of many giving circles' operations. It takes place informally, through the running of the giving circle and distributing money, and formally, through workshops, seminars, and discussions with guest speakers. This educational process seems to happen more intentionally and intently within formal organizations than in small groups or loose networks.

Giving circle members also learn by taking part in the giving circle's operations and governance. This may be shared, as in the case of small groups, or there may be a board or committee to which members can volunteer. Either way, members have the chance to learn how to run and govern an organization. Even in cases where there is some staff support, giving circles are largely led by volunteers. Finally, some giving circle members learn through direct volunteer engagement with nonprofit agencies. Members get to share their expertise while building leadership skills and knowledge areas about community issues and nonprofit operations.

Part of the capacity-building effects of giving circles also involves empowering members. This is an important element of citizen capacity building, because individuals need to feel as if they have the power to make a difference if they are going to participate and be effective in civic life.[28] Empowerment was an issue that came up for all types of giving circles, but it was mentioned most frequently in relation to loose networks and small groups. For example, several women who helped start Womenade groups commented that this was something they could do. One woman also brought up her efforts to help start another Womenade in an adjacent town in order to empower women and discussed her efforts within her own group to encourage members to take on leadership roles. Marsha Wallace, founder of Dining for Women, pointed out the power that comes from a network of women joining together to fund particular causes:

> Most of the time the problems of the world seem overwhelming and I struggle with feelings of helplessness and impotence that comes from knowing that I am only one person with limited time, resources, and power to effect a change in the injustices and pain in lives of women of the world. Then I think of all of the Dining for Women members across the country and power that women united can wield, and I feel a glimmer of hope.[29]

Likewise, Bread for the Journey members also have "their own idea of what they want to do," seeing the BFJ model as a way to give people doing good work a small amount of money and support to enable them to be "useful and helpful in some kind of creative and intelligent way."[30]

One member said, "The thing I liked about the circle concept is that it's very empowering—people are completely in control of how it goes."[31] Members gain even more power through the leverage they create by combining resources. A man from a small group African American giving circle noted that the circle offered him a direct avenue to empowered participation in the community at a time when "he found that many of his friends had a passion to do something but didn't know where to start."[32] Indeed, some giving circles, especially those formed around racial, ethnic, or other nonwhite identities, may see the giving circle as a tool not only for helping their communities but also for "gaining a seat at the table."[33] One indication of this is that several giving circle members have been asked to join the boards of nonprofit organizations funded by the giving circle.

In sum, opportunities for democratic participation within giving circles is substantial, but it varies for different types of giving circles. In small groups, everyone seems to be involved in deliberation, decision-making, and capacity-building activities. In formal organizations and loose networks, because of the size and structure of the groups, members can choose to opt in or out of these activities. Formal organizations are the most systematic and comprehensive in efforts to educate and engage members with others in the community, while loose networks seem to empower individuals and connect members more directly to individuals in need, even if only through the organization's leadership.

Broadening Identification with the Needs of Others

Democracy's success also depends on linking citizens across boundaries of social and economic differences so that they can understand one another and arrive at some notion of the common good. This relates to Tocqueville's emphasis on the importance of cultivating meaningful relationships through voluntary association. It also extends our understanding of these relationships to connections among individuals beyond the group, connecting to theories of social capital and social ethics.[34] Thus another aspect of democratizing voluntarism is the degree to which it might provide opportunities for individuals to identify with others, especially people different from themselves. The degree to which individuals identify with others through giving circles is examined below by looking at how members relate to each other, to nonprofit professionals in funded (or potentially funded) organizations, and to individuals in need or clients who are served by nonprofit funding recipients.

Identification with Other Giving Circle Members

Examining the identification giving circle members have with one another is important because it gives some indication of the level of bonding or bridging taking place within giving circles. Putnam explains that *bonding* social capital is inward looking and tends to reinforce exclusive identities and homogeneous groups, whereas *bridging* social capital is outward looking and encompasses people across diverse social cleavages.[35] The data from interviews and documentation suggest that a good deal of bonding takes place *within* giving circles. For example, one member of a small group giving circle described how she has "gotten to see a more compassionate side of some of my coworkers that I hadn't known existed before. So I guess it has helped me develop a more well-rounded understanding of certain individuals."[36] Women in particular, who spoke of bonding with their group, saw this as valuable in its own right but also discussed the need to rationalize this socialization process. Some talked about the "excuse" that the giving circle gave them and others to be social and to take time out for themselves while helping others in need. In other words, the giving circle allowed them not to feel guilty about socializing or bonding with others in the group because they were also "doing something good" while they were meeting.

Sometimes the bonding or socializing in the group can take over its charitable aspect. For instance, a philanthropic professional and member of a small group giving circle said:

> It's amazing how fast the group has bonded. We all have commented on that. Some of the people knew one another quite well, and others only knew a couple of people. It took us about two meetings, I would say, at most three, and everybody was just like, I don't know if we're even going to have time to hear about the charity because there was just wonderful synergy that happened.[37]

Other members, especially those in formal organizations, also commented on the social aspects of the group, but they seemed to have a much more instrumental view of its importance: seeing it as a means for networking to enable peer learning, fostering collaboration, and creating positive outcomes in the community. According to a philanthropic professional affiliated with Social Venture Partners (SVP):

> Through the power of this network, and the power of our connections, and the power of our convictions, and we're not going to dictate what those convictions are, we are helping to organically get people connected who are driven to make a difference and who don't want to be on the other end of the faucet just getting the drips but who really want to understand why the plumbing leaks all the time.[38]

Conversely, a study of SVP Seattle found that many of the partners interviewed felt little affinity for other members and felt more affinity with the nonprofit professionals they worked with as volunteers.[39] This may be because formal organization giving circles like SVP put less emphasis on the social aspect of the giving circle and more on education and volunteering.

The bonding that seems to occur in many giving circles is important for building community in the group and pockets of community in larger society. Even though some members were often already friends and colleagues before the giving circle was created, there were also many members who met for the first time through the giving circle. As far as Putnam is concerned, in his analysis of social capital, this is a positive thing. The giving circle can provide members who are new to the community with an opportunity to meet people and connect to the wider community. For example, the Arizona Five Arts Circle provides opportunities, through the arts, for individuals new to the area to socialize and meet people with similar backgrounds. Whether or not this is good for democracy in its full or substantive sense is another matter discussed in more depth in the next chapter.

Identification with Nonprofit Professionals

Giving circle members are also making new connections directly with nonprofit professionals. This takes place within the giving circle because several nonprofit professionals participate in giving circles as members, as well as through interactions between giving circle members and nonprofit staff who head organizations funded by the giving circle. In the latter case, interactions with nonprofit professionals take place through site visits, guest speaking or presentations at meetings, or informal meetings over lunch; at receptions or events; or when a giving circle member volunteers with a nonprofit organization. Some giving circle members also work directly with nonprofit professionals as they create proposals to submit to the giving circle for funding. Through these encounters, giving circle members become networked into the nonprofit and philanthropic sector to a degree open only to major donors previously and in what appears to typically be a more hands-on fashion. Giving circle members see this as a substantial benefit. Indeed, for some members, their connection with the nonprofit staff is greater than that within the giving circle, as in the case of SVP Seattle.[40] As one interviewee stated, in some ways giving circles serve to "break down sector worlds" by bringing together people from the nonprofit and for-profit worlds.[41]

Several of those interviewed, as well as case studies and other documents, confirmed that these new relationships seem to be changing the way that some giving circle members think about nonprofit organizations. For example, giving circle members coming from a for-profit business background, who may have started out with the idea that they could influence nonprofit organizations to be more "businesslike," soon realized that things were not so simple and straightforward in the nonprofit world as compared with the for-profit world. A member of SVP Seattle described his impressions this way:

> It is a very humbling thing to realize that these organizations play for much higher stakes than we do. We think because we deal with numbers with a lot of zeros after them that those are high stakes. But when you see some of the situations that these nonprofits face, you begin to wonder if you are a big enough person to do the job.[42]

Thus giving circle members seem to be more knowledgeable and aware of nonprofit organizations in the community because of their experiences in the giving circle. As a philanthropic professional and member of a small group giving circle put it:

> Some of the most philanthropic women in the community are in our particular giving circle, so even though they're well informed about many organizations, I'm sure they would all tell you they've learned a lot about nonprofit organizations they didn't know much about or more about the ones they did.[43]

This product of giving circle participation seems to be more prevalent in formal organizations and small groups than in loose networks, probably because in loose networks, members are connecting more directly with individuals in need than with nonprofit professionals.

Identification with Individuals in Need

The data suggest that there is relatively limited interaction taking place directly between giving circle members and clients served by nonprofit funding recipients and/or individuals in need. Especially in the case of small group and formal organization giving circles, the main interaction outside the group takes place on the administrative level between giving circle members and the nonprofit staff. Even when giving circle members volunteer with an organization, they tend to do so at a management or administrative level. There are exceptions. With Community Capital Alliance, a young leader fund, members go out of their way to find volunteer opportunities that put them in direct contact with clients served by nonprofit organizations. Some giving circle members also interact with clients during site visits or at educational meetings. The impact of these activities is not insignificant. A member of one formal organization giving circle described how participation has influenced members:

> You don't really know what it is like to be somebody who is coming out of jail and trying to reestablish their life. You don't really know what it is like to be 34 and living in poverty and struggling to find a job. But you go on a site visit and you meet these people, and it is a very different story than what you might see in the newspaper or on television.[44]

For loose networks, there is much greater direct interaction with those in need, though the interaction seems to be limited largely to that between the board or organizers of the loose network and the individuals in need—that is, except on special occasions like Christmas or Thanksgiving. Interactions take place mainly when a giving circle member delivers money or in-kind gifts directly to the person in need. This provides members with an opportunity to connect with the individuals they are helping. As one loose network member described it: "I love that idea because it puts a face to your giving, and so it means more."[45]

Another avenue through which giving circle members identify with nonprofit clients and individuals in need is through their increased awareness of issues faced by these individuals. Through the formal and informal educational processes that take place to varying degrees within giving circles, especially within small groups and formal organizations, members are exposed to issues and problems in the community. Engagement with the issues, in turn, exposes giving circle members to people and places they would not have been exposed to otherwise. This is the case for the Quality of Life Giving Circle members, who are now visiting poor neighborhoods in Baltimore and discovering that there are good things going on there.[46]

Exposure to new issues and areas seems to bring about a new awareness level for giving circle members about what is going on in the "real world." As one small group member described it:

> It is a way of feeling like, okay, I can be connected to the problem, I can be aware of it, which makes me a better citizen, and I can actually contribute to solving it. It has raised my awareness level because I just walked around dumb and happy for a long time. Not really aware of a lot of the problems in my community and the organizations that put programs on to try and help those people.[47]

Another small group member said, "I think it has helped me to get out of my own head a little bit and understand better not just my community but what it means to not be me."[48] Similarly, a loose network giving circle member said that she has a whole new perspective on things when she sees someone, such as a homeless person, walking down the street. She has a new understanding about the difficulties that person might face as well as the difficulties in helping them. As another loose network member put it: "The little bit that we do is wonderful. I mean, we feel good about it, and it is nice to see that happening. But it is just a drop in the bucket."[49]

In sum, identification is being created among giving circle members and between giving circle members and nonprofit professionals. In the latter case, this has served to expand the understanding giving circle members have of the needs of and difficulties faced by nonprofit organizations. There seems to be less contact between giving circle members and individuals in need, except perhaps between leaders of loose networks and individual gift recipients. However, identification does seem to be created between giving circle members and individuals in need through the members' increased knowledge and awareness about issues and problems faced by these individuals in the community.

Expanding Who Benefits from Voluntarism

The final area to examine in the context of creating a more democratic voluntarism is the need to expand who benefits from voluntary action. This is important because a more equitable distribution of resources may help in creating an environment more conducive to a full or substantive democracy: in which disparities are not so great and enable individuals to understand one another. A full democracy depends not just on procedural fairness but also on fairness in outcomes. The degree to which giving circles expand who benefits from voluntarism is examined below in relation to types of funding recipients, areas of support, and the impact on individual members' giving and volunteering.

Types of Funding Recipients

Funding smaller grassroots organizations may indicate a desire by giving circles members for a more equitable distribution of funds and support for local self-help initiatives essential to democratic self-governance. Giving circles give to nonprofit organizations, individuals doing good work (who are not affiliated with a particular nonprofit), and individuals in need. Formal organizations and small groups primarily give to and volunteer at nonprofit organizations, and these organizations tend to be small and locally based. However, rather than explicitly supporting grassroots self-governance, giving circles give to small organizations because, according to those interviewed, they want to have a bigger impact with their resources. Additionally, a focus on funding local organizations is preferred because members want to see for themselves what is going on and do some good in their own communities.

The organizations funded by giving circles are described by members as high risk and entrepreneurial, well run with strong leadership, or a mixture of both. For example, the Chicago Young Leader Fund looks for "innovative and entrepreneurial nonprofits flying under the radar of larger foundations. The nonprofits must be less than five years old, have a maximum operating budget of $250,000, and receive no major funding from organizations like the United Way."[50] At the other extreme, the Everychild Foundation, a formal organization women's giving circle, requires that applicants for funding be acknowledged leaders in their field and have a "documented history of successfully implementing major projects and properly administering large grants."[51] Combining both strategies, formal organizations like the Hestia Fund and SVP seem to have a "mixed portfolio" approach to their funding. According to one SVP member:

> Where other groups might be reluctant to fund some of these high-risk ideas, a group like ours can invest. But we also invest in some blue chips in the community—solid, reputable organizations that have been in the community for years, but who may have new ideas or programs that they are hoping to launch. We look for a mix of investments: some smaller, riskier ideas, coupled with organizations that have a proven track record of success.[52]

For those giving circles that feature direct engagement with nonprofit organizations, in particular SVP, an important criterion in selecting funding recipients is also the ability of the organization to utilize the expertise of the giving circle members.

Loose networks also give to nonprofit organizations but just as or more often their funding recipients are individuals who either are doing good work or are in need of direct assistance. There are several examples in which Bread for the Journey chapters have given people money to implement good ideas: like the high school student rebuilding computers for foster children, the retired man who makes stained-glass angels in his garage and takes them to children's hospitals, and the teacher who created an organic garden to educate her students. As a Bread for the Journey member described it, they mostly fund "individuals who want to do something. They are the ones who don't have all the big ways to raise funds and get money. They just have an idea." If they fund an organization, they do as much as they can to ensure that *all* of the money goes to an individual or club within the organization. According to the same Bread for the Journey member, recalling a children's program, "It took us months to figure out how to give money to just this one little club, this one little department, because we were supposed to write it to the recreation department, but we wanted to be sure that it went right to them. So we had to do all this stuff to make sure it got there instead of to the whole city."[53]

There is also at least one formal organization—a young leader fund—that gives money directly to individuals doing good work. The B'More Fund gives money to "individuals who, through their work, enrich the lives of Baltimore's residents."[54] Womenade gives directly to individuals in need. They give Christmas gifts, Thanksgiving dinners, diapers, gift cards, checks for rent or utility bills, furniture, cars, and so on. These individuals are identified through giving circle member referrals and newspaper stories or through working with nonprofit organizations such as homeless shelters and emergency clinics.

Finding funding and volunteer opportunities can be a struggle for all types of giving circles. Small groups like Shared Giving have had difficulty finding the "best" organizations that have a real need for their help. Part of the difficulty of finding appropriate funding recipients, according to several of those interviewed, is due to members' lack of capacity to search for small organizations. Jovanovic, Carlone, and Massood also found that members of young leader funds lamented the lack of time available to do all the investigative work to find the right organizations to fund.[55] Another problem is that the nonprofit organizations that giving circle members approach about funding frequently do not seem ready for the help. For example, one SVP affiliate was unable to persuade nonprofit organizations to even apply for funding. A member described their experience this way:

> In that year, since it was our first, we did invite applications. We designated a list of about sixty early childhood centers. The invitation said we're a new grant maker and we will be dispersing between $30,000 and $50,000 for general operating support; come find out about it. And two people said they would come. I had our investment committee call the other fifty-eight, and some of the organizations hung up on them! This is one of the biggest lessons learned. We can bring in all kinds of great things to our centers—programs, fieldtrips, computers. But unless we have the staff to back it up and implement it all, we might as well not bother.[56]

Loose networks have also struggled to make nonprofit organizations understand their intentions, as in the case of the Womenade in Nixa, Missouri. It found several nonprofit organizations "less than enthusiastic about the Womenade idea" when they approached them to give away the money they had raised.[57] Another Womenade group had a hard time at first persuading local nonprofit organizations to help connect them with people in need because the nonprofit organization did not understand that they wanted to *give* money away rather than get something from the organization. Similarly, a member of a young leader fund commented on the difficulty they have each year finding substantive volunteer experiences for members.

Nonprofit professionals, for their part, admit that the giving circle model focused on high engagement is not always a great fit for their organization. For instance, sometimes organizations might be in a stage when they do not need volunteers. According to one executive director who leads an organization that has been funded by two formal organization giving circles:

> I would discourage giving circles from saying, "Okay, we're going to give money, *and* we're going to get involved." I think they should say, "We're going to give money and get involved if that's what the nonprofit needs." You know, like in our history there have been times when we really needed volunteers, like in the beginning, and now we are up and running, and we don't really use volunteers for much of anything because we would prefer not to do it that way.[58]

Based on the evidence above, giving circles seem to be expanding who benefits in comparison with traditional voluntarism in several ways. The focus on giving to and volunteering at smaller organizations certainly goes against the grain of traditional philanthropy. As noted earlier, though representing 80 percent of charitable institutions, smaller organizations with budgets under $2 million typically receive the least amount of private funding, and the largest charitable gifts—those of $1 million or more—tend to go to the wealthiest organizations.[59] Loose network giving circles also give to individuals in need or doing good work, which is unusual for today's organized philanthropy, although it appears that giving circles that want to give directly to individuals face some difficulties in doing so. In both cases, giving to smaller organizations and to individuals implies that giving circles support local and individual grassroots governance and empowerment, even if unintentionally.

Where Giving Circles Provide Resources

Giving circles give in a wide range of areas. The most popular groups, based on 2005 data for 114 giving circles, appear to be children/youth and women/girls. In addition, data from a study completed in 2006, focusing on nonprofit organization funding recipients, show that giving circles made about 40 percent of total number of grants to human service organizations and over 50 percent of the amount of total funding to education-related organizations (see table 5.2).[60] There was not enough data to analyze where giving circle members volunteer.

It is difficult to find data on areas of funding, and because many giving circles, especially formal organizations, give or volunteer in more than one

Table 5.2 Giving circle nonprofit funding recipients by field, 1996–2005

	Education	Human services	Arts and culture	Public benefit	Environment and animals	Health	International	Religion
# Grants (N=1,288)	237	518	176	139	50	100	46	22
% Total grants	18.4%	40.2%	13.7%	10.8%	3.9%	7.7%	3.6%	1.7%
$ Received (N=28,406,948)	15,692,772	7,446,769	2,663,939	876,934	562,284	566,098	328,965	269,187
% Total $	55.3%	26.2%	9.4%	3.1%	2.0%	1.9%	1.2%	1.0%

funding area, it is difficult to compare types of giving circles. However, a few observations can be made. Children/youth and education seem to be the most popular areas of funding for formal organizations. It appears that formal organizations are also the most likely types of giving circles to volunteer with an organization that they fund, so we can assume that they volunteer for the most part in these areas as well. In addition, most targeted giving to identity groups (such as women, African Americans, etc.) appears to be done by formal organizations, which by far include most of the giving circles made up of these same identity groups. In other words, when a group is formed around a certain identity, they tend to fund (and volunteer) in relation to that identity group. For example, women's giving circles tend to provide funding to women/girls, and African American giving circles tend to give to the African American community. It is no surprise as well that children/youth receive a good deal of attention from giving circles, since giving circle members tend to be younger, most likely at a stage in their life where they have younger children at home and so have greater connection to and awareness of this group.

However, it should also be noted that these giving and volunteering patterns are not universal for all giving circles. Loose networks, which are overwhelmingly female, tend to *not* focus on giving only to women and girls' issues, although they do help many women. The largest area of funding for these giving circles, primarily because of the focus of most Womenade groups, is for emergency relief such as paying utility bills, providing money for food, and the like. Women, men, and children benefit from this funding. In addition, some groups do not specifically target identity groups but do give to these groups. For example, Shared Giving's focus is on social justice issues, but it has funded a women's domestic violence center and a Latino resource center.

How do these areas of support measure up to trends for other private giving and volunteering? The funding (and volunteering) patterns of giving circles indicate on the one hand that groups not typically funded by traditional philanthropy or most attractive to volunteers are being resourced by giving circles: such as women/girls or organizations serving nonwhites (thus expanding who benefits). Private giving overall—which includes giving by individuals, corporations, and foundations—went predominantly to religion (36 percent), education (15 percent), human services (10 percent), and health (9 percent) in 2005.[61] Thus, if comparing giving circles with all private giving, which is dominated by individual contributions (over 80 percent), the main similarity is a shared interest in education and human services, though giving circles seem to focus more on each of these two areas. The most noticeable difference is that most giving circles tend to *not* fund religious or health-related organizations.[62] As for volunteering, data from the Corporation for National and Community Service showed that in 2006, people volunteered mainly in the areas of religion (35.3 percent), educational or youth services (27 percent), and social and community service (13.1 percent).[63] If we assume that areas of volunteering are similar to areas of giving for most giving circles, and that formal organizations produce the majority of volunteers, then giving circle members are most likely to volunteer in the areas of children/youth, women/girls, and education, not in the area of religion.

Because more detailed data are available, a comparison can also be made between foundation and giving circle funding areas. Foundation giving represents approximately 8 percent of all private giving.[64] In 2004, foundations funded (as a percentage of total dollars predominantly in the areas of education (23 percent), health (23 percent), human services (14 percent), public affairs/ society benefit (11 percent), and arts and culture (12 percent). Religion received only 2 percent of total foundation dollars. Regarding particular populations, foundations gave, as a percent of total dollars in 2006, to the economically disadvantaged (15.7 percent), children and youth (18.1 percent), ethnic or racial minorities (8.2 percent), and women and girls (6.4 percent).[65] Thus it appears that giving circles and foundations share many similarities in funding distribution, especially in the areas of education and human services. There are also similarities in funding the economically disadvantaged and minority groups. The major difference seems to be giving circles' greater emphasis on funding children/youth and women/girls.

Based on the evidence above, we can conclude that giving circles do seem to be expanding, at least to some degree, who and what groups benefit from giving and volunteering. But these patterns also indicate that people do tend to give to whom and to what they know and with which they are familiar. Identity-based giving circles are not always expanding giving beyond the direct familiarity of the membership.

Effects on Members' Giving

Giving circle members do appear to be giving to new organizations and issue areas because of their participation in a giving circle. This was a frequent theme that emerged in interviews, case studies, and other documentation and seemed to be true for all types of giving circles. Giving circle members say they have a new awareness of issues and organizations because of the giving circle. For example, according to a small group member when asked if they have changed where they give since being in the giving circle: "Yes, definitely. I give to a broader set of organizations now because I've learned about some of them only through the giving circle. I think that everybody in the room when we meet is broadened."[66] Several members of Shared Giving brought up how they learned about and were forced to think about issue areas they would not have otherwise thought much about if not for the giving circle, such as domestic violence, seniors and prescription drugs, K–12 education and at-risk youth, and early childhood education. These were issues that members did not know much about before their participation in the giving circle.

Due to this exposure, members seem to be redirecting or increasing their personal giving, beyond the giving circle, to organizations they were introduced to through the giving circle. For instance, according to a case study done for SVP Seattle, at least forty of the approximately seventy partners who worked with the nonprofit investees examined in the capacity building part of the study also made individual donations to those nonprofits.[67] A philanthropic professional working with SVP affiliates also noted:

> I've heard repeatedly in talking with partners that they've given money outside of SVP to nonprofits that SVP funded because there is no way that they would have ever heard about them or had the deep enriching experience of working with them unless SVP had introduced them to them. It is kind of a matchmaker of sorts.[68]

Silicon Valley Social Venture Fund (SV2) found as well that when it asked its members how much they gave to organizations beyond what was given through the giving circle, it was $450,000 beyond the $125,000 made in grants by SV2.[69]

SVP-type organizations are not the only giving circles where this is taking place. Contributing time and money beyond the giving circle was also noted by members of formal organizations such as the Hestia Fund, Baltimore Women's Giving Circle, the Everychild Foundation, Quality of Life Giving Circle, and Arizona Five Arts Circle; small groups such as the Sacramento Women's Action Network and Shared Giving; and loose networks such as Womenade. Some members have even been inspired to create new organizations, including charities and giving circles, or changed careers to work in nonprofit organizations because of their giving circle experience. Nonprofit professionals noted as well that they have received substantial (and often ongoing) gifts from a member or members of the giving circle beyond the gift provided by the giving circle itself and recruited new volunteers and board members for their organization beyond gifts made by the giving circle.[70]

It appears that members are giving more money and in a different fashion because of their experience in the giving circle. For those who were already philanthropic, to what degree they have increased their giving is unclear, but there is a good deal of evidence to suggest that participating in a giving circle increases their level of giving and their commitment to giving. For example, a recent study of twelve SVP affiliates found that nearly 75 percent of survey respondents indicated that their total giving increased after joining SVP.[71] For some, although they were philanthropic before, the giving circle minimum fee forced them to stretch beyond what they were used to. As one member of a young leader fund put it: "It seems like in the beginning $250 seems like so much money to give away, but once you get used to it, what we're seeing is average member contributions go up as you become part of this group."[72] In addition, some members end up increasing their giving because of exposure to new organizations and issues—they give in these areas as well as to the areas they had given to before. This coincides with the literature showing that people who are more engaged tend to give more money.[73] That is, when people are able to build a significant relationship with a cause or organization, they will increase their giving.

Beyond the amount, the giving circle may influence to an even larger degree *how* members give their money. Members say they are more informed and thoughtful about their giving because of the giving circle; they are more interested in knowing where their gift is going—either through the giving circle or beyond the giving circle—and what it is used for. This seems to be the case across the different types of giving circles. For example, according to a member of the Hestia Fund, a formal organization:

> I know just in my case that I take this money much more personally, because I feel so involved in where it's going, whereas if I write a check to an art museum, I'm not nearly as clear about what that money is going to be used for. I understand why I'm giving it, but I'm not as linked to where it's going.[74]

A small group giving circle member said:

> I think it has influenced me to ask tougher questions about the outfits that I give to, and that is a good thing. To ask, well, how much of my dollar really goes to support the thing that you say you are doing rather than more fundraising? I was loose about that before.[75]

Members also seem to be more focused and strategic in their giving. Because they begin to see their giving in the context of issues and needs in the community, in which they want to have some impact, their donations are more targeted. Thus members say they give fewer but larger gifts. As one small group member interviewed said, "We are through writing $25 checks" in response to direct mail.[76] Or, according to a philanthropic professional affiliated with SVP:

> As a result of engagement with SVP, people not only give smarter, they give more. Smarter as in they are more focused, which means they might give bigger checks to fewer nonprofits and they are giving in such a way that they are more satisfied with their philanthropy. They don't feel scattered. They feel like they are making a difference. They feel like they are giving to the causes that matter to them.[77]

This is supported by survey evidence showing that across a dozen SVP affiliates, members increase their strategic giving practices in several areas.[78] This impact on members seems to exist predominantly in small groups and formal organizations, but less so or not at all in loose networks. In fact, one member of a loose network commented that she is now *more* likely to respond to direct mail from a homeless shelter because she has a much greater awareness of the needs in the community.[79]

We may be able to conclude from the data that giving circle members are expanding the amount that they give and the variety of organizations to which they give their time and money because of their experience in the giving circle. They are also more thoughtful and strategic about these gifts of time and money and have a greater awareness about needs in the community. What is still a bit unclear is the degree to which members give beyond their own familiarities. Loose networks may do the most to stretch members in this area, while small groups and formal organizations may do the most to increase the level and strategic intention of this giving.

Conclusion

This chapter has examined the potential democratic effects of giving circles and the degree to which they might serve to counter some of the anti-democratic aspects of voluntarism as well as ameliorate some of the negative effects of modernization, that is, the degree to which giving circles serve to democratize voluntarism. Given the above analysis, what do giving circles reveal about the ability for voluntary associations and philanthropy to enhance the capacities of citizens to contribute to the civic education and participation of members while also meeting social needs and solving community problems in an environment of governance beyond the state? This question is addressed in the next and final chapter.

6 Voluntarism and Governing beyond the State

In this final chapter, I discuss themes and conclusions, based on evidence from the giving circle context, about the role of voluntarism in a democratic society. Beyond attempting to portray the dimensions of the giving circle landscape, this book has also been concerned with broad-based questions about the role of philanthropy and voluntary association in democratic society. As with many voluntary associations, giving circles can serve two needs that are not necessarily mutually exclusive but are not always in alignment either. One is serving the needs of members—for camaraderie, education about the philanthropic process and issues in the community, or ease of use—and the other is meeting the needs of the larger community, including supporting nonprofits and their clients or individuals in need or doing good work. As internally democratic groups, giving circles can do much to enhance the civic education and participation of members, thus countering some of the negative aspects of voluntarism, including the effects of modernization. They can also expose members to issues and areas outside of their typical frame of reference, bring more diverse groups to the philanthropic table, and influence members to be more strategic and committed, thus helping to overcome some of the antidemocratic aspects of voluntarism, such as a narrow and short-term foci, elite hegemony, and asymmetry in the philanthropic relationship. However, giving circles do not seem to have the ability, even among the largest and most organized, to fully counter issues of fragmentation and provide for the adequate redistribution of resources to places where they are most needed. This seems to be emblematic of voluntary associations generally, which leads to the conclusion that, although voluntarism contributes much to civic engagement and enhancing the quality of life, it cannot adequately provide for basic, ongoing needs in society. I conclude the chapter with a discussion of implications for philanthropic and nonprofit professionals and public policy.

A Recap of What We Know about Giving Circles

The previous two chapters have shown that giving circles involve individuals pooling money and other resources and then deciding together where to give these away. Through regular meetings and events, giving circles frequently serve to educate members about community issues, engage members in voluntary efforts, provide social opportunities, and maintain donor independence from any particular charity. Three "ideal" types of giving circles were identified through an examination of the giving circle landscape. These include small groups, loose networks, and formal organizations.

Small groups pool their funds to give to worthy causes. Because the group is small, leadership is frequently shared, and all are able to participate in the agenda-setting and decision-making processes. The major focus seems to be on informal social and educational activities; there is less emphasis on engagement with funding recipients. These groups often begin as groups of friends who use the giving circle as an opportunity to socialize while doing good.

Loose networks are typically run by a core group that does the organizing and makes grant decisions while others, who may or may not consider themselves to be members, participate intermittently, usually attending special events like potluck dinners or social gatherings. Their meetings tend to be more social than educational. Individual participants can make funding recommendations to the core group, but typically they do not make funding decisions or otherwise interact with funding recipients. Members praise these groups for their flexibility and organic, nonbureaucratic nature. Unlike the other types of giving circles, these groups give a good deal of their resources to individuals rather than to organizations. Loose networks are especially attractive to women, who see the group as an opportunity to fit "doing good" into their busy lives.

Formal organizations are larger and more formal in their structure and decision-making processes than the other two types of giving circles. They look very much like a traditional voluntary organization structure with a board, committees, often professional staff support, and a core membership. The membership size of formal organizations tends to be larger, and the cost to join is higher than the other types of giving circles. The grant-making process is also more formalized than in the other giving circles. It typically involves committees or investment teams making grant decisions directly or making recommendations to the membership, who then vote on these recommendations for funding. Within the committees themselves, there is often much deliberation, but outside of the committees, member votes, if taken, are often a formality. The focus is on education and engagement. Nearly all formal organizations have some formal educational programming in addition to grant making and informal educational opportunities, and about half provide opportunities for members to volunteer with nonprofit organizations, especially with funding recipients. In most cases, members volunteer their expertise at the administrative level rather than through direct service.

Giving circles are attractive to various types of donors. Those who participate are overwhelmingly young and white and predominately from professional or upper-middle-class backgrounds. Giving circles are also growing in popularity among other racial and ethnic communities and other identity groups. They attract people who are somewhat new to philanthropy (or at least the giving side of voluntarism and traditional organized philanthropy), and they tend to attract like-minded individuals with shared backgrounds, so there is often little diversity within these groups. This is significant for considering the degree to which giving circles create identification between giving circle members and the needs of others. Identification with others is certainly being created *among* giving circle members as well as between members and nonprofit professionals.

In the latter case, this has served to expand members' understanding of the needs of nonprofit organizations. Identification with others in need is more tenuous. There seems to be little contact, except for leaders of loose networks, between giving circle members and individuals in need; however, identification does seem to be created between giving circle members and individuals in need through the members' increased knowledge and awareness about issues and problems in the community.

Opportunities for democratic participation within giving circles are substantial but the form varies for different types of giving circles. For small groups, everyone seems to be involved in deliberation, decision-making and capacity building activities. In formal organizations and loose networks, because of the size and structure of the groups, members can choose to opt in or out of these activities. Formal organizations are the most systematic and comprehensive in efforts to educate and engage members with others in the community while loose networks seem to do the most to empower individuals and connect members more directly to individuals in need, even if only for the most part through the organization's leadership.

Giving circles are also funding the types of organizations that are not typically funded by traditional philanthropy: small, locally based grassroots organizations. They are also funding individuals doing good work and individuals in need directly, thereby attempting to bypass the organized voluntary infrastructure completely. The areas funded by giving circles also seem to be somewhat different from mainstream philanthropy. If comparing giving circles to all private giving, the main similarity is a shared interest in education and human services, though giving circles seem to focus more on these than other areas. Giving circles and foundations also share many similarities in what they fund, especially in the areas of education and human services. There are also similarities in funding the economically disadvantaged and minority (nonwhite) groups. The major difference seems to be giving circles' greater emphasis on funding children/youth and women/girls. Identity-based giving circles tend to fund in areas that match their identity focus. Perhaps most important, giving circle members appear to be exposed to and giving to new organizations and issue areas because of their participation in the giving circle, and they seem to be giving more and in a more strategic fashion.

The data suggest, then, that giving circles do democratize voluntarism to varying degrees depending on their size and structure and primary activities. For example, what seems to be most advantageous about small group giving circles is their small size. This allows for everyone to participate in agenda setting, deliberation, and decision making. It also allows for an intimacy—or bonding—to take place among members to a degree that may not be possible within other types of giving circles. However, their small size and informality may prevent them from becoming systematic about identifying needs in the community and finding appropriate funding opportunities. Small groups also seem to have less direct engagement with individuals in need.

At the base of the loose network giving circle is a sense of empowerment—

doing something on one's own and doing it outside of the bureaucracy or traditional power structure—especially for women. What is also special about these types of giving circles is their focus on helping individuals outside of the typical nonprofit institutional structure. Yet loose networks frequently have weak ties among members, who only participate intermittently in events or respond to fundraising appeals. That is, except for the leaders of the group, who in many ways become a small group within a larger network setting, there is much less participation among members in agenda setting, deliberation, and decision making. There is also less emphasis on educating members about needs in the community, as compared with small groups and formal organizations (except perhaps through an informal sharing of stories). The focus, rather, is on discovering and responding to the needs of individuals and socializing with (new and old) friends. There is no systematic scan of what the needs in the community are or systematic discussion of how best to address these. Rather, giving is done in an ad hoc fashion to individuals who are in need or doing good work. Some members also seem to see their giving through the group as an alternative to volunteering, so there may be little engagement beyond that with the individual in need or doing good work.

Formal organizations are much more structured than the other types of giving circles—and more bureaucratic. Compared with small groups and loose networks, formal organizations seem to look and act the most like traditional funding models. Members do not seem to enjoy the equal participation and intimacy of a small group and the informal, nonbureaucratic structure of the loose network. On the other hand, formal organizations are the most systematic about identifying needs in the community, educating members about these needs, finding appropriate funding recipients, and enabling members to engage directly with recipients. They also seem to be the most dedicated to attracting diverse populations to participate.

In summary, giving circles generally seem to do much to democratize voluntarism. However, if one looks deeper, it becomes apparent that each type of giving circle has its strengths and weaknesses regarding internal and external democratization. Small groups seem to do the most for creating equal opportunities for democratic participation for members; loose networks provide the most opportunities for broadening identification through direct, one-on-one contact between giving circle members and others in need and empowering members; and formal organizations seem to have the most impact on educating members about problems in the community and distributing resources where they appear to be needed the most.

Giving Circles and Degrees of Democratization

Giving circles have emerged at the nexus of several important social, political, and economic trends that have led to shifts in voluntarism and the way people relate to community in the midst of government cutbacks, devolution, and privatization, which coincide with a drive to increasingly rely on voluntary institutions to address community needs. I set out in this book to answer these two questions in this context: (1) In what ways do giving circles contribute to the civic education and participation of members? and (2) What do giving circles reveal about the capacity of voluntary associations and philanthropy to meet social needs and solve community problems in an environment of governance beyond the state? Answering these questions enables us to also consider what role voluntarism can or should play in a democratic society.

Do giving circles contribute to the civic education and participation of members? The answer to this question is clearly "yes," as indicated by the data discussed in earlier chapters, but it is useful to qualify this "yes" in the context of modernization and the changing nature of voluntary action in the United States. As discussed in chapter 3, people seem to be changing the ways in which they want to, or have to, participate in their community in the context of a shift to a posttraditional society. Beck describes our society today as increasingly characterized by the dissolution of traditional parameters and a differentiation of lifestyles.[1] It is a social transformation from collectivistic to individualistic and institutionalized to self-organized.[2] Part of the reaction by individuals to this shift has been to seek out more engagement in community, but in ways that match their personal interests, that they can control, and in the context of their hectic lives. In this context, voluntarism may be appealing to individuals "suspended in [the] glorious, but terrifying isolation" of a posttraditional society because it promises a kind of nostalgic community.[3]

These changes in society are reflected in newer forms of association and organization—different from traditional voluntary associations—that seem to bring about different democratic effects than those envisioned by Tocqueville and others. Some of these associations are more informal in nature, consisting of few institutional links transcending the local level, no clear center of authority, and limited, project-oriented objectives. Giving circles seem to fall very much in this category. Like informal associations that are small in scale and more grassroots in nature, they appear to encourage more people to become involved in the community in a meaningful way, but also in a new way that is more episodic or objectives-focused or both. Small group, loose network, and even formal organization giving circles act as an alternative to mainstream or traditional bureaucratic voluntary organizations, especially attracting younger and female participants, thus bringing more diversity to voluntarism generally.

Giving circles offer an alternative experience to community interaction that is different from that offered (or not offered) by large-scale modern, bureaucratic institutions, one that *does* seem to be more connected to grassroots civic action and more collectivist and democratic in structure and processes. Comparing each giving circle type with Rothschild-Whitt's ideal typical dimensions of collectivist-democratic organizations shows this to be the case (see table 6.1).[4] The collectivist-democratic model is premised on the logic of value or substantive rationality rather than formal instrumental rationality as is the case with bureaucratic organizations (discussed in chapter 2). Substantive rationality emphasizes values or substantive goals such as peace, equality or de-

Table 6.1 Comparison of the dimensions of giving circle ideal types with Rothschild-Whitt's (1979) ideal typical dimensions of collectivist-democratic organizations

Dimension	Collectivist-democratic organizations	Small group giving circles	Loose network giving circles	Formal organization giving circles
Authority	Resides in collective as a whole; delegated, if at all, only temporarily; consensus decision making	Resides in collective as a whole; consensus decision making	Resides with core group of leaders; consensus decision making within core group	Resides with volunteer or elected lead group and/or committees; consensus decision making or vote within these groups
Rules	Minimal stipulated rules; operations and decisions conducted in ad hoc manner	Minimal to no rules; decisions made on case-by-case basis	Minimal to no rules; decisions made on case-by-case basis	Few stipulated rules; established process for decision making
Social control	Primarily based on personal or moral appeals and the selection of homogeneous personnel	Personal and moral appeals; voluntary membership; largely homogeneous membership	Personal and moral appeals; voluntary membership; largely homogeneous membership	Personal and moral appeals; voluntary membership; largely homogeneous membership
Social relations	Ideal of community; relations holistic, affective, and of value in themselves (even leading to goal displacement)	Community building key aspect of group; heavy focus on social relations	Empowerment key aspect of group; heavy focus on social relations	Networking key aspect of group; some focus on social relations, especially with nonprofit funding recipients

Recruitment and advancement	Employment based on friends, social-political values, personality attributes, and informally assessed knowledge and skills	Work is voluntary; paid staff, if any, on loan to group	Work is voluntary	Work is mostly voluntary; paid staff, if any, on loan to group or usually hired based on formal criteria
Incentive structure	Normative and solidarity incentives are primary; material incentives secondary	Normative incentives; few or no material incentives	Normative incentives; few or no material incentives	Normative incentives; few or no material incentives
Social stratification	Egalitarian; reward differentials, if any, are strictly limited by the collectivity	Egalitarian	Largely egalitarian; core group has more influence	Largely egalitarian; lead group and committee members have more influence
Differentiation	Minimal division of labor; demystify expertise	Minimal to no division of labor; role rotation and task sharing	Core group stays in leadership position; task sharing	Leadership roles rotated based on volunteer availability; task sharing

mocracy rather than instrumental activity, formal laws, and procedural regularity, as is the case with formal rationality.[5] While Rothschild-Whitt's focus was on work rather than voluntary organizations, the model is useful for understanding the democratic contributions of giving circles. As table 6.1 indicates, small groups seem to come closest to a collectivist-democratic organization, while formal organizations are farthest away, yet they share similarities with collectivist-democratic organizations.

As evidence of this alternative avenue for involvement, giving circle members frequently noted their desire to be more engaged with community issues, but in their own way and outside of the bureaucratic structure of traditional philanthropy and voluntary association. This is similar to the reasons members interviewed by Wuthnow say they are attracted to support groups or the Everyday Maker's new way of participating in civic affairs, which is directed toward concrete problem solving in everyday life rather than membership that is full time and for life.[6] At the same time, however, many giving circle members said that their giving circle offered a relatively *easy* way to participate in voluntarism. Many women saw the giving circle as a way to fit "doing good" into their busy lives. Like Wuthnow's findings with support groups, giving circles seem to be based on weak obligations to others in the group and community, that is, a form of community that is obtained at relatively little social or personal cost.[7]

Nonetheless, giving circle members seem to be motivated to go beyond passive consumption and private concerns to create a new civic space where debate and deliberation are generally encouraged, especially during the grant making process. Members also learn about and discuss important social and political issues (but usually not personally controversial issues like abortion or gun control). In this regard then, giving circles share similarities to Fung's minipublics in their frequent encouragement of deliberative discussion among members.[8] This is especially the case for formal organization giving circles that very consciously help members create informed opinions about public or community issues and also implement action (through funding and volunteering) to address these issues. Alternatively, Wuthnow found that support groups tend to discourage debate or criticism of others' opinions and explicitly rule out discussions of social and political issues.[9]

One of the shortcomings of giving circles may be the limited degree to which their work is explicitly tied to political actions and outcomes and thus to larger social change efforts. Giving circles generally do not extend their work into the political or advocacy arena. There seem to be only a handful of giving circles that specifically conduct advocacy efforts beyond providing resources to organizations or individuals. Only one giving circle included in the study sought to influence public policy related to early childhood development for low-income children. It is less clear what impact participation in giving circles has on members' political or civic actions. In a study of young leader funds, Jovanovic, Carolone, and Massood found that several members saw their participation in the giving circle as their "principal political outlet."[10] There is yet little information or evidence about how the effects of participating in giving circles extend beyond voluntarism into the voting booth and to other political acts. Indeed, it may be that giving circles, as a kind of self-help/mutual aid group, provide members with an avenue for *avoiding* direct political participation. Giving circle members may see their actions through the giving circle as their act of good citizenship as well as an opportunity to support the community outside of the bureaucratic structure of government or organized philanthropic institutions. This is an area in need of further investigation.

Who participates in giving circles may also be problematic in the context of democratic effects. Giving circles do seem to be attractive to women and relatively younger individuals who have not participated as much in the giving side of traditional organized voluntarism. However, it appears that, even though a greater number of racial, ethnic, and other identity-based giving circles are emerging, their numbers are still small. Giving circles are also limited in diversity *within* groups: homogeneous in their race/ethnicity and perhaps less so but still homogenous in their socioeconomic levels, and these characteristics seem to exist for all types of giving circles. This is not surprising. For example, research has already shown that people in higher status occupations are typically more active in voluntary associations, and active membership in voluntary associations is often positively correlated with income and educational and occupational status levels.[11] These findings also coincide with McPherson and Smith-Lovin's assertions that homogeneity tends to occur generally in voluntary associations.[12] Rothschild-Whitt also found that collectivist-democratic organizations "may require from the outset substantial homogeneity" to be created and then sustained.[13] In this regard, then, giving circles are not very different from many voluntary associations that entrench social and cultural differences rather than bridge them.[14]

Given the homogeneous nature of these groups, it is not clear if there is more *bonding* among members or *bridging* between members and individuals in need taking place. Recall that Putnam defines bonding social capital as inward looking and tends to reinforce exclusive identities within homogeneous groups, while bridging social capital is outward looking and encompasses bringing people together across diverse social cleavages.[15] There is a good deal of networking and connecting taking place within giving circles. Some giving circle members, especially women, talk about the bonding that has occurred and deepened relationships. In fact, the level of socialization among members sometimes nearly takes over the charitable aspects of the group. Such bonding probably reinforces the like-mindedness and shared identities of the groups. Contrary to Gutmann's point of view—that the more economically, ethnically, and religiously heterogeneous the membership of an association, the greater may be its capacity to cultivate public discourse and deliberation conducive to democratic citizenship—this bonding around an identity may be a way to empower individuals, particularly those who traditionally have had less say in how resources are distributed in their communities.[16] As Putnam and Feldstein note, (bonding) social capital is often higher in smaller settings because these settings enable members to get to know one another more easily and hence make listening and trusting easier—"smaller is better for forging and sustaining connections."[17] Many do see giving circles as means for networking to enable peer learning, fostering collaboration, and creating positive outcomes in the community.

Yet bridging does seem to be taking place to some degree. On the most direct level, some giving circle members, specifically those in loose networks, are increasing their identification with individuals in need through direct relief. This is reminiscent of the premodern voluntarism practiced in colonial America,[18] but with a twist: loose network members must rely on a nonprofit organization or news outlet to help them find and connect to the individuals in need. Through small groups and formal organizations, giving circle members have increased awareness of and interaction with issues faced by individuals in need. Through panels, guest speakers, site visits, or independent research, members engage with the issues and learn about the problems in the community and who is working to solve these problems. In this way, small groups and formal organizations create a new kind of mediated relationship between donors and recipient. Direct engagement or engagement with the issues has in turn exposed giving circle members to people and places they would not have been exposed to otherwise. This certainly seems to be a beneficial effect of giving circles that may serve to change members' civic and political points of view, although it is hard to say if these enlarged horizons result in an "outward-bound spiral of social bonds" and what influence it has on democratic outcomes.[19]

What is the capacity of giving circles to address underlying societal problems (rather than taking a fragmented, short-term approach to community problem solving)? This question gets at the heart of understanding the proper role of voluntarism in a democratic society, especially in a society increasingly governed beyond the state. In the United States and elsewhere we have seen a shift from an age of *government* to one of *governance,* that is, a shift from state-centered action to one of governance beyond the state. While this shift is not exactly new, it is "increasingly regarded as an effective and legitimate form of societal governance."[20] In conjunction with a move to governance beyond the state have been calls for voluntary associations to play a more central role in addressing collective problems, including implementing what were once considered *public* social welfare policies, and for private philanthropy to provide more support to social welfare organizations. Can voluntarism "replace" government in this way? Giving circles offer some evidence that it would be improbable or nearly impossible for voluntarism to do so, and even if it were possible, the case of giving circles helps us to examine if we would want voluntarism to do so anyway. Let us examine this by looking at the capacity for different types of giving circles to distribute resources and how these resources are distributed.

Formal organization giving circles probably do the most to address underlying societal problems. Generally, members in formal organizations take a systematic approach to becoming educated about an *issue area* and who is doing what within that area. They then try to focus their resources on filling gaps in a particular area (see figure 6.1). Small group members, though still attempt-

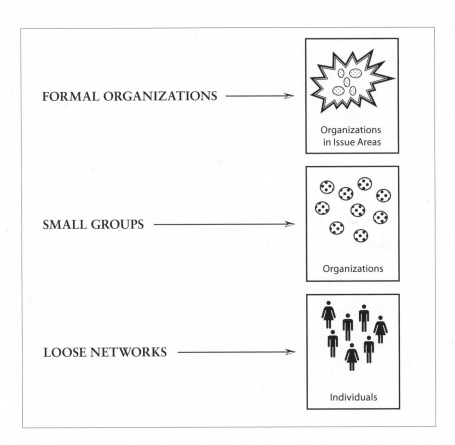

FORMAL ORGANIZATIONS ⟶ Organizations in Issue Areas

SMALL GROUPS ⟶ Organizations

LOOSE NETWORKS ⟶ Individuals

Figure 6.1. The funding focus of giving circles by type.

ing to educate themselves, are less comprehensive in trying to understand an issue area. Generally, they are more focused on *organizations* than on issues. They look closely at whatever organization happens to come across their radar screen, so to speak, and then the issues related to that organization and decide on funding based on this limited information. Finally, loose network giving circles are for the most part focused on funding *individuals*. They are generally not systematic at all about understanding issues or organizations; rather, they provide (often emergency) assistance in reaction to referrals or stories about individuals in need or doing good work.

Ultimately, while there is some degree of resource redistribution from giving circles to small grassroots organizations or individuals, it is not clear that these resources are going where they are most needed. Even for formal organizations, giving circles frequently have a difficult time finding the best areas and organizations to fund, partly because giving circles focus on giving to small, less well known, and local organizations (or to individuals). In addition, the resources that giving circles bring to bear on issues or problems amounts to only a fraction of what is likely needed. Recent research by Bearman estimates that giving circles have given more than $68 million so far; however, this is only a fraction of the $260 billion given privately in the United States in 2005 alone and an even tinier percentage of what government has spent on social welfare areas.[21] This raises important questions about the ability of giving circles, and voluntarism more generally, to meet basic needs in the community. Giving circles may be good for enhancing citizenship, but not good enough, it seems, for adequately addressing needs in the community.

The Tensions and Limits of Voluntary Action

Several conclusions and implications for civic engagement and democratic outcomes emerge from the giving circle context, which reveal some of the tensions and limits of voluntarism in a democratic society. One area to consider is the tension between bonding and bridging social capital and their democratic effects. We see a competing tension between these two—with bonding dominant in many giving circles.[22] Both are important to enhancing democracy, so it seems that the most beneficial state of this tension is to find a balance.

How might we tip the scales in favor of bridging over bonding among giving circles and other small efforts at voluntary community action, so as to combat the potential atomization and fragmentation that occurs with the creation of such independent, homogeneous groups, which are now becoming so prevalent in posttraditional society? Weisinger and Salipante argue that bonding in such groups is inevitable but could be leveraged to eventually create bridging situations.[23] For example, if one wanted to attract minority groups and preserve their comfort level without forced assimilation to the majority group, they suggest creating a sequence of bonding in small groups first and then creating opportunities for groups to mix and temporarily recategorize through engaged, structured interactions involving routine tasks. Likewise, Fung and Wright suggest a system of centralized supervision and coordination among voluntary associations, involving a form of "coordinated decentralization" for the models of governance such as the minipublics described by Fung. In this context, they suggest that local spheres of action be connected to superordinate bodies to help coordinate and distribute resources, solve problems that local units cannot address on their own, rectify pathological or incompetent decision making, and diffuse innovation and learn across boundaries.[24] Fung calls this "accountable autonomy."[25] This idea is similar to Putnam and Feldstein's suggestion to build a federation of small groups within a larger group to counter the dilemma of size and scope indicative of social capital. There have been a few efforts to create what I would call very loosely structured federations within the giving circle movement. One is Dining for Women (DFW), which has a network of chapters across the country. Chapters receive information about nonprofit organizations featured for the month and send money to the headquarters located in Greenville, South Carolina. However, there does not seem to be much interaction between the chapters, except perhaps via email and newsletter. Bread for the Journey (BFJ) also follows a federated model to some degree, where chapters are affiliated with the international office in Mill Valley, California, and send a small percentage of their funds raised each year there. These chapters do get together each year to share stories, learn to operate a neighborhood charity, and evaluate programs.[26] However, the data available on BFJ chapters suggests they are not very diverse in terms of race/ethnicity. The Community Investment Network (CIN) is a network of nine African American giving circles located mainly in the American south. It provides education and a platform for ongoing dialogue and support among these giving circles.[27] CIN also holds an annual conference each year, but because of its focus, there seems to be relatively little diversity across these groups in terms of race/ethnicity. Finally, the Giving Circles Network is a nonprofit organization that assists giving circles to better network among themselves, leverage their resources, and enhance the impact of their giving. It is a relatively new organization that has just started signing up members and will hold its first annual meeting in 2008. It is too early to tell if this group can influence its giving circle members to occasionally work together across race and class lines. This might mean creating some kind of a federated movement where homogeneous, locally based giving circles are created independently, but on occasion groups work together across race and class lines, temporarily recategorizing around specific tasks.

This may be difficult to achieve, however. The federated model is increasingly irrelevant in today's posttraditional environment. The new small-scale avenues to civic engagement and individualized lifestyle politics discussed in chapter 3 are antithetical in many ways to any kind of centralized structure. In the case of giving circles, there is a grassroots element to them that a centralized authority may not be able to force or structure as it would like. Giving circle members describe their attraction to the independent nature of the giving circle, a place where they feel empowered to act on their own and can control how things go. For those in small groups and loose networks, members want a simple, nonbureaucratic structure. Giving circle members are similar to support group members who are fed up with large-scale institutions and prefer to help themselves.[28]

Would we want some kind of federated structure or coordinated decentralization to occur even if it could be created? Fung and Wright would most likely argue "yes" in the case of reform in public agencies such as schools and police departments, and rightly so.[29] There are legal and public interest obligations that must be ensured within these public agencies. However, for private groups (that should be) beyond the pale of public authority, as with voluntary associations such as giving circles, such a goal is problematic. One of the key aspects of giving circles within the today's philanthropic environment is their independence from a higher authority. This independence, indeed, exemplifies the nature of voluntary associations so admired by Tocqueville. As Barber notes, we go to them voluntarily and join as freely associated individuals and groups, but they also afford a common ground and enable collaborative modes of action.[30] They have a public feel without being coercive. Similarly, Warren and Rosenblum write that voluntary associations contribute most to democracy because people are free to associate within them. *Freedom of association* is integral to free human life and thus to creating a democratic society.[31] It follows logically that because the point of many kinds of association is precisely their freedom and spontaneity, intervention from a higher authority cannot help but damage their effects.[32] The irony here is that to rely to a greater degree on voluntarism to address collective social needs, exit from collective action "must be foreclosed in particular for [voluntary] groups commanding resources that are crucial for building a successful community"; that is, voluntary groups must no longer be free to associate as they see fit.[33]

A real problem, then, lies in the trade-off between the grassroots independence and noncoercive collaborative action that enables voluntary institutions to contribute to democratic governance and the ability of these institutions to adequately and comprehensively address community problems. This is not a grave issue if voluntarism's role is solely that of enhancing quality of life while government (perhaps in collaboration with other entities) addresses community problems. However, when voluntary institutions are increasingly relied upon and left on their own to address social problems, this tradeoff is extremely problematic; voluntary institutions become minigovernments (rather than just minipublics), and either their noncoercive independent democratic nature or the public good must be compromised.

In the context of governance beyond the state, we must come to terms with the tension between voluntary associations' internally democratic effects and their democratic outcomes. Giving circles expose the need to examine this tension. For example, small groups seem to be the most democratic internally: they provide the most opportunities for all members to participate in decision making, agenda setting, deliberation, and citizen capacity building efforts within the group. However, creating these opportunities depends largely on having a small, informal structure and taking the time to sustain such a process, which also serves to limit activities that take place beyond the group. In many cases, small groups are unable to have a comprehensive view of the needs of the community, and they have fewer resources to fill in gaps appropriately. Loose networks are even less comprehensive in their approach to finding funding opportunities because they respond to individual needs (although they do have the redeeming quality of empowering members within the group).

One could argue, considering the internal democratization effects of small groups, that democracy and bureaucracy are in opposition to each other: the more bureaucratic the group, in the sense described by Weber, the less democratic it must be.[34] Certainly, many scholars would agree with this assessment.[35] This does seem to be the case if one focuses *only* on the internal organizational aspects of democratization. Yet if one also considers democratic outcomes, the bureaucracy versus democracy dichotomy is much more complicated. For example, in the case of giving circles, formal organizations, though the most bureaucratic and hierarchical in structure, do a much better job of systematically educating members about needs in the community and trying to fill those needs. They also tend to offer more opportunities for members to engage directly with community organizations, which in turn, with their more formal educational component, may lead to greater identification with others beyond the group and ultimately to a distribution of resources to more diverse beneficiaries.

One conclusion from the giving circle context, then, may be that democracy within the organization does not necessarily lead to democracy in society, especially if one is concerned with substantive democratic outcomes. This is somewhat contrary to those who argue, primarily in the context of the workplace, that democracy within the organization is necessary for democracy at the macro or national level.[36] This may be true from a procedural view of democracy, but it is much more complicated if one's interest is also in addressing problems in the community, a concern that increases for voluntary associations in an environment of governance beyond the state. Here again, a federated system may help to balance these contradictions but still has the difficulties discussed above.

Is it possible, then, to balance the competing demands for voluntary associations to enhance the democratic effects on members while also addressing basic social problems in the community? The evidence suggests that this would be a difficult balance to reach and maintain. Lichterman found in a study of small church groups that "instituting bridges beyond a group often, though not always, threatened the solidarity of the groups—even groups that defined themselves as bridge builders."[37] Sørensen and Torfing also show that organizations have difficulty maintaining internal democracy when their leadership also participates in political networks around larger societal issues.[38] If such a balance is so difficult to reach, should the benefit of giving circles, and voluntary associations more generally, be seen in what they do for members or what they do for the organizations and individuals they help and the community? Should the emphasis be on the process or the outcomes, the supply or the demand?[39] In my own experience participating in giving circles, I have seen the tension that arises in placing the value of the giving circle on the member participation and process itself instead of on the outcomes and needs that may be met in the community through the giving circle. For example, in the New River Valley Change Network, we struggled with the desire to create an inclusive giving circle where people of all backgrounds and income levels could participate— with the assumption that it is the internal process and act of participation that is important—and the desire to try to meet substantive needs in the community and create broader social change. We needed more money to do the latter, which contradicted keeping the membership fee low so that all who wanted to might participate.

There is also a tension between encouraging giving circle members to participate and use a process that is most beneficial to them as members—such as enabling members to learn about needs in the community and perhaps get excited about funding a particular project or learning about how nonprofit organizations work—and meeting the needs of funding recipients and the community—such as funding for general operating costs or for needs that are not of special interest to members. As one nonprofit professional noted in an interview:

> The giving circles' motivations are a little more complex. They need to keep a membership interested and engaged and all that stuff, and people say, "Ah, we've been funding [organization name] for three years. Let's go fund some other group. You know, I heard of this one great group, blah, blah, blah," and then they're off onto the next thing.[40]

So what is good for the giving circle member from an educational or personal interest perspective is not necessarily good for organizations or issue areas that need to depend on more regular sources of income to be effective and address deep-seated problems.

Indeed, while there have been calls for an increasing reliance on voluntarism to govern beyond the state, there has also been a growing demand by donors, to participate in the community in their own way and to appease their own interests. Can such fragmented and individualized approaches to community action actually address community problems and create broader social change and betterment? It does not seem promising. Wuthnow writes that the increasing porousness of family, economy, and community means that more needy are falling through the cracks. More people are isolated and cut off from the informal ties that give them social support, motivate them to care about others, and mobilize them to take an active part in their communities. People are very aware that families are homeless in their community or that crime is increasing, but they are generally aroused by individual cases rather than broader social conditions. They are less motivated to do something about poverty or crime in general. Those who volunteer stress how good it feels to be helpful, and they feel more worthwhile about themselves, but this reinforces the sense that loose connections may not be the same as deep loyalty to community.[41]

Conclusion

Volunteers, philanthropists, citizens, and policy makers need to discuss what the role for voluntarism should be in our society. Should voluntarism be relied upon to provide for basic human needs? Voluntarism seems to do well at addressing small, short-term problems and enhancing quality of life. It does not do so well at reducing, preventing, or eliminating large community needs. Rather, voluntarism's most important role in society may be nothing more or less than enabling people to be philanthropic or charitable: to liberate the "human aspiration to give" and "enable human beings to develop their full human potential."[42] Indeed, Aristotle believed generosity to be one of the paradigm virtues. He saw philanthropy as allowing individuals a chance to enact this and other virtues such as benevolence, kindness, compassion, justice, and reciprocity.[43] Likewise, Payton and Moody see philanthropy as the "primary vehicle people use to implement their moral imagination and to shape and advance the moral agenda of our society."[44] This is an important role to play in society and much needed. So is it appropriate to require voluntarism to do something different; something that would potentially compromise its contributions to human development? Voluntary associations and philanthropy may contribute the most to democracy if they are allowed the freedom to do as they wish while the state is made strong enough to develop and enforce a system of fundamental rights, protect zones of freedom within which associational life grows, and support citizens with enough basic income and services.[45] Levy argues that essential services such as emergency aid, food, health care, and so on that "make possible the development of a range of human possibilities" should be a fundamental right rather than a voluntary contribution.[46] We should encourage a flourishing of philanthropic associations such as giving circles, but realize that their biggest contribution to democratic governance is more about what they *enable* members to give back to their communities rather than what funding recipients and the community gain from these gifts.

Appendix: Research Methodology

The data on giving circles used in this book come from two phases of research. The first phase was completed in 2005 and involved an exploratory study of the giving circle movement and gathered qualitative and quantitative data from thirty personal and telephone interviews with giving circle leaders and members and philanthropic professionals, news articles and other documentation, and secondary data. The second phase of the research involved interviewing eighteen nonprofit professionals (primarily executive and development directors from seventeen nonprofit organizations) about their experience receiving funding from and working with giving circles.

Phase I Research Data Collection

This phase of the study started by creating a database of giving circles. This database, created in 2005, included information in part or in whole for 188 giving circles. Groups included in the database were those that described themselves, or were described by others, as giving circles. Excluded were donor circles—fundraising efforts initiated by a particular charity where donors have no significant voice in how the funds are used. The characteristics of membership fee, organizational structure and size, and giving circle activities were used to preliminarily categorize the giving circles in the database in order to choose an interview sample. Membership fee was important to consider because it represents the socioeconomic status of the member in the giving circle (i.e., a giving circle with a $5,000 fee attracts people from a higher socioeconomic level than one with a $100 fee or no fee), and this may influence democratic participation and identification with others. Organizational structure and size were included because they may have an influence on whether or not participation is meaningful. For example, a larger, more bureaucratic giving circle may provide fewer opportunities for participation in agenda setting and decision making. What activities the giving circle offers was also used because of its importance for level of participation and identification with others. For instance, a giving circle that focuses on social activities may have different impacts on participants than one that focuses on education or engagement with nonprofit organizations.

From this categorization, a sample was drawn to gain maximum information about giving circles' processes and impacts across different types of giving circles, and the individuals from several giving circles were interviewed. Giving circle members (23) were located in Baltimore, Md., Boston, Mass., Durham, N.C., Grand Rapids, Mich., Irvine, Calif., Jacksonville, Fla., Minneapolis, Minn., Omaha, Neb., San Jose, Calif., Seattle, Wash., and Wilmington, Del. They represented leaders or founders of some groups, staff and members of some groups, and most of the members in one case study giving circle. Philanthropic professionals (7) were also interviewed, purposefully selected based on their reputation in working with giving circles or because they were referred, through snowball sampling, by other philanthropic professionals. They were located in Baltimore, Md., Boston, Mass., Omaha, Neb., Mill Valley, Calif., San Francisco, Calif., Seattle, Wash., and Washington, D.C.

Interviews took place between April 24, 2004, and September 15, 2004, and ranged in length from twenty minutes to two hours. When possible, interviews were audio-taped.[1] An interview protocol was used, and notes were taken during and after each interview. Questions were conversational in an attempt to get the participant to discuss further something he/she had mentioned related to the research questions.[2] See below for a list of interview questions. In addition, news articles, websites, and other documents written about giving circles were found through Google, Lexus-Nexus, and other article database searches. Secondary data came from a survey conducted by the Forum of Regional Associations of Grantmakers' New Ventures in Philanthropy Initiative.[3] The survey was web-based, and individuals were asked to participate via email. Responses were obtained for sixty giving circles. The other major sources of secondary data were from case studies of several giving circles: Social Venture Partners (SVP) Seattle,[4] SVP Calgary,[5] Hestia Fund,[6] Baltimore Women's Giving Circle,[7] and the Women's Giving Circle of Howard County.[8] Additionally, participant observation was used to inform the design and structure of the study. The author participated for one year in the Omaha Venture Group (OVG) prior to beginning data collection. For more information on OVG, see the case study in chapter 4.

Although a sample of giving circles was chosen to represent many of the key characteristics among giving circles, it is impossible to know and account for every giving circle attribute. It is likely that the data available are skewed to the larger formal giving circles that are more strongly affiliated with community foundations and other organized philanthropic organizations. These are the types of giving circles that have received the most attention from the news media and researchers, perhaps because they are most intimately connected to organized philanthropy. However, I did my best to gather and consider data from a cross-section of giving circles and from various sources to minimize this problem. In addition, interviewing many giving circle leaders, members who were also in some cases staff personnel, and philanthropic professionals may have skewed the data. For example, it may be that those who start or lead giving circles come to the giving circle with a great deal of philanthropic experience, and this may influence the perceptions they have of their giving circle experience. The data might also be skewed in that those participating in giving circles may be more prone to volunteerism. The study did not include interviews with individuals who no longer participate in giving circles. However, I feel confident that many of these shortcomings were addressed through the triangulated use of multiple interviews, case studies, and document analysis, which help to ensure greater trustworthiness of the findings.[9]

Phase II Research Data Collection

The methodological process for the second phase of research involved updating the giving circle database created in 2005 and then creating a new database of grantees that have received funding from giving circles. Information for this new database was obtained from interviews and documents from earlier studies of giving circles as well as through a new search for information using the Internet and article search engines. The newly created grantee database included data for 1,333 grants made to 878 nonprofit (and a few public or quasi-public) organizations and 160 individuals, given by 116 giving circles. At the time, this number (116) represented about half of the giving circles identified in the giving circle database. Of the 1,333 grants in the database, 1,295 were provided by giving circles for which we could identify the type of giving circle: formal organizations provided 860 (66%) of these gifts, loose networks provided 358 (28%) grants, and small groups provided 77 (6%) grants.

Complete information was not available for the amounts of all grants (we were able to find this information for 987, or 52%, of the funding recipients). At least $28,406,948 was given by the giving circles identified in the database. This represented an average gift of $28,781, but gifts ranged from $90 to $715,000. Grants were awarded between 1996 and 2005. Given that some of the grants were made to cover several years at a time, it is difficult to be exact, but we estimated that 57 grants were given in 2000, 70 grants were given in 2001, 231 grants were given in 2002, 230 grants were given in 2003, 301 grants were given in 2004, and 272 grants were given in 2005.

From the newly created funding recipient database, a purposefully selected sample of organizations was chosen. This sample represented organizations funded by the three types of giving circles—small groups, loose networks, and formal organizations—and giving circles of varying identity groups (e.g., women-only, young leaders, etc.), as well as different organizational budget sizes and fields (e.g., arts, human services, education). The sample included seventeen organizations: four of these were funded by two giving circles, and one was funded by three giving circles. Thus these seventeen nonprofit organizations were funded by twenty-three giving circles. The breakdown of giving circles in the sample providing funding by type included: twelve formal organizations (52.2%), three loose networks (13%), and eight small groups (34.7%). The nonprofit funding recipients in the sample represented the fields of human services, education, arts, health, environment, and public benefit, though some of these organizations were involved in more than one field of interest. Specifically, three of the organizations were related to education and human services, and one was education- and arts-related. The sample nonprofit organizations ranged in size from small to large in organizational and budget size, and the amount they received ranged from $1,000 to $167,000 (in one year; some organizations did receive multiyear gifts). These organizations were located across the United States.

One shortcoming of our sample was that we were not able to get a proportionate representative sample of organizations funded by the various types of giving circles. For example, only one public benefit organization was represented in the sample, although these types of organizations represent almost 20 percent of the identified funding recipient population. Efforts were made to include more public benefit organizations in the sample but proved unsuccessful. The low representation of organizations funded by loose networks in the sample may also be attributed to the fact that several funding recipient organizations could not be reached by email or telephone. This may be because, based on knowledge gained in earlier studies, loose networks are much less organized (looser if you will) and less bureaucratic in nature and in many ways seek out more grassroots-oriented organizations or individuals to fund. All combined, this made it difficult to reach the population funded by loose networks. Ultimately, the organizational representatives included in the study had to be found and then be willing to spend the time to participate in the study. Furthermore, we did not attempt to choose sample nonprofit organizations according to race or ethnic background. As with earlier studies of giving circles, this is a major gap in the research that needs to be addressed.

A representative from each of the nonprofit funding recipients in the sample was interviewed: a total of seventeen interviews (including one interview with both the executive director and development director of one organization) by telephone.

Interviews ranged from twenty minutes to an hour and seventeen minutes. Eleven executive-level directors, six development directors or personnel, and one board secretary were interviewed. All interviews were audio-taped and transcribed with the consent of the interviewee.[10] Articles, websites, and other documentation on giving circles and their funding recipients were also used for data collection.

Data Analysis

For both phases of the study, MAX qualitative data analysis (QDA) software was used to systematically organize, code, and analyze data from interviews, case studies, documents, and notes. Analysis followed a strategy set out by Maxwell that involved an iterative process of contextualizing and categorizing strategies.[11] This process included reading interviews and other documents completely through to get a sense of the whole, rereading interviews and coding segments, and recoding and grouping codes into broad clusters of similar topics or nodes, primarily around the research questions though allowing for emergent topics. These clusters were then iteratively recoded into more specific and simplified nodes, creating "trees."[12] This process continued until no new codes emerged. Tables and matrices were constructed from the data and used to identify patterns, comparisons, trends, and paradoxes across cases.[13] Microsoft Excel and Access were also used to track data within the giving circle databases.

In the context of a qualitative framework, trustworthiness is essential to demonstrate the reliability and objectivity of the study. Lincoln and Guba write that such research must be able to "establish confidence in the 'truth' of the findings of a particular inquiry."[14] The triangulated use of multiple interviews and document analysis, as well as looking for and analyzing negative cases in the data and using more than one researcher to analyze and discuss the data, helped to ensure greater trustworthiness of the data.[15] Theoretical validation was also sought through regular presentation and discussion of emerging conclusions with colleagues.[16]

Interview Questions

Giving Circle Members

1. What is your role within the giving circle?
2. Before your involvement in the giving circle, how active were you philanthropically?
   a. Has participation in the giving circle changed your level of philanthropic participation? Please explain.
   b. Have you used other modes of giving? How do they compare with your experience in the giving circle?
3. What are the rules for grant making in your giving circle, and how were they established?
   a. Who is involved in the decision-making process within the circle?
   b. What role do you play in decision making within the circle?
   c. Are there opportunities for discussion/deliberation before decisions are made?
   d. Do you think there is a better process for decision making?
4. Has your participation in the giving circle influenced your relationship with others in the community? How?
5. Has your participation in the giving circle changed your attitude about others in the community? Please explain.

6. What types of organizations or groups have been funded by your giving circle?
   a. Has your participation in the giving circle influenced where or to whom you give your own time and/or money? Please explain.
   b. What is your impression of the funding recipients?
7. Is there anything else you would like to tell me about your experience participating in a giving circle?

Philanthropic Professionals

1. In your experience, what kinds of people participate in giving circles?
   a. Do giving circles attract individuals who are new to philanthropy?
2. What kind of impact does participation in a giving circle have on members' philanthropy?
   a. Are there different impacts among different types of giving circles?
   b. Do you think giving circles differ from other modes of philanthropy? How?
3. How are decisions typically made in the giving circles with which you are familiar?
   a. Who is involved in the decision-making process?
   b. Are there opportunities for discussion/deliberation before decisions are made?
4. What do you think makes a good or successful giving circle?
5. Do you think participation in a giving circle influences members' relationships with others in the community? Please explain.
   a. Does it change their attitude about others in the community? Please explain.
6. What types of organizations or groups are funded by giving circles?
7. Do you have any other information or data about giving circles that you would be willing to share?
8. Are there any other philanthropic professionals knowledgeable about giving circles that I should talk to? Can I use your name as an introduction?
9. Is there anything else you would like to tell me about giving circles?

Nonprofit Professionals

1. Could you first tell me a little bit about your organization?
2. What kinds of interactions have you had with giving circles?
   a. What has been your experience working with giving circles?
      i. How was initial contact made?
      ii. Have you worked with more than one giving circle? How do they compare?
   b. What are your impressions of giving circles and members?
   c. Have they been successful in your opinion? [outcomes?]
3. Is there anything specific about your organization that you think is attractive to giving circles and their members?
4. How does your experience with the giving circle compare with other types of fundraising?
   a. How are they similar or different from other fundraising that you do?
5. Do you see giving circle members as different from other types of donors?
   a. How would you describe their characteristics?
   b. Are there generational differences?
   c. How do they compare with other types of "new" [younger generation] donors?
   d. Do you relate differently to these types of funders? Is the role of executive director or fundraiser different?

6. What strategies have you used to cultivate giving from giving circles and their members?
7. How has giving circle funding and/or the new philanthropy influenced or impacted your organization?
   a. Its mission?
   b. Structure?
   c. Budget?
   d. Have you changed the way you do fundraising because of your interaction with giving circles and their funding?
8. What do you recommend to other fundraisers as ways to attract funding from giving circles and their members [or new donors]?
9. What advice would you give to giving circle members about giving to and working with your organization?
10. Is there anything else you would like to tell me about the funding you have received from the giving circle(s) or your experience with new donors?

Notes

Preface

1. Gunderman, "Giving and Human Excellence," 9–10.
2. Warren, *Democracy and Associations*, 28.

Introduction

1. Venture philanthropy is defined by Gingold as "the application of venture capital principles and practices to achieve social change." Gingold, "New Frontiers in Philanthropy." See also Letts, Ryan, and Grossman, "Virtuous Capital," and Moody, " 'Building a Culture.' "

2. As some indication of this, Giving New England distributed hundreds of "Giving Circle Starter Kits" (Kong, "Fortunate Seek Guidance in Giving Away Their Wealth"), the Women's Philanthropy Institute has published a popular handbook, Shaw-Hardy, *Creating a Women's Giving Circle*, and New Ventures in Philanthropy at the Forum of Regional Associations of Grantmakers has created an online Giving Circle Knowledge Center (at www.givingforum.org/s_forum/sec.asp?CID=611&DID=2661). This is matched with the effort by several philanthropic institutions across the country to promote giving circles as a means for improving and increasing philanthropy in their communities. See, e.g., Baltimore Giving Project, "Information on Local Giving Circles"; "Start a Giving Circle."

3. Earlier institutions such as women's clubs and Rotaries often did not start or sustain such a focus; the philanthropic aspect either emerged later or was secondary to the main intent of the group. See Charles, *Service Clubs in American Society*, 3; Stivers, *Bureau Men, Settlement Women*, 50.

4. Philanthropy's meaning and manifestations have changed a good deal throughout history as Merle Curti articulates in "Philanthropy." It has come to be defined as the act of giving money and other resources, including time, to aid individuals, causes, and organizations. Payton and Moody, in *Understanding Philanthropy*, 27, define it as "voluntary action for the public good." Philanthropy is distinct from nonprofit and tax-exempt organizations and voluntary associations, though all three are interrelated. Nonprofit organizations are those designated by a state as a nonprofit corporation and often by the U.S. Internal Revenue Service as tax-exempt. The term *nonprofit*, then, designates a legal and regulatory status for an organization that typically does work related to the arts, education, health care, and social welfare. Nonprofit organizations can be quite diverse, ranging from small human service organizations (such as homeless shelters) to large federated organizations (like the American Red Cross or Salvation Army) and substantially endowed universities, hospitals, and foundations. Voluntary associations predate (as those described by Alexis de Tocqueville in *Democracy in America*), continue to exist alongside, or sometimes become nonprofit-designated organizations. They are groups of individuals who voluntarily come together to accomplish a purpose, and they range

from informal self-help or study groups such as book clubs and Bible study groups to more formal organizations like the Kiwanis or League of Women Voters.

5. See, e.g., Bianchi, "Serving Nonprofits"; Byrne, "The New Face of Philanthropy"; Cobb, "The New Philanthropy"; Schweitzer, "Building on New Foundations"; Streisand, "The New Philanthropy."

6. Schervish and Havens, "The New Physics of Philanthropy"; Eikenberry, "Promoting Philanthropy"; McCully, *Philanthropy Reconsidered*.

7. Philanthropic Initiative, *What's a Donor to Do?* chap. 4.

8. Another indication of a more individualized, low commitment, less engaged practice to emerge within the new philanthropy is "consumption philanthropy," a practice in which there is a charitable element associated with purchasing a service or product. For example, today one can buy an iPod or other Product (RED) merchandise while also alleviating the spread of AIDS in Africa because a percentage of the purchase of the product will go to the Global Fund to Fight AIDS, Tuberculosis, and Malaria, or one can purchase soup, candy, and other "pink" products to support breast cancer research and awareness. See Nickel and Eikenberry, "A Critique of the Discourse of Marketized Philanthropy."

9. Hustinx and Lammertyn, "Collective and Reflexive Styles of Volunteering," 168.

10. Cited in Ellison, "Towards a New Social Politics," 711–12.

11. Cobb, "The New Philanthropy," 126.

12. See, e.g., Borkman, *Understanding Self-Help/Mutual Aid;* Clary, "Study Circles"; Katz, *Self-Help in America;* and Wuthnow, *Sharing the Journey*.

13. Wuthnow, *Sharing the Journey,* 40, 45.

14. Gundelach and Torpe, "Voluntary Associations"; Wuthnow, *Loose Connections*.

15. Bang and Sørensen, "The Everyday Maker"; Bennett, "The Uncivic Culture"; Lichterman, *The Search for Political Community;* Macduff, "Societal Changes and the Rise of the Episodic Volunteer."

16. Wuthnow, *Loose Connections,* 8.

17. Gundelach and Torpe, "Voluntary Associations," 13.

18. Paulson, "A Pooling of Funds to Boost Donors' Impact," 18; Matson, "The New Face of Social Capital."

19. Community Wealth Ventures, *Venture Philanthropy 2002;* Jovanovic, Carolone, and Massood, "Voice and Community Engagement."

20. Ahn, "The Hestia Fund"; Elias, "Social Venture Partners"; Sbarbaro, "Social Venture Partners Replication."

21. Guthrie, Preston, and Bernholz, "Transforming Philanthropic Transactions"; Orloff, "Social Venture Partners Calgary."

22. Bearman, *More Giving Together;* Clohesy, *Donor Circles;* Rutnik and Bearman, *Giving Together;* Rutnik and Beaudoin-Schwartz, "Growing Philanthropy through Giving Circles."

23. Though a contested term, Michael Walzer defines civil society as "the space of uncoerced human association and also the set of relational networks—formed for the sake of family, faith, interest, and ideology—that fill this space." Barber, *A Place for Us,* 4. See also chapter 2 in this book.

24. See, e.g., Baccaro, "Civil Society Meets the State"; Chandoke, *The Conceits of Civil Society;* Cohen and Rogers, "Secondary Associations and Democratic Governance" and *Associations and Democracy;* Fung, "Associations and Democracy"; Fung and Wright, "Deepening Democracy"; Hirst, *Associative Democracy* and "Renewing Democracy through Associations"; Sørensen, "Democratic Governance and the Changing Role of

Users of Public Services"; Streeck, "Inclusion and Secession"; Szasz, "Progress through Mischief"; Young, "Social Groups in Associative Democracy."

25. Warren, *Democracy and Associations*, 10.

26. Hirst, *Associative Democracy*, 6, 26.

27. Hirst, "Democracy and Governance"; Peters and Pierre, "Governance without Government?"; Pierre, *Debating Governance;* Rhodes, "The New Governance."

28. Milward and Provan, "Governing the Hollow State," 359.

29. Kettl, *Government by Proxy;* Wolch, *The Shadow State;* Milward and Provan, "Governing the Hollow State"; Peters, "Managing the Hollow State"; Salamon, "Of Market Failure, Voluntary Failure, and Third-Party Government" and *Partners in Public Service;* Sørensen, "Democratic Theory and Network Governance"; Sørensen and Torfing, "Network Governance and Post-Liberal Democracy."

30. Streeck, "Inclusion and Secession," 513.

31. Peters, *The Future of Governing*, 22–28

32. Prasad, *The Politics of Free Markets,* 7; Hacker, *The Divided Welfare State,* 6.

33. Cited in Prasad, *The Politics of Free Markets,* 10.

34. Hacker, *The Divided Welfare State,* 7; Olasky, *The Tragedy of American Compassion.*

35. Giddens, *Beyond Left and Right;* Hirst, *Associative Democracy* and "Renewing Democracy through Associations."

36. It should be noted that such initiatives are only recent manifestations of deep-seated values held by Americans: mistrust of a strong state that might impede personal liberties and individual choice coupled with a desire for maintaining community and quality of life. Bellah and colleagues in *Habits of the Heart* describe this as the tension between our "first language" of moral discourse—the individualism of classical liberalism—and our "second language" of moral discourse—the traditions of self-government and community of classical republicanism.

37. According to Habermas, the public sphere is "a space of institutions and practices between the private interests of everyday life . . . and the realm of state power." In Kellner, "Habermas, the Public Sphere, and Democracy."

38. Stivers, "The Public Agency as Polis," 87.

39. Glassman, *Democracy and Equality,* 16.

40. Held, *Models of Democracy,* 59.

41. Putnam, *Making Democracy Work.*

42. Gundelach and Torpe, "Voluntary Associations," 6.

43. Tocqueville, *Democracy in America.*

44. Fung, "Associations and Democracy."

45. Almond and Verba, *The Civic Culture;* Barber, *A Place for Us;* Evans and Boyte, *Free Spaces;* Skocpol, *Diminished Democracy;* Verba, Schlozman and Brady, *Voice and Equality.*

46. Putnam, "Bowling Alone," 67.

47. Putnam, *Bowling Alone,* 22.

48. Putnam and Feldstein, *Better Together,* 277.

49. Wuthnow, "The United States," 67.

50. Skocpol, *Diminished Democracy,* 13.

51. Putnam, "Bowling Alone," 71; Skocpol, "The United States," 132.

52. Salamon, "Of Market Failure, Voluntary Failure, and Third-Party Government" and *Partners in Public Service;* Frumkin, *Strategic Philanthropy.*

53. Hodgkinson, "Individual Giving and Volunteering."

54. Boris and Steuerle, "What Charities Cannot Do"; Burke, "Establishing a Context"; Salamon, *Partners in Public Service;* Skocpol, *Diminished Democracy,* 12; Wolpert, "Decentralization and Equity in Public and Nonprofit Sectors."

55. May, "Introduction," xxii.

56. Arnove, "Introduction"; Fisher, "The Role of Philanthropic Foundations"; Whittington, "Revisiting Tocqueville's America," 24.

57. Poppendieck, *Sweet Charity?* 255.

58. See Rutnik and Bearman, *Giving Together,* 42–45, for survey questions.

59. Gunderman, "Giving and Human Excellence," 9–10.

1. Democracy, Voluntary Association, and Philanthropy

1. Held, *Models of Democracy;* McSwain, "Administrators and Citizenship," 137, 139; Bellah et al., *Habits of the Heart,* 334; Sandel, *Democracy's Discontent.*

2. Bellah et al., *Habits of the Heart,* 28–31; Box, *Citizen Governance,* 12–13; McSwite, *Legitimacy in Public Administration,* chaps. 3 and 4.

3. McCarthy, *American Creed,* 16.

4. Kemmis, *Community and the Politics of Place,* 11.

5. Box, *Public Administration and Society,* 26–27.

6. Adams, Bowerman, Dolbeare, and Stivers, "Joining Purpose to Practice," 228–29. It should be noted here that even democratic theorists agree that a genuine democracy has never existed in the United States and that egalitarian democracy can only be an ideal. See Wiebe, *Self-Rule,* 6. Yet, as Agger argues in *Postponing the Postmodern,* 21, democracy cannot remain only an ideal; it must be worked through by families, colleagues, citizens, and others in everyday lives, notably through dialogue, the underlying principle of democracy. In "The Ethics of Democracy," Dewey saw democracy not as a mere form of government but as a way of being, relating, and living. Working toward an ideal form of democracy and the degree to which society realizes this ideal is the best measure of its quality.

7. Krugman, "For Richer."

8. Phillips, *Wealth and Democracy,* 43; Cagetti and De Nardi, "Wealth Inequality"; Diaz-Gimenez, Quadrini, and Ríos-Rull, "Dimensions of Inequality," 5.

9. Hall, "A Charitable Divide."

10. Tobin and Weinberg, *Mega-Gifts in American Philanthropy.*

11. DeNavas-Walt, Proctor, and Smith, *Income, Poverty, and Health Insurance Coverage in the United States.*

12. U.S. Census, "Poverty."

13. U.S. Conference of Mayors, "Hunger and Homelessness Continues to Rise in U.S. Cities."

14. Hall, "A Charitable Divide."

15. Havens and Schervish, "Why the $41 Trillion Wealth Transfer Is Still Valid."

16. Heying, "Civic Elites and Corporate Delocalization"; Uslaner, "Volunteering and Social Capital," 114–15; Wuthnow, "The United States," 67.

17. See Havens and Schervish, "Millionaires and the Millennium."

18. Passey and Tonkiss, "Trust, Voluntary Association, and Civil Society," 33; Lichterman, "Social Capital or Group Style?" 534.

19. See, e.g., Eberly, *The Soul of Civil Society.*

20. Warren, *Democracy and Association,* 18–25.

21. See, e.g., Fung and Wright, "Thinking about Empowered Participatory Governance"; Ventriss, "A Substantive View of Ethical Citizenship in Public Affairs."

22. Gross, "Giving in America," 30.

23. Tocqueville, *Democracy in America*, 630.

24. Fung, "Associations and Democracy," 515.

25. Walzer cited in Barber, *A Place for Us*, 4.

26. Barber, *A Place for Us*, 6.

27. Dekker and van den Broek, "Civil Society in Comparative Perspective."

28. Edwards and Foley, "Civil Society and Social Capital: A Primer."

29. Ibid., 6.

30. Berry, "Nonprofits and Civic Engagement," 568.

31. Edwards and Foley, "Civil Society and Social Capital: A Primer," 5.

32. Clarke, "The Prospects of Local Democratic Governance," 141.

33. Newton, "Social Capital and Democracy," 579; Warren, *Democracy and Association*, 9.

34. Berger and Neuhaus, *To Empower People*; Dewey, *The Public and Its Problems*; Durkheim, *The Division of Labor in Society*; Rawls, *A Theory of Justice*, 471–72.

35. Almond and Verba, *The Civic Culture*; Barber, *A Place for Us*; Skocpol, *Diminished Democracy*; Verba, Schlozman, and Brady, *Voice and Equality*.

36. Putnam, *Making Democracy Work*, 167.

37. Frumkin, *Strategic Philanthropy*, 1, 14, 17, 18. See also Payton and Moody, *Understanding Philanthropy*, chap. 6.

38. Warren, *Democracy and Association*, 32.

39. Eliasoph, *Avoiding Politics*, 7–28, found in her ethnographic study of voluntary organizations that in voluntary group contexts she participated in for two and a half years—volunteer, recreational, and activist groups—discussion of politics was almost always considered inappropriate and out of place. Volunteer meetings she attended did not involve discussion. They were short, to the point, and task-oriented. There was little or no respect for discussion itself and willingness to debate about troubling issues that might not be resolved immediately.

40. Chambers and Kopstein, "Bad Civil Society"; Berman, "Civil Society and the Collapse of the Weimer Republic"; Kwon, "Associations, Civic Norms, and Democracy"; Sargent, *Extremism in America*.

41. Tamir, "Revisiting the Civic Sphere," 218–19.

42. Eikenberry and Nickel, "Towards a Critical Social Theory of Philanthropy," 9. See also Frumkin, *Strategic Philanthropy*, 13.

43. Roelofs, "The Third Sector as Protective Layer for Capitalism."

44. Diaz, "For Whom and for What?" 517.

45. Urban Institute, *The Nonprofit Sector in Brief*, 2.

46. Independent Sector, *The New Nonprofit Almanac and Desk Reference*, 3; Giving USA Foundation, *Giving USA 2006*.

47. Hodgkinson, "Individual Giving and Volunteering," 391.

48. Wolpert, "How Federal Cutbacks Affect the Charitable Sector," 106; Wolpert, "Decentralization and Equity in Public and Nonprofit Sectors"; Wolpert, "Communities, Networks, and the Future of Philanthropy," 238.

49. Giving USA Foundation, *Giving USA 2006*; Hodgkinson, "Individual Giving and Volunteering," 396; Wolpert, "How Federal Cutbacks Affect the Charitable Sector," 101; The Center on Philanthropy, "Patterns of Household Charitable Giving by Income Group," 2; Tobin and Weinburg, *Mega-Gifts in American Philanthropy*.

50. See, e.g., Ostrander and Schervish, "Giving and Getting," 74; Schervish, "Gentle as Doves and Wise as Serpents"; Schervish and Havens, "The Mind of the Millionaire"; Schervish and Herman, *Empowerment and Beneficence.*

51. Schervish and Havens, "The Mind of the Millionaire," 91.

52. Odendahl, *Charity Begins at Home,* 67; Ostrower, *Why the Wealthy Give;* Wolpert, "Decentralization and Equity in Public and Nonprofit Sectors," 7.

53. Wolpert, "How Federal Cutbacks Affect the Charitable Sector," 101.

54. Diaz, "For Whom and for What?" 519.

55. Salamon, "Social Services."

56. Galaskiewicz et al., "Funding Sources, Auspices, and Location of Youth Services."

57. Burke, "Establishing a Context"; Hammack, "Foundations in the American Polity"; Salamon, *Partners in Public Service;* Skocpol, *Diminished Democracy,* 12.

58. Wolpert, "Decentralization and Equity in Public and Nonprofit Sectors," 2.

59. Burke, "Nonprofit History's New Numbers," 185, 187.

60. Hodgkinson, "Individual Giving and Volunteering," 395.

61. Burke, "Establishing a Context," 94.

62. Urban Institute, *The Nonprofit Sector in Brief.*

63. Hodgkinson, "Individual Giving and Volunteering," 402.

64. Abramson, Salamon and Steuerle, "The Nonprofit Sector and the Federal Budget," 114.

65. Joulfaian, "Basic Facts on Charitable Giving," 12.

66. MacDonald, "Where Are All the Charitable Bequests?"

67. Hodgkinson, "Individual Giving and Volunteering," 403.

68. Ibid., 412.

69. Hall, "A Charitable Divide."

70. Wolpert, "How Federal Cutbacks Affect the Charitable Sector," 100.

71. Hodgkinson and Weitzman, *Giving and Volunteering in the United States,* 11; Urban Institute, *The Nonprofit Sector in Brief,* 4.

72. Poppendieck, *Sweet Charity?* 3.

73. Ibid., 213–22.

74. Wolpert, "How Federal Cutbacks Affect the Charitable Sector," 106.

75. Wagner, *What's Love Got to Do with It?* chap. 5.

76. May, "Introduction," xx, xxii.

77. Lichterman, *Elusive Togetherness,* 170.

78. Ostrander, "The Problem of Poverty and Why Philanthropy Neglects It," 228.

79. Poppendieck, *Sweet Charity?* chap. 9.

80. Fischer, "Philanthropy and Injustice in Mill and Addams," 281–82.

81. Cohen and Rogers, *Associations and Democracy,* 7.

82. Poppendieck, *Sweet Charity?* 6, 12, 26–27, 38, 302. See also Eikenberry and Nickel, "Towards a Critical Social Theory of Philanthropy."

83. Hall, "Resolving the Dilemmas of Democratic Governance," 9.

84. Ibid., 9–10; Whittington, "Revisiting Tocqueville's America," 24.

85. Warren, *Democracy and Association,* 11.

86. Odendahl, *Charity Begins at Home,* 3.

87. Frumkin, *Strategic Philanthropy,* 2.

88. Nevarez, "Corporate Philanthropy in the New Urban Economy," 199–200. See also Heying, "Civic Elites and Corporate Delocalization"; Hunter, *Community Power Structure;* Schulze, "The Role of Economic Dominants in Community Power Structure"; Schulze and Blumberg, "The Determination of Local Power Elites."

89. Logan and Molotch, *Urban Fortunes*, 204.

90. Nielsen, *The Big Foundations*, 5–6.

91. Brilliant, *Private Charity and Public Inquiry*, 11.

92. Nielsen, *The Big Foundations*, 6.

93. See, e.g., Fisher, "The Role of Philanthropic Foundations"; Roelofs, "The Third Sector as a Protective Layer for Capitalism."

94. Arnove, "Introduction," 1.

95. Jenkins, "Social Movement Philanthropy and American Democracy"; Faber and McCarthy, "Introduction."

96. Warren, *Democracy and Association*, 26.

97. Poppendieck, *Sweet Charity?* 303.

98. Katz, *The Undeserving Poor*, 194.

99. Menninger, "Observations on the Psychology of Giving and Receiving Money," 211.

100. May, "Introduction," xxi.

101. Wagner, *What's Love Got to Do with It?* chaps. 2 and 3; Ferguson, *Empire*, chap. 3; Halstead, *The Second British Empire*.

102. Wagner, *What's Love Got to Do with It?* 5.

103. Vogel, "Who's Making Global Civil Society."

104. Poppendieck, *Sweet Charity?* 255.

105. Fischer, "Philanthropy and Injustice in Mill and Addams," 286–87. See also Addams, *Democracy and Social Ethics*.

106. Warren, *Democracy and Association*; Rosenblum, *Membership and Morals*.

107. Tamir, "Revisiting the Civic Sphere."

108. Frumkin, *Strategic Philanthropy*, 33.

109. Warren, *Democracy and Association*, 18.

2. The Modernization and Marketization of Voluntarism

1. Staeheli, "Citizenship and the Search for Community."

2. Putnam, *Bowling Alone*, 283–84.

3. Putnam, *Bowling Alone*. See also Etzioni, *The Spirit of Community*.

4. Best and Kellner, *The Postmodern Turn*, 18.

5. Jacques, *Manufacturing the Employee*, 37; Adams, "Enthralled with Modernity."

6. Halfpenny, "Trust, Charity, and Civil Society," 135.

7. Jaffee, *Organization Theory*, 89.

8. Weber, *The Theory of Social and Economic Organization*.

9. Jaffee, *Organization Theory*, 91–92.

10. Denhardt, *In the Shadow of Organization*, 28. See also Hummel, *The Bureaucratic Experience*.

11. Olson, *The Logic of Collective Action*, 33–52.

12. Kellner, "Habermas, the Public Sphere, and Democracy."

13. Habermas, *The Structural Transformation of the Public Sphere*, 176.

14. Kellner, "Habermas, the Public Sphere, and Democracy."

15. Anderson, "The Ethical Limitations of the Market." See also Zimmerman and Dart, *Charities Doing Commercial Ventures*.

16. Nickel and Eikenberry, "A Critique of the Discourse of Marketized Philanthropy," 14. See also Eliasoph, *Avoiding Politics*; Ferrell, "Remapping the City"; King, *Pink Ribbons, Inc.*, xxx.

17. Nickel and Eikenberry, "A Critique of the Discourse of Marketized Philanthropy."

18. Berger and Neuhaus, *To Empower People;* Durkheim, *The Division of Labor in Society.*

19. Berry, "Native American Philanthropy"; Bremner, *American Philanthropy,* 5.

20. Adamson, "Smoothing Out the Road," 32.

21. Friedman, "Philanthropy in America," 6.

22. McCarthy, *American Creed,* 3.

23. Gross, "Giving in America," 30.

24. McGarvie, "The Dartmouth College Case and the Legal Design of Civil Society," 93.

25. Ibid.

26. Gross, "Giving in America," 43.

27. Skocpol, "The United States," 109.

28. Lubove, *The Professional Altruist,* vii.

29. Sealander, "Curing Evils at Their Source."

30. Rose-Ackerman, "United Charities," 136.

31. Lubove, *The Professional Altruist,* 172.

32. Davis, *Spearheads for Reform;* Hays, *The Response to Industrialism;* Hofstadter, *The Age of Reform.*

33. Knight, "Jane Addams and Hull House," 137.

34. Husock, "Bringing Back the Settlement House," 16.

35. Trolander, *Professionalism and Social Change.*

36. McCully, *Philanthropy Reconsidered.*

37. Ibid.

38. Salamon, "The Marketization of Welfare." See also Weisbrod, *To Profit or Not to Profit?*

39. Young and Salamon, "Commercialization, Social Ventures, and For-Profit Competition," 425–26; Weitzman et al., *The New Nonprofit Almanac and Desk Reference,* 8.

40. Backman and Smith, "Healthy Organizations, Unhealthy Communities?" 360; Crimmins and Keil, *Enterprise in the Nonprofit Sector.*

41. Salamon, "Holding the Center."

42. Kerlin, "Nonprofit Commercial Revenue."

43. Weitzman et al., *The New Nonprofit Almanac and Desk Reference,* 91.

44. Kettl, "The Global Revolution in Public Management"; Osborne and Gaebler, *Reinventing Government;* Peters, *The Future of Governing;* Smith, "Managing the Challenges of Government Contracts."

45. Ryan, "The New Landscape for Nonprofits," 130.

46. Nightingale and Pindus, "Privatization of Public Social Services."

47. Ryan, "The New Landscape for Nonprofits," 129.

48. Skloot, "Evolution or Extinction," 319.

49. Foster and Bradach, "Should Nonprofits Seek Profits?" 94.

50. Pozorski, "Social Venture Partners," 24.

51. Gingold, "New Frontiers in Philanthropy."

52. Roberts Enterprise Development Fund website, emphasis added.

53. Dees, Emerson, and Economy, *Enterprising Nonprofits,* 5.

54. Reis and Clohesy, "Unleashing New Resources and Entrepreneurship for the Common Good," 5.

55. Ibid.

56. Young, "Commercialism in Nonprofit Social Service Associations," 202.

57. Nickel and Eikenberry, "A Critique of the Discourse of Marketized Philanthropy"; King, *Pink Ribbons Inc.*

58. Salamon, "Holding the Center."

59. Gross, "Giving in America," 44.

60. Lubove, *The Professional Altruist,* 172.

61. Katz, *The Undeserving Poor,* 162.

62. Lichterman, *Elusive Togetherness,* 58.

63. Lichterman, "Social Capital or Group Style," 540.

64. Lubove, *The Professional Altruist,* 158.

65. Ibid., 51.

66. Katz, *In the Shadow of the Poorhouse,* 162.

67. Milofsky, "Structure and Process in Community Self-Help Organizations," 211.

68. Hodgkinson, "Individual Giving and Volunteering," 389.

69. Pratt, "Bowling Together," 251.

70. Milofsky, "Structure and Process in Community Self-Help Organizations," 208.

71. Kaufman, *For the Common Good?*

72. Skocpol, "The United States." Skocpol also notes that though getting individuals of all social-economic backgrounds—especially the middle class—involved in voluntarism, these voluntary associations have also often been exclusionary of certain groups—such as women and African Americans. Charles, *Service Clubs in American Society,* also notes that the focus of these groups typically has been less on philanthropic social welfare than on promoting social and business benefits.

73. Skocpol, *Diminished Democracy,* 113.

74. Gundelach and Torpe, "Voluntary Associations," 27; Putnam, *Bowling Alone,* 53–58; Skocpol, "The United States," 130.

75. Gundelach and Torpe, "Voluntary Associations," 32.

76. Nonprofit Sector Strategy Group, *The Nonprofit Sector and the Market.*

77. Salamon, "Holding the Center."

78. Jeavons, "When Management Is the Message," 409.

79. Alexander and Weiner, "The Adoption of the Corporate Governance Model," 235.

80. Adams and Perlmutter, "Commercial Venturing," 30.

81. Ibid., 31.

82. Alexander, Nank and Stivers, "Implications of Welfare Reform," 460.

83. Dart, "Being 'Business-Like' in a Nonprofit Organization," 303.

84. Cooney, "The Institutional and Technical Structuring of Nonprofit Ventures."

85. Salamon, "Holding the Center."

86. Ryan, "The New Landscape for Nonprofits," 136.

87. Skloot, "Evolution or Extinction," 323; see also Alexander, "The Impact of Devolution on Nonprofits."

88. Wagner, *What's Love Got to Do with It?* 107.

89. Backman and Smith, "Healthy Organizations, Unhealthy Communities," 362.

90. Zimmerman and Dart, *Charities Doing Commercial Ventures.*

91. Wang, "Money and Autonomy," 4.

92. Backman and Smith, "Healthy Organizations, Unhealthy Communities," 356.

93. Nonprofit Sector Strategy Group, *The Nonprofit Sector and the Market,* 6.

94. James, "Commercialism among Nonprofits."

95. Zimmerman and Dart, *Charities Doing Commercial Ventures,* 27–29.

96. Alexander, Nank and Stivers, "Implications of Welfare Reform," 462.

97. Ibid.; Milofsky, "Structure and Process in Community Self-Help Organizations"; Ryan, "The New Landscape for Nonprofits," 135.

98. Ryan, "The New Landscape for Nonprofits," 135.

99. Alexander, Nank and Stivers, "Implications of Welfare Reform," 462.

100. Backman and Smith, "Healthy Organizations, Unhealthy Communities," 369.

101. Adams and Perlmutter, "Commercial Venturing"; Backman and Smith, "Healthy Organizations, Unhealthy Communities"; Guo, "Government Funding and Community Representation."

102. Dicke, "Ensuring Accountability in Human Services Contracting." See also: Eikenberry and Pautz, "Administrative Reform in the United States."

103. DiMaggio, *Nonprofit Enterprise in the Arts;* Grønbjerg, *Understanding Nonprofit Funding;* Smith and Lipsky, *Nonprofits for Hire.*

3. The Democratization and New Shape of Voluntarism

1. Nagai, Lerner, and Rothman, *Giving for Social Change,* 4.

2. Warren, *Democracy and Association,* 4. For various models of democracy, see Held, *Models of Democracy.*

3. Alter, "An Education in Giving"; Paulson, "A Pooling of Funds to Boost Donors' Impact"; Hodgkinson, "Individual Giving and Volunteering," 389; Salamon, "The Resilient Sector," 35; *Sharing the Wealth.*

4. Hodgkinson and Weitzman, "Overview," 109; Schervish, Havens, and O'Herlihy, "Charitable Giving," 18.

5. Urban Institute, *The Nonprofit Sector in Brief,* 6.

6. Center on Philanthropy, "Average and Median Amounts of Household Giving & Volunteering"; Weitzman et al., *The New Nonprofit Almanac and Desk Reference.*

7. Anft and Lipman, "How Americans Give"; National Association of Children's Hospitals and Related Institutions, *Different Strokes for Different Folks;* Chao, "Asian American Philanthropy"; Ramos, "Latino Philanthropy."

8. DeNavas-Walt, Proctor and Smith, *Income, Poverty, and Health Insurance Coverage in the United States.*

9. Eckstein, "A Theory of Stable Democracy," 282.

10. Gastil, "A Definition of Small Group Democracy," 284.

11. Gutmann, "Freedom of Association."

12. Lichterman "Social Capital or Group Style," 534, 535.

13. Bachrach and Botwinick, *Power and Empowerment;* Barber, *Strong Democracy;* Follett, *The New State;* Passey and Tonkiss, "Trust, Voluntary Association and Civil Society," 47; Pateman, *Participation and Democratic Theory;* Stivers, "The Public Agency as Polis"; Verba, Schlozman and Brady, *Voice and Equality.*

14. Independent Sector, "Giving and Volunteering in the United States"; Jackson, Bachmeier, Wood, and Craft, "Volunteering and Charitable Giving"; Putnam, *Bowling Alone;* Reddy, "Individual Philanthropy and Giving Behavior"; Schervish and Havens, "Social Participation and Charitable Giving"; Schervish and Herman, *Empowerment and Beneficence.*

15. Lichterman, *Elusive Togetherness,* 25.

16. Putnam, "Bowling Alone," 67. For a discussion of various definitions of social capital, see Edwards and Foley, "Civil Society and Social Capital beyond Putnam";

Putnam, *Making Democracy Work* and *Bowling Alone*; Putnam and Goss, "Introduction"; and Schuller, Baron, and Field, "Social Capital."

17. Putnam, *Bowling Alone*, 22.

18. Putnam and Feldstein, *Better Together*, 277.

19. Granovetter, "The Strength of Weak Ties."

20. Wuthnow, "The United States," 670.

21. Fischer, "Philanthropy and Injustice in Mill and Addams," 287.

22. Schervish and Herman, *Empowerment and Beneficence*; Schervish, O'Herlihy and Havens, *Agent Animated Wealth and Philanthropy*, 71.

23. Burke, "Establishing a Context," 12; McCully, *Philanthropy Reconsidered*, 55; Tobin and Weinberg, *Mega-Gifts in American Philanthropy*.

24. It should be noted that Salamon's study of human service–related organizations showed that these organizations do not always help the poor or most in need. See Salamon, "Social Services."

25. Tobin and Weinberg, *Mega-Gifts in American Philanthropy*; Giving USA Foundation, *Giving USA 2006*.

26. Center on Philanthropy, "Center on Philanthropy Panel Study—Household Giving and Volunteering Reports."

27. Saxon-Harold, Wiener, McCormack, and Weber, "America's Religious Congregations," 5.

28. Foundation Center, "Foundation Giving Trends."

29. Lenkowsky, "Foundations and Corporate Philanthropy," 366.

30. Foundation Center, "Foundation Giving Trends"; Dorfman, "Creating a Philanthropic Sector That Is More Responsive to the Needs of Diverse Communities"; Aguilar et al., "Fairness in Philanthropy," 2; DeNavas-Walt, Proctor, and Smith, *Income, Poverty, and Health Insurance Coverage in the United States*.

31. Weitzman et al., *The New Nonprofit Almanac and Desk Reference*.

32. Grimm et al., *Volunteering in America*.

33. Odendahl, *Charity Begins at Home*; Ostrower, *Why the Wealthy Give*; Wolpert, "Decentralization and Equity in Public and Nonprofit Sectors."

34. Tobin and Weinberg, *Mega-Gifts in American Philanthropy*.

35. Best and Kellner, *The Postmodern Turn*, 255–58.

36. Catlaw, "Authority, Representation, and the Contradictions of Posttraditional Governing," 261; Heelas, "Introduction," 2; Gundelach and Torpe, "Social Reflexivity," 54; Beck, *Risk Society*, 92.

37. Ellison, "Towards a New Social Politics," 711.

38. Bellah et al., *Habits of the Heart*, 6.

39. Catlaw, "Authority, Representation, and the Contradictions of Posttraditional Governing," 269.

40. Loseke, "The Whole Spirit of Modern Philanthropy," 438; Wuthnow, *Loose Connections*, 212.

41. Wuthnow, *Loose Connections*, 149.

42. Gundelach and Torpe, "Voluntary Associations," 12; Kemmis, *Community and the Politics of Place*.

43. Hustinx and Lammertyn, "Collective and Reflexive Styles of Volunteering," 176, 179.

44. Ellison, "Towards a New Social Politics," 712; Wuthnow, *Loose Connections*, 7–8.

45. Skocpol, *Diminished Democracy*, 156–58.

46. Skocpol, "The United States," 132.

47. Putnam, "Bowling Alone," 71.

48. Putnam, *Bowling Alone*, 49–53.

49. See also Borkman, *Understanding Self-Help/Mutual Aid*; Clary, *Study Circles*; Katz, *Self-Help in America*; Putnam, *Bowling Alone*.

50. Wuthnow, *Sharing the Journey*, 45.

51. Gundelach and Torpe, "Voluntary Associations"; Wuthnow, *Loose Connections*.

52. Bang and Sørensen, "The Everyday Maker."

53. Fung, "Survey Article," 339–41. For more information on deliberative polls, see http://cdd.stanford.edu/polls/docs/summary; for National Issues Forms, see www.nifi .org; and for study circles, see www.studycircles.org/en/index.aspx. For more information on Oregon Health Decisions, see www.oregonhealthdecisions.org, and for the Washington, D.C., Citizen Summit, see www.citizensummit.dc.gov. For information on grassroots ecosystem management collaborative, see Weber, *Bringing Society Back In*, and for neighborhood involvement in public administration, see Fung, *Empowered Participation*.

54. For other criticisms of Putnam's thesis, see Lemann, "Kicking in Groups"; Levi, "Social and Unsocial Capital"; Skocpol, "Unravelling from Above"; and Schudson, "What If Civic Life Didn't Die?" For alternatives to Putnam's thesis, see Bang and Sorensen, "The Everyday Maker"; Bennett, "The Uncivic Culture"; Gundelach and Torpe, *Voluntary Associations*; Inglehart, *Modernization and Postmodernization*; Norris, *Democratic Phoenix*; and Wuthnow, *Loose Connections*.

55. Nunn, "Building the Bridge from Episodic Volunteerism to Social Capital," 117.

56. Hustinx and Lammertyn, "Collective and Reflexive Styles of Volunteering," 168.

57. Macduff, "Societal Changes and the Rise of the Episodic Volunteer," 55.

58. Grace and Wendroff, *High Impact Philanthropy*, chap. 7; The Philanthropic Initiative, *What's a Donor to Do?* chap. 4; Schervish, O'Herlihy, and Havens, *Agent Animated Wealth and Philanthropy*, 44.

59. Reis and Clohesy, "Unleashing New Resources and Entrepreneurship for the Common Good," 120–21.

60. Lubove, *The Professional Altruist*, 49.

61. Wuthnow, *Sharing the Journey*, 40.

62. Wuthnow, *Loose Connections*, 207.

63. Lichterman, *Elusive Togetherness*, 83.

64. Walsh, *Talking About Politics*. See also Kaufman, *For the Common Good?*

65. Wuthnow, *Sharing the Journey*, 319.

66. Ibid., 320.

67. Wuthnow, *Loose Connections*, 166.

68. Fine and Harrington, "Tiny Publics," 343; Silver, "The Curious Importance of Small Groups," 65.

69. Fung, "Survey Article."

70. Wuthnow, *Sharing the Journey*, 319.

71. Wuthnow, *Loose Connections*, 110.

72. Lichterman, *Elusive Togetherness*, 68.

4. The Giving Circle Landscape

1. Schweitzer, "Building on New Foundations," 32.

2. Bearman, *More Giving Together*.

3. Interview with philanthropic professional #6, July 7, 2004. All names of those interviewed are withheld to maintain anonymity. For a discussion of those interviewed, see the appendix.

4. Rutnik and Bearman. *Giving Together,* 11.

5. Everychild Foundation, "Where the Money Will Go and How to Be Involved."

6. Interview with member of Omaha Venture Group, September 3, 2004.

7. Kennedy, "Clubs with a Cause," 75.

8. Schervish and Havens, "The New Physics of Philanthropy."

9. Eikenberry, "Fundraising or Promoting Philanthropy?"

10. For a discussion of these and a study of one university-affiliated giving circle, see Beeson, "Women's Giving Circles."

11. Selinsky, "The Power of Giving."

12. Interview with member #1 of Shared Giving, May 17, 2004.

13. Interview with member #8 of Shared Giving, May 20, 2004.

14. Interview with member #1 of Shared Giving, May 17, 2004.

15. Interview with member #8 of Shared Giving, May 20, 2004.

16. Interview with member #6 of Shared Giving, May 19, 2004.

17. Interview with member #7 of Shared Giving, May 19, 2004.

18. Interview with member #8 of Shared Giving, May 20, 2004.

19. Forum of Regional Associations of Grantmakers, "AsiaNextGen Giving Circle Profile"; AsiaNextGen, "Join Us."

20. AsiaNextGen, "Grantees."

21. Forum of Regional Associations of Grantmakers, "Asian Giving Circle Brings Hope to New York Children."

22. "AsiaNextGen Made Its First Donation."

23. Chao, "Asian American Philanthropy."

24. Bernstein, "Class Divide in Chinese-Americans' Charity."

25. Womenade is derived from the saying: "When life hands you a lemon, make lemonade." If you have women, make Womenade.

26. Korelitz, "Second Helpings."

27. Interview with member of Womenade, August 10, 2004.

28. Ibid.

29. Ibid.

30. Interview with staff member of Bread for the Journey, August 16, 2004.

31. Bread for the Journey, *Stories of Kindness and Generosity,* cover, 1; "Interview with Rev. Wayne Muller."

32. Interview with member of Bread for the Journey, August 30, 2004.

33. Interview with staff member of Bread for the Journey, August 16, 2004.

34. Bole, "More Than a Handout."

35. Elias, "Social Venture Partners," 1.

36. Ibid., 2.

37. Ibid., 14.

38. Interview with staff member of Social Venture Partners Seattle, July 19, 2004.

39. Ibid.

40. Social Venture Partners Seattle, "History."

41. Interview with staff member of Social Venture Partners Seattle, July 19, 2004.

42. Ibid.

43. Guthrie, Preston, and Bernholz, "Transforming Philanthropic Transactions," 2.

44. Elias, "Social Venture Partners," 3.

45. Interview with member of Omaha Venture Group, September 3, 2004.

46. Interview with member of Women's Giving Alliance, August 25, 2004.

47. See also Beeson, "Women's Giving Circles," 77.

48. Lynch, "Generosity Grows with Women's Fund Giving Circles," 17.

49. Interview with staff member of Silicon Valley Social Venture Fund, September 3, 2004. Beeson, "Women's Giving Circles," 96, also found this to be true in her case study.

50. Interview with philanthropic professional #5, July 12, 2004.

51. Interview with giving circle member #8 of Shared Giving, May 20, 2004.

52. Charles, *Service Clubs in American Society,* 3; Stivers, *Bureau Men, Settlement Women,* 50.

53. Interview with member of the Red Heart Society, August 2, 2004.

54. Interview with staff member of Social Venture Partners Seattle, July 14, 2004.

55. Interview with nonprofit professional #5, June 16, 2006.

56. Interview with nonprofit professional #1, May 15, 2006.

57. Interview with nonprofit professional #7, June 19, 2006.

58. Interview with nonprofit professional #9, June 28, 2006.

59. Interview with nonprofit professional #4, June 14, 2006.

5. The Democratic Effects of Giving Circles

1. Gastil, "A Definition of Small Group Democracy"; Gutmann, "Freedom of Association."

2. Alter, "An Education in Giving"; Paulson, "A Pooling of Funds to Boost Donors' Impact"; Hodgkinson, "Individual Giving and Volunteering," 389; Salamon, "The Resilient Sector," 35; *Sharing the Wealth.*

3. It is difficult to determine clear differences among the three types of giving circles regarding members' ages because of the incomplete data available. Data is especially limited for loose networks.

4. Hodgkinson and Weitzman, *Giving & Volunteering in the United States,* 109; Schervish, Havens, and O'Herlihy, "Charitable Giving," 18.

5. Urban Institute, *The Nonprofit Sector in Brief,* 6. Janoski and Wilson, "Pathways to Voluntarism," 290, found that, early in adulthood, individuals are more likely to participate in "self-oriented" associations (e.g., professional associations) than they are in "community-oriented" organizations (e.g., neighborhood and service organizations).

6. Interview with member of Omaha Venture Group, September 3, 2004.

7. Interview with philanthropic professional #6, July 7, 2004.

8. Weitzman et al., *The New Nonprofit Almanac and Desk Reference,* 73.

9. The Center on Philanthropy, "Patterns of Household Charitable Giving by Income Group."

10. Kaminski, "Women as Donors," 206; Shaw and Taylor, *Reinventing Fundraising,* 90, 102.

11. Hartman, *Grassroots Giving Circles Survey Report;* Jovanovic, Carolone, and Massood, "Voice and Community Engagement."

12. The current (updated in 2007) database includes approximately 600 giving circles, but in-depth data from surveys, interviews, and documentation are only available for about 165 groups.

13. Hartman, "Grassroots Giving Circles Survey Report."

14. Babchuk and Edwards, "Voluntary Associations and the Integration Hypothesis."

15. Gastil, "A Definition of Small Group Democracy."

16. Ibid., 284.

17. At least one exception regarding members' say in funding recipients is the Arizona Five Arts Circle, through which the five arts organizations funded remain the same each year.

18. Interview with member of Shared Giving #7, May 19, 2004.

19. Guthrie, Preston, and Bernholz, "Transforming Philanthropic Transactions," 11.

20. Jovanovic, Carolone, and Massood, "Voice and Community Engagement," 11.

21. Gastil, "A Definition of Small Group Democracy," 285–86.

22. Interview with member of Omaha Venture Group, September 3, 2004.

23. Interview with member of Social Venture Partners Delaware, July 19, 2004.

24. Eliasoph, *Avoiding Politics;* Lichterman, *The Search for Political Community* and "Social Capital or Group Style?"

25. Interview with member of Bread for the Journey, August 30, 2004.

26. Lichterman, "Social Capital or Group Style?" 535.

27. Verba, Schlozman, and Brady, *Voice and Equality.*

28. Verba, Schlozman, and Brady also note that beyond political efficacy and other factors such as interest and information, time, money, and skills are needed to provide the wherewithal to be civically engaged. Ibid., 354.

29. From the Dining for Women Web Blog, October 8, 2007: www.diningforwomen .org/?page_id=8/.

30. Interview with staff member of Bread for the Journey, August 16, 2004; "Interview with Rev. Wayne Muller."

31. Toussaint, "Giving Circle Finds a Way to Help."

32. Lewis, "Blacks Build New Legacy of Giving."

33. See, e.g., the New Mountain Climbers brochure at www.scribd.com/doc/425922/ New-Mountain-Climbers-brochure.

34. Putnam, *Bowling Alone;* Addams, *Democracy and Social Ethics.*

35. Putnam, *Bowling Alone,* 22.

36. Interview with member of ACI Worldwide Giving Circle, May 10, 2004.

37. Interview with philanthropic professional #1, April 22, 2004.

38. Interview with philanthropic professional #5, July 12, 2004.

39. Guthrie, Preston, and Bernholz, "Transforming Philanthropic Transactions," 16.

40. Ibid.

41. Interview with philanthropic professional #3, August 5, 2004.

42. Elias, "Social Venture Partners," 6.

43. Interview with philanthropic professional #1, April 22, 2004.

44. Interview with member of the Quality of Life Giving Circle, September 15, 2004.

45. Interview with member of Womenade, August 10, 2004.

46. Interview with member of the Quality of Life Giving Circle, September 15, 2004.

47. Interview with member of ACI Worldwide Giving Circle, May 10, 2004.

48. Interview with member of Shared Giving #8, May 20, 2004.

49. Interview with member of Bread for the Journey, August 30, 2004.

50. Matson, "The New Face of Social Capital?" 54.

51. Everychild Foundation, "Information for Applicants."

52. Sbarbaro, "Social Venture Partners Replication," 3.

53. Interview with member of Bread for the Journey, August 30, 2004.

54. B'More Fund brochure, 2.

55. Jovanovic, Carlone, and Massood, "Voice and Community Engagement," 12.

56. Interview with member of Social Venture Partners Delaware, July 19, 2004.

57. Atteberry Smith, "Missouri Friends Raise Funds for Medical Clinic."

58. Interview with nonprofit professional #7, June 19, 2006. This interview was conducted as part of a study of nonprofit organizations that received funding from giving circles. For more information about the study methodology, see the appendix, phase II.

59. Burke, "Establishing a Context," 12; McCully, *Philanthropy Reconsidered*, chap. 1; Tobin and Weinberg, *Mega-Gifts in American Philanthropy.*

60. For information on study methodology for this study, see the appendix, phase II. Several of the nonprofit organizations included in the data for table 5.2 worked in multiple fields, so we had to make judgments about the area to which the gift was given as best we could based on data available. In the table, public benefit includes civil rights and social action, community improvement and development, philanthropy and voluntarism, and public affairs.

61. Giving USA Foundation, *Giving USA 2006.*

62. That is, unless a giving circle is formed around a particular religious identity such as Natan, an all Jewish giving circle, focused on benefiting the Jewish community. Even their gifts, however, tended to not go to religious institutions per se.

63. Grimm et al., "Volunteering in America."

64. Giving USA Foundation, *Giving USA 2006.*

65. Foundation Center, "Foundation Giving Trends."

66. Interview with member of ACI Worldwide Giving Circle, May 10, 2004.

67. Guthrie, Preston, and Bernholz, "Transforming Philanthropic Transactions," 16.

68. Interview with philanthropic professional #5, July 12, 2004.

69. Interview with staff member of Silicon Valley Social Venture Fund, August 11, 2004.

70. This data is from a 2006 study of nonprofit professionals that received funding from giving circles. For information on the methodology of this study, see the appendix, phase II.

71. Hemmings Kahn, "Demonstrating Social Venture Partners' Impact."

72. Interview with member of Community Capital Alliance, August 30, 2004.

73. Independent Sector, "Giving and Volunteering in the United States"; Jackson, Bachmeier, Wood, and Craft, "Volunteering and Charitable Giving"; Putnam, *Bowling Alone;* Reddy, "Individual Philanthropy and Giving Behavior"; Schervish and Havens, "Social Participation and Charitable Giving"; Schervish and Herman, *Empowerment and Beneficence.*

74. Ahn, "The Hestia Fund," 21.

75. Interview with member of Shared Giving #8, May 20, 2004.

76. Interview with member of Shared Giving #1, May 17, 2004.

77. Interview with philanthropic professional #5, July 12, 2004.

78. Hemmings Kahn, "Demonstrating Social Venture Partners' Impact."

79. Interview with member of Womenade, August 10, 2004.

6. Voluntarism and Governing beyond the State

1. Beck, *Risk Society.*

2. Hustinx and Lammertyn, "Collective and Reflexive Styles of Volunteering," 168.

3. Bellah et al., *Habits of the Heart*, 6.

4. Rothschild-Whitt, "The Collectivist Organization."

5. Rothschild and Whitt, *The Cooperative Workplace*, 49.

6. Bang and Sørensen, "The Everyday Maker"; Wuthnow, *Sharing the Journey.*

7. Wuthnow, *Sharing the Journey.*

8. Fung, "Survey Article."

9. Wuthnow, *Sharing the Journey*, 319.

10. Jovanovic, Carolone, and Massood, "Voice and Community Engagement," 23.

11. Axelrod, "Urban Structure and Social Participation," 40; Babchuk and Booth, "Voluntary Association Membership," 26; McPherson, "A Dynamic Model of Voluntary Affiliation," 718; Pearce, *Volunteers*, 65.

12. McPherson and Smith-Lovin, "Homophily in Voluntary Organizations."

13. Rothschild-Whitt, "The Collectivist Organization," 520.

14. Kaufman, *For the Common Good?*

15. Putnam, *Bowling Alone*, 22.

16. Gutmann, "Freedom of Association."

17. Putnam and Feldstein, *Better Together*, 277.

18. See Gross, "Giving in America."

19. Lichterman, *Elusive Togetherness*, 8.

20. Sørensen and Torfing, "Network Governance and Post-Liberal Democracy," 205.

21. Bearman, *More Giving Together;* Giving USA Foundation, *Giving USA 2006;* Boris and Steuerle, "What Charities Cannot Do."

22. It appears that small self-help groups are similarly better at creating bonding than bridging social capital, according to Wuthnow, *Sharing the Journey.*

23. Weisinger and Salipante, "A Grounded Theory for Building Ethnically Bridging Social Capital in Voluntary Organizations."

24. Fung and Wright, "Deepening Democracy"; Fung, "Survey Article," 22.

25. Fung, *Empowered Participation.*

26. Bread for the Journey, "Starting a Bread for the Journey Chapter."

27. Community Investment Network, "History."

28. Wuthnow, *Sharing the Journey.*

29. Fung and Wright, "Deepening Democracy."

30. Barber, *A Place for Us*, 49.

31. Warren, *Democracy and Association;* Rosenblum, *Membership and Morals.*

32. Tamir, "Revisiting the Civic Sphere."

33. Streeck, "Inclusion and Secession," 514.

34. Weber, *The Theory of Social and Economic Organization.*

35. See, e.g., Rothschild-Whitt, "The Collectivist Organization," and Rothschild and Whitt, *The Cooperative Workplace.*

36. Bachrach and Botwinick, *Power and Empowerment;* Haque, "Threats to Public Workplace Democracy"; Pateman, *Participation and Democratic Theory.*

37. Lichterman, *Elusive Togetherness*, 15.

38. Sørensen and Torfing, "Network Politics, Political Capital, and Democracy," 621–22.

39. Schervish and Havens, "The New Physics of Philanthropy." See also Eikenberry, "Fundraising or Promoting Philanthropy?"

40. Interview with nonprofit professional #7, June 19, 2006.

41. Wuthnow, *Loose Connections*, 72, 89.

42. Gunderman, "Giving and Human Excellence," 9-10.

43. Levy, "Against Philanthropy, Individual and Corporate."

44. Payton and Moody, *Understanding Philanthropy*, 99.

45. Warren, *Democracy and Association*, 28.

46. Levy, "Against Philanthropy, Individual and Corporate," 163.

Appendix

1. Because of technical difficulties, five interviews were not recorded.

2. Kvale, *InterViews,* 237.

3. See Rutnik and Bearman, *Giving Together,* 42–45, for survey questions.

4. Elias, "Social Venture Partners"; Guthrie, Preston, and Bernholz, "Transforming Philanthropic Transactions"; Sbarbaro, "Social Venture Partners Replication."

5. Orloff, "Social Venture Partners Calgary."

6. Ahn, "The Hestia Fund."

7. Rutnik and Beaudoin-Schwartz, *Growing Philanthropy through Giving Circles.*

8. Ibid.

9. Berg, *Qualitative Research Methods for the Social Sciences,* 5; Lincoln and Guba, *Naturalistic Inquiry.*

10. That is, with the exception of one interview in which half the recording was lost.

11. Maxwell, "Designing a Qualitative Study," 90.

12. Coffey and Atkinson, *Making Sense of Qualitative Data,* 29.

13. Miles and Huberman, *Qualitative Data Analysis.*

14. Lincoln and Guba, *Naturalistic Inquiry,* 290.

15. Berg, *Qualitative Research Methods for the Social Sciences,* 5; Borman, LeCompte, and Goetz, "Ethnographic and Qualitative Research Design and Why It Doesn't Work," 44.

16. Creswell, *Qualitative Inquiry and Research Design,* 202.

Bibliography

Abramson, Alan J., Lester M. Salamon, and C. Eugene Steuerle. "The Nonprofit Sector and the Federal Budget: Recent History and Future Directions." In *Nonprofits and Government,* ed. Elizabeth T. Boris and C. Eugene Steuerle, 99–139. Washington: Urban Institute, 1999.

Adams, Carolyn, and Felice Perlmutter. "Commercial Venturing and the Transformation of America's Voluntary Social Welfare Agencies." *Nonprofit and Voluntary Sector Quarterly* 20 (1991): 25–38.

Adams, Guy B. "Enthralled with Modernity: The Historical Context of Knowledge and Theory Development in Public Administration." *Public Administration Review* 52 (1992): 363–73.

Adams, Guy B., Priscilla V. Bowerman, Kenneth M. Dolbeare, and Camilla Stivers. "Joining Purpose to Practice: A Democratic Identity for the Public Service." In *Images and Identities in Public Administration,* ed. Henry D. Kass and Bayard L. Catron, 219–40. Newbury Park: Sage, 1990.

Adamson, Rebecca L. "Smoothing Out the Road." *Foundation News & Commentary* 42, July/August 2001, 32–35.

Addams, Jane. *Democracy and Social Ethics.* New York: Macmillan, 1902.

Agger, Ben. *Postponing the Postmodern: Sociological Practices, Selves, and Theories.* Lanham, Md.: Rowman & Littlefield, 2002.

Aguilar, Orson, Tomasa Duenas, Brenda Flores, Lupe Godinez, Hilary Joy, and Isabel Zavala. "Fairness in Philanthropy. Part I: Foundation Giving to Minority-Led Nonprofits." Berkeley, Calif.: Greenlining Institute, November 2005, available at www.philanthropy.iupui.edu/Millennium/usefulInformation/Fairness%20in%20Philanthropy.pdf.

Ahn, Roy. "The Hestia Fund," John F. Kennedy School of Government Case Program, CR16-03-1691.0. Cambridge: Harvard University, 2003.

Alexander, Jeffrey A., and Bryan J. Weiner. "The Adoption of the Corporate Governance Model by Nonprofit Organizations." *Nonprofit Management & Leadership* 8 (1998): 233–42.

Alexander, Jennifer. "The Impact of Devolution on Nonprofits: A Multiphase Study of Social Service Organizations." *Nonprofit Management & Leadership* 10 (1999): 57–70.

Alexander, Jennifer, Renee Nank, and Camilla Stivers. "Implications of Welfare Reform: Do Nonprofit Survival Strategies Threaten Civil Society?" *Nonprofit and Voluntary Sector Quarterly* 28 (1999): 452–75.

Almond, Gabriel A., and Sidney Verba. *The Civic Culture: Political Attitudes and Democracy in Five Nations.* Princeton, N.J.: Princeton University Press, 1963.

Alter, Jonathan. "An Education in Giving: Teacher's Web Site Lets You Choose Which Projects You Want to Donate To." *Newsweek,* April 24, 2002.

Anderson, Elizabeth. "The Ethical Limitations of the Market." *Economics and Philosophy* 6 (1990): 179–205.

Anft, Michael, and Harvy Lipman. "How Americans Give: Chronicle Study Finds that Race Is a Powerful Influence." *Chronicle of Philanthropy,* May 1, 2003.

Arnove, Robert F. "Introduction." In *Philanthropy and Cultural Imperialism: The Foundations at Home and Abroad,* ed. Robert F. Arnove, 1–24. Bloomington: Indiana University Press, 1980.

AsiaNextGen. "Grantees," 2007, available at www.asianextgen.org/grantees.html.

AsiaNextGen. "Join Us," 2007, available at www.asianextgen.org/join_us.html.

"AsiaNextGen Made Its First Donation," *Epoch Times,* September 25, 2006.

Atteberry Smith, Susan. "Missouri Friends Raise Funds for Medical Clinic." *Hannibal Courier Post,* October 12, 2002.

Axelrod, Morris. "Urban Structure and Social Participation." In *Social Participation in Urban Society,* ed. John Edwards and Alan Booth, 39–44. Cambridge, Mass.: Schenkman, 1973.

Babchuk, Nicholas, and Alan Booth. "Voluntary Association Membership: A Longitudinal Analysis." In *Social Participation in Urban Society,* ed. John Edwards and Alan Booth, 23–37. Cambridge, Mass.: Schenkman, 1973.

Babchuk, Nicholas, and John N. Edwards. "Voluntary Associations and the Integration Hypothesis." *Sociological Inquiry* 35 (1965): 149–62.

Baccaro, Lucio. "Civil Society Meets the State: Towards Associational Democracy." *Socio-Economic Review* 4 (2006): 185–208.

Bachrach, Peter, and Aryeh Botwinick. *Power and Empowerment: A Radical Theory of Participatory Democracy.* Philadelphia: Temple University Press, 1992.

Backman, Elaine V., and Steven Rathgeb Smith. "Healthy Organizations, Unhealthy Communities?" *Nonprofit Management & Leadership* 10 (2000): 355–73.

Baltimore Giving Project. "Information on Local Giving Circles," available at www.baltimoregivingproject.org.

Bang, Henrik P., and Eva Sørensen. "The Everyday Maker: A New Challenge to Democratic Governance." *Administrative Theory & Praxis* 21 (1999): 325–41.

Barber, Benjamin R. *A Place for Us: How to Make Society Civil and Democracy Strong.* New York: Hill and Wang, 1998.

———. *Strong Democracy: Participatory Politics for a New Age.* Berkeley: University of California Press, 1984.

Bauman, Zygmunt. *The Individualized Society.* Cambridge: Polity, 2001.

Bearman, Jessica E. *More Giving Together: The Growth and Impact of Giving Circles and Shared Giving.* Washington, D.C.: Forum of Regional Associations of Grantmakers, 2007. Available at www.givingforum.org/s_forum/bin.asp?CID=611&DID=5316&DOC=FILE.PDF.

Beck, Ulrich. *Risk Society: Towards a New Modernity.* New Delhi: Sage, 1992.

Beck, Ulrich, and Elisabeth Beck-Gernsheim. "Individualization and 'Precarious Freedoms': Perspectives and Controversies of a Subject-Oriented Sociology." In *Detraditionalization: Critical Reflections on Authority and Identity,* ed. Paul Heelas, Scott Lash, and Paul Morris, 23–48. Cambridge, Mass.: Blackwell, 1996.

Beeson, Melisa Jane Ellis. "Women's Giving Circles: A Case Study in Higher Education Philanthropy." EdD diss., Indiana University, 2006.

Bellah, Robert N., Richard Madsen, William M. Sullivan, Ann Swidler, and Steven M. Tipton. *Habits of the Heart: Individualism and Commitment in American Life.* New York: Harper & Row, 1985.

Berg, Bruce L. *Qualitative Research Methods for the Social Sciences.* 4th ed. Boston: Allyn and Bacon, 2001.

Berger, Peter L., and Richard J. Neuhaus. *To Empower People: From State to Civil Society.* Ed. Michael Novak. 2nd ed. Washington, D.C.: AEI Press, 1996.

Berman, Sheri. "Civil Society and the Collapse of the Weimar Republic." *World Politics* 49 (1997): 401–29.

Bernstein, Nina. "Class Divide in Chinese-Americans' Charity." *New York Times,* January 20, 2007.

Berry, Jeffrey M. "Nonprofits and Civic Engagement." *Public Administration Review* 65 (2005): 568–78.

Berry, Mindy L. "Native American Philanthropy and Expanding Social Participation and Self-Determination." In *Cultures of Caring: Philanthropy in Diverse American Communities,* ed. J. Scanlon, 29–105. Washington, D.C.: Council on Foundations, 1999.

Best, Steven, and Douglas Kellner. *The Postmodern Turn.* New York: Guilford Press, 1997.

Bianchi, Alessandra. "Serving Nonprofits: The New Philanthropy." *Inc.,* October 2000, 23–25.

B'More Fund. Brochure. Baltimore Community Foundation, n.d.

Bole, Robert. "More Than a Handout: High Tech Giving Starts at the Bottom." *Horizon* (online magazine). Columbia, Md.: Enterprise Foundation, 1999.

Boris, Elizabeth, and C. Eugene Steuerle. "What Charities Cannot Do." *Christian Science Monitor,* October 1, 1999.

Borkman, Thomasina Jo. *Understanding Self-Help/Mutual Aid: Experiential Learning in the Commons.* New Brunswick: Rutgers University Press, 1999.

Borman, Kathryn M., Margaret D. LeCompte, and Judith P. Goetz. "Ethnographic and Qualitative Research Design and Why It Doesn't Work." *American Behavioral Scientist* 30 (1986): 42–57.

Box, Richard C. *Citizen Governance: Leading American Communities into the Twenty-first Century.* Thousand Oaks: Sage, 1998.

———. *Public Administration and Society: Critical Issues in American Governance.* Armonk, N.Y.: M. E. Sharpe, 2004.

Brainerd, Paul. "Social Venture Partners: Engaging a New Generation of Givers." *Nonprofit and Voluntary Sector Quarterly* 28 (1999): 502–7.

Brakman, Dana. "Dismembering Civil Society: The Social Cost of Internally Undemocratic Nonprofits." *Oregon Law Review* 82 (2003): 865–86.

Bread for the Journey International. *Stories of Kindness and Generosity.* Mill Valley, Calif.: Bread for the Journey International, 2002.

Bremner, Robert H. *American Philanthropy.* 2nd ed. Chicago: University of Chicago Press, 1988.

Brilliant, Eleanor L. *Private Charity and Public Inquiry: A History of the Filer and Peterson Commissions.* Bloomington: Indiana University Press, 2000.

Brody, Evelyn. "Entrance, Voice, and Exit: The Constitutional Bounds of the Right of Association." *University of California Davis Law Review* 35 (2002): 821–32.

Burke, Colin C. "Establishing a Context: The Elusive History of America's Nonprofit Domain—Numbers Count—If Someone Counted." Working paper 261. Yale University Program on Non-Profit Organizations, November 2000.

———. "Nonprofit History's New Numbers (and the Need for More)." *Nonprofit and Voluntary Sector Quarterly* 30 (2001): 174–203.

Byrne, John A. "The New Face of Philanthropy." *Business Week,* December 2002, 282–94.

Cagetti, Marco, and Mariacristina De Nardi. "Wealth Inequality: Data and Models."

Working paper 2005-10. Federal Reserve Bank of Chicago, August 17, 2005. Available at www.chicagofed.org/publications/workingpapers/wp2005_10.pdf.

Catlaw, Thomas J. "Authority, Representation, and the Contradictions of Posttraditional Governing." *American Review of Public Administration* 36 (2006): 261-87.

Center on Philanthropy at Indiana University. "Average and Median Amounts of Household Giving & Volunteering in 2002." March 2006, available at www .philanthropy.iupui.edu.

———. "Center on Philanthropy Panel Study—Household Giving and Volunteering Reports," March 2006, available at www.philanthropy.iupui.edu.

———. "Patterns of Household Charitable Giving by Income Group, 2005." Summer 2007, available at www.philanthropy.iupui.edu.

Chambers, Simone, and Jeffrey Kopstein. "Bad Civil Society." *Political Theory* 29 (2001): 837–65.

Chandoke, Neera. *The Conceits of Civil Society.* New Delhi: Oxford University Press, 2003.

Chao, Jessica. "Asian American Philanthropy: Expanding Circles of Participation." In *Cultures of Caring: Philanthropy in Diverse American Communities.* Washington, D.C.: Council on Foundations, June 1999. Available at www.cof.org/files/ Documents/Publications/Cultures_of_Caring/asianamerican.pdf.

Charles, Jeffrey A. *Service Clubs in American Society: Rotary, Kiwanis, and Lions.* Urbana: University of Illinois Press, 1993.

Clarke, Susan E. "The Prospects for Local Democratic Governance: The Governance Roles of Nonprofit Organizations." *Policy Studies Review* 18 (2001): 129–45.

Clary, Bruce. "Study Circles, Deliberative Discourse, and Civic Education: 'Learning to Bowl Together.'" Paper presented at the annual meeting of the National Association of Schools of Public Affairs and Administration, Los Angeles, October 2002.

Clohesy, Stephanie J. *Donor Circles: Launching and Leveraging Shared Giving.* Women's Funding Network, 2004. Available at www.wfnet.org/resource/publication/ donor-circles-launching-and-leveraging-shared-giving.

Cobb, Nina K. "The New Philanthropy: Its Impact on Funding Arts and Culture." *Journal of Arts Management, Law, and Society* 32 (2002): 125–43.

Coffey, Amanda, and Paul Atkinson. *Making Sense of Qualitative Data.* Thousand Oaks: Sage, 1996.

Cohen, Joshua, and Joel Rogers. *Associations and Democracy.* London: Verso, 1995.

———. "Secondary Associations and Democratic Governance." *Politics & Society* 20 (1992): 393–472.

Community Investment Network. "History," 2006, available at www .thecommunityinvestment.org.

Community Wealth Ventures, Inc. *Venture Philanthropy 2002: Advancing Nonprofit Performance through High-Engagement Grantmaking.* Washington, D.C.: Venture Philanthropy Partners, 2002.

Cooney, Kate. "The Institutional and Technical Structuring of Nonprofit Ventures: Case Study of a U.S. Hybrid Organization Caught between Two Fields." *Voluntas* 17 (2006): 143–61.

Creswell, John. W. *Qualitative Inquiry and Research Design: Choosing among Five Traditions.* Thousand Oaks: Sage, 1998.

Crimmins, James C., and Mary Keil. *Enterprise in the Nonprofit Sector.* New York: Rockefeller Brothers Fund, 1983.

Crotty, Michael. *The Foundations of Social Research: Meaning and Perspective in the Research Process.* London: Sage, 1998.

Curti, Merle. "Philanthropy." In *Dictionary of the History of Ideas: Studies of Selected Pivotal Ideas,* vol. 3, ed. Philip P. Wiener, 486–93. New York: Charles Scribner's Sons, 1973.

Dahl, Robert A. *Democracy and Its Critics.* New Haven: Yale University Press, 1989.

Dart, Raymond. "Being 'Business-Like' in a Nonprofit Organization: A Grounded and Inductive Typology." *Nonprofit and Voluntary Sector Quarterly* 33 (2004): 290–310.

Davis, Allen F. *Spearheads for Reform: The Social Settlements and the Progressive Movement, 1890–1914.* New York: Oxford University Press, 1984.

Dees, J. Gregory, Jed Emerson, and Peter Economy. *Enterprising Nonprofits: A Toolkit for Social Entrepreneurs.* New York: Wiley, 2001.

Dekker, Paul, and A. van den Broek. "Civil Society in Comparative Perspective: Involvement in Voluntary Associations in North America and Western Europe." *Voluntas* 9 (1998): 11–38.

Delanty, Gerard. *Modernity and Postmodernity: Knowledge, Power, and the Self.* London: Sage, 2000.

DeNavas-Walt, Carmen, Bernadette D. Proctor, and Jessica Smith. *Income, Poverty, and Health Insurance Coverage in the United States, 2006.* Current Population Reports, P60-233. U.S. Census Bureau. Washington, D.C.: U.S. Government Printing Office, August 2007. Available at www.census.gov/prod/2007pubs/p60-233.pdf.

Denhardt, Robert B. *In the Shadow of Organization.* Lawrence: Regents Press of Kansas, 1981.

Dewey, John. "The Ethics of Democracy." In *The Early Works, 1882–1898.* Carbondale: Southern Illinois University Press, 1967–72.

———. *The Public and Its Problems.* Chicago: Swallow Press, 1954.

Diaz, William. "For Whom and for What? The Contributions of the Nonprofit Sector." In *The State of Nonprofit America,* ed. Lester M. Salamon, 517–36. Washington, D.C.: Brookings Institution Press, 2002.

Diaz-Gimenez, Javier, Vincenzo Quadrini, and José-Victor Ríos-Rull. "Dimensions of Inequality: Facts on the U.S. Distributions." *Quarterly Review* 21 (1997): 3–21.

Dicke, Lisa A. "Ensuring Accountability in Human Services Contracting: Can Stewardship Theory Fill the Bill?" *American Review of Public Administration* 32 (2002): 455–70.

DiMaggio, Paul J. *Nonprofit Enterprise in the Arts.* New York: Oxford University Press, 1986.

Dorfman, Aaron. "Creating a Philanthropic Sector That Is More Responsive to the Needs of Diverse Communities." Comments to the U.S. House Committee on Ways and Means, Subcommittee on Oversight. Washington, D.C.: National Committee for Responsive Philanthropy, September 25, 2007. Available at www.ncrp.org/downloads/RP-Fall%202007-NCRPComments-lowres.pdf.

Durkheim, Emile. *The Division of Labor in Society.* New York: Free Press, 1984.

Eberly, Don E. *The Soul of Civil Society: Voluntary Associations and the Public Value of Moral Habits.* Lanham, Md.: Lexington Books, 2002.

Eckstein, Harry. *A Theory of Stable Democracy.* Princeton: Princeton University Center of International Studies, 1961.

Edwards, Bob, and Michael W. Foley. "Civil Society and Social Capital beyond Putnam." *American Behavioral Scientist* 42 (1998): 124–39.

Edwards, Bob, and Michael W. Foley. "Civil Society and Social Capital: A Primer." In *Beyond Tocqueville: Civil Society and the Social Capital Debate in Comparative Perspective*, ed. Bob Edwards, Michael W. Foley, and Mario Diani, 1–14. Hanover: University Press of New England, 2001.

Eikenberry, Angela M. "Promoting Philanthropy: A Qualitative Study of the Massachusetts Catalogue for Philanthropy." *International Journal of Nonprofit and Voluntary Sector Marketing* 10 (2005): 137–49.

Eikenberry, Angela M., and Patricia M. Nickel. "Towards a Critical Social Theory of Philanthropy in an Era of Governance." In *Theorizing Power Post 9/11*, ed. Wolfgang Natter. Blacksburg: Virginia Tech, forthcoming.

Eikenberry, Angela M., and Michelle C. Pautz. "Administrative Reform in the United States: Toward Partnership in Governance." In *Handbook of Administrative Reform: An International Perspective*, ed. Jerri Killian and Niklas Ekland, 197–214. Boca Raton, Fla.: CRC Press, 2008.

Elias, Joan. "Social Venture Partners (draft v3.01)." Kansas City, Mo.: Ewing Marion Kauffman Foundation, 1998.

Eliasoph, Nina. *Avoiding Politics: How Americans Produce Apathy in Everyday Life*. Cambridge: Cambridge University Press, 1998.

Ellis L. Phillips Foundation. "The Paradigm-Shift in Philanthropy." In *The Catalogue for Philanthropy*. Boston: Ellis L. Phillips Foundation, 2000.

Ellison, Nick. "Towards a New Social Politics: Citizenship and Reflexivity in Late Modernity." *Sociology* 31 (1997): 697–717.

Etzioni, Amitai. *The Spirit of Community: Rights, Responsibilities, and the Communitarian Agenda*. New York: Crown, 1993.

Evans, Sara. M., and Harry C. Boyte. *Free Spaces: The Sources of Democratic Change in America*. New York: Harper & Row, 1986.

The Everychild Foundation. "Information for Applicants." Available at www.everychildfoundation.org/grant.cfm.

The Everychild Foundation. "Where the Money Will Go and How to Be Involved." Available in 2004 at www.everychildfoundation.org/involvement.cfm.

Faber, Daniel R., and Deborah McCarthy. "Introduction." In *Foundations for Social Change: Critical Perspectives on Philanthropy and Popular Movements*, ed. Daniel R. Faber and Deborah McCarthy, 3–32. Lanham, Md.: Rowman & Littlefield, 2005.

Feminist Majority Foundation. *Empowering Women in Philanthropy*. Arlington, Va.: Feminist Majority Foundation, 1991.

Ferguson, Niall. *Empire: The Rise and Demise of the British World Order and the Lessons for Global Power*. New York: Basic Books, 2002.

Ferrell, Jeff. "Remapping the City: Public Identity, Cultural Space, and Social Justice." *Contemporary Justice Review* 4 (2001): 161–80.

Fine, Gary A., and Brooke Harrington. "Tiny Publics: Small Groups and Civil Society." *Sociological Theory* 22 (2004): 341–56.

Fischer, Marilyn. "Philanthropy and Injustice in Mill and Addams." *Nonprofit and Voluntary Sector Quarterly* 24 (1995): 281–92.

Fisher, Donald. "The Role of Philanthropic Foundations in the Reproduction and Production of Hegemony." *Sociology* 17 (1983): 206–33.

Foley, Michael W., John D. McCarthy, and Mark Chaves. "Social Capital, Religious Institutions, and Poor Communities." In *Social Capital and Poor Communities*, ed.

Susan Saegert, J. Phillip Thompson, and Mark R. Warren, 215–45. New York: Russell Sage Foundation, 2001.

Follett, Mary P. *The New State.* University Park: Pennsylvania State University Press, 1998. First published 1918.

Forum of Regional Associations of Grantmakers. "AsiaNextGen Giving Circle Profile," 2008, available at www.givingforum.org.

———. "Asian Giving Circle Brings Hope to New York Children," 2008, available at www.givingforum.org.

Foster, William, and Jeffrey Bradach. "Should Nonprofits Seek Profits?" *Harvard Business Review,* February 2005, 92–100.

Foundation Center. "Foundation Giving Trends: Update on Funding Priorities, 2008 Edition." New York: Foundation Center, 2008.

Fox, Charles J., and Hugh T. Miller. *Postmodern Public Administration.* Thousand Oaks: Sage, 1995.

Friedman, Lawrence J. "Philanthropy in America: Historicism and Its Discontents." In *Charity, Philanthropy, and Civility in American History,* ed. Lawrence J. Friedman and Mark D. McGarvie, 1–21. New York: Cambridge University Press, 2003.

Frumkin, Peter. *Strategic Philanthropy: The Art and Science of Philanthropy.* Chicago: University of Chicago Press, 2006.

Fung, Archon. "Associations and Democracy: Between Theories, Hopes, and Realities." *Annual Review of Sociology* 29 (2003): 515–39.

———. *Empowered Participation: Reinventing Urban Democracy.* Princeton, N.J.: Princeton University Press, 2004.

———. "Survey Article: Recipes for Public Spheres: Eight Institutional Design Choices and Their Consequences." *Journal of Political Philosophy* 11 (2003): 338–67.

Fung, Archon, and Erik O. Wright. "Deepening Democracy: Innovations in Empowered Participatory Governance." *Politics & Society* 29 (2001): 5–41.

———. "Thinking about Empowered Participatory Governance." In *Deepening Democracy: Institutional Innovations in Empowered Participatory Governance,* ed. Archon Fung and Eric O. Wright, 3–44. London: Verso, 2003.

Galaskiewicz, Joseph, Paola Molina, Olga Mayorova, and Joy Inouye. "Funding Sources, Auspices, and Location of Youth Services." Paper presented at the 2005 ARNOVA conference, Washington, D.C., November 17–19, 2005.

Gastil, John. "A Definition of Small Group Democracy." *Small Group Research* 23 (1992): 278–301.

Giddens, Anthony. *Beyond Left and Right: The Future of Radical Politics.* Cambridge: Polity Press, 1994.

Gingold, Diane. "New Frontiers in Philanthropy." *Fortune.com,* July 2000.

Giving USA Foundation. *Giving USA 2006.* Glenview, Ill.: Giving USA Foundation, 2006.

Glassman, Ronald M. *Democracy and Equality: Theories and Programs for the Modern World.* New York: Praeger, 1989.

Grace, Kay S., and Alan L. Wendroff. *High Impact Philanthropy: How Donors, Boards, and Nonprofit Organizations Can Transform Communities.* New York: Wiley, 2001.

Granovetter, Mark. "The Strength of Weak Ties." *American Journal of Sociology* 78 (1973): 1360–80.

Grimm, Robert, Jr., et al. "Volunteering in America: 2007 State Trends and Rankings in

Civic Life." Washington, D.C.: Corporation for National and Community Service, April 2007.

Grønbjerg, Kirsten A. *Understanding Nonprofit Funding: Managing Revenues in Social Services and Community Development Organizations.* San Francisco: Jossey-Bass, 1993.

Gross, Robert. "Giving in America: From Charity to Philanthropy." In *Charity, Philanthropy, and Civility in American History,* ed. Lawrence J. Friedman, and Mark D. McGarvie, 29–48. New York: Cambridge University Press, 2003.

Gundelach, Peter, and Lars Torpe. "Social Reflexivity, Democracy, and New Types of Citizen Involvement in Denmark." In *Private Groups and Public Life: Social Participation, Voluntary Associations, and Political Involvement in Representative Democracy,* ed. Jan W. Van Deth, 47–63. London: Routledge, 1997.

———. "Voluntary Associations: New Types of Involvement and Democracy." Paper presented at the ECPR Joint Sessions of Workshops. Oslo, Norway, 1996. Available at www.aub.aau.dk/phd/department02/text/1996/35031996_2.pdf.

Gunderman, Richard B. "Giving and Human Excellence: The Paradigm of Liberal Philanthropy." Working paper 9, Philanthropic Enterprise, December 2003. Available at www.thephilanthropicenterprise.org/main/library.php/87/p.

Guo, Chao. "Government Funding and Community Representation on Nonprofit Boards: The Bargain We Strike." *Nonprofit Quarterly* 14 (2007): 70–76.

Guthrie, Kendall, Alan Preston, and Lucy Bernholz. 2003. "Transforming Philanthropic Transactions: An Evaluation of the First Five Years at Social Venture Partners Seattle." Blueprint Research and Design, Inc., 2003. Available at www.blueprintrd .com/text/svp.pdf.

Gutmann, Amy. "Freedom of Association: An Introductory Essay." In *Freedom of Association,* ed. Amy Gutmann, 3–32. Princeton: Princeton University Press, 1998.

Habermas, Jürgen. *The Structural Transformation of the Public Sphere: An Inquiry into a Category of Bourgeois Society.* Cambridge: MIT Press, 1989.

Hacker, Jacob S. *The Divided Welfare State: The Battle over Public and Private Social Benefits in the United States.* Cambridge: Cambridge University Press, 2002.

Halfpenny, Peter. "Trust, Charity, and Civil Society." In *Trust and Civil Society,* ed. Fran Tonkiss and Andrew Passey, 132–50. New York: St. Martin's Press, 2000.

Hall, Holly. "A Charitable Divide." *Chronicle of Philanthropy,* January 10, 2008.

Hall, Peter D. "Resolving the Dilemmas of Democratic Governance: The Historical Development of Trusteeship in America, 1636–1996." In *Philanthropic Foundations: New Scholarship, New Possibilities,* ed. Ellen Condliffe Lagemann, 3–42. Bloomington: Indiana University Press, 1999.

Halstead, John P. *The Second British Empire: Trade, Philanthropy, and Good Government, 1820–1890.* Westport, Conn.: Greenwood Press, 1983.

Hammack, David C. "Foundations in the American Polity, 1900–1950." In *Philanthropic Foundations: New Scholarship, New Possibilities,* ed. Ellen Condliffe Lagemann, 43–68. Bloomington: Indiana University Press, 1999.

Hartman, Marilyn. "Grassroots Giving Circles Survey Report." Manuscript, Research Triangle Park, N.C., August 18, 2004.

Haque, M. Shamsul. "Threats to Public Workplace Democracy." *Peace Review* 12 (2000): 237–41.

Havens, John J., and Paul G. Schervish. "Millionaires and the Millennium: New Estimates of the Forthcoming Wealth Transfer and the Prospects for a Golden Age of Philanthropy." Boston College Social Welfare Research Institute, October 19, 1999. Available at www.bc.edu/research/cwp/meta-elements/pdf/m_m.pdf.

———. "Why the $41 Trillion Wealth Transfer Is Still Valid: A Review of Challenges and Questions." *Journal of Gift Planning* 7 (2003): 11–5, 47–50.

Hays, Samuel P. *The Response to Industrialism, 1885–1914.* Chicago: University of Chicago Press, 1958.

Heelas, Paul. "Introduction: Detraditionalization and Its Rivals." In *Detraditionalization: Critical Reflections on Authority and Identity,* ed. Paul Heelas, Scott Lash, and Paul Morris, 1–20. Cambridge, Mass.: Blackwell, 1996.

Heelas, P., Scott Lash, and Paul Morris, eds. *Detraditionalization: Detraditionalization: Critical Reflections on Authority and Identity.* Cambridge, Mass.: Blackwell, 1996.

Held, David. *Models of Democracy.* Stanford, Calif.: Stanford University Press, 1996.

Hemmings Kahn, Erin. "Demonstrating Social Venture Partners' Impact: 2007 Philanthropy Development Report." Seattle, Wash.: Social Venture Partners International, September 10, 2007.

Heying, Charles H. "Civic Elites and Corporate Delocalization." *American Behavioral Scientist* 40 (1997): 657–68.

Hirst, Paul. *Associative Democracy: New Forms of Economic and Social Governance.* Amherst: University of Massachusetts Press, 1994.

———. "Democracy and Governance." In *Debating Governance: Authority, Steering, and Democracy,* ed. Jon Pierre, 13–35. New York: Oxford University Press, 2000.

———. "Renewing Democracy through Associations." *Political Quarterly* 73 (2002): 409–21.

Hodgkinson, Virginia A., with Kathryn E. Nelson and Edward D. Sivak Jr. "Individual Giving and Volunteering." In *The State of Nonprofit America,* ed. Lester M. Salamon, 387–420. Washington, D.C.: Brookings Institution Press, 2002.

Hodgkinson, Virginia A., and Murray S. Weitzman. *Giving and Volunteering in the United States.* Washington, D.C.: Independent Sector, 1994.

———. "Overview: The State of Independent Sector." In J. S. Otto, ed., *The nature of the nonprofit sector,* 9–22. Boulder: Westview Press.

Hofstadter, Richard. *The Age of Reform.* New York: Knopf, 1955.

Hummel, Ralph P. *The Bureaucratic Experience: The Post-Modern Challenge.* 5th ed. Armonk, N.Y.: M. E. Sharpe, 2007.

Hunter, Floyd. *Community Power Structure: A Study of Decision Makers.* Chapel Hill: University of North Carolina Press, 1953.

Husock, Howard. "Bringing Back the Settlement House." *Public Welfare* 51 (1993): 16–25.

Hustinx, Lesley, and Frans Lammertyn. "Collective and Reflexive Styles of Volunteering: A Sociological Modernization Perspective." *Voluntas* 14 (2003): 167–87.

Independent Sector. "Giving and Volunteering in the United States." Survey conducted by the Gallup Organization. Washington, D.C.: Independent Sector, 1996.

———. *The New Nonprofit Almanac and Desk Reference: The Essential Facts and Figures for Managers, Researchers, and Volunteers.* Washington, D.C.: Independent Sector, 2002.

Inglehart, Ronald. *Modernization and Postmodernization.* Princeton, N.J.: Princeton University Press, 1997.

"Interview with Rev. Wayne Muller." *Pathways Magazine,* September/October 1997. Available at www.breadforthejourney.org/history.htm.

Jackson, Elton F., Mark D. Bachmeier, James R. Wood, and Elizabeth A. Craft. "Volunteering and Charitable Giving: Do Religious and Associational Ties Promote Helping Behavior?" *Nonprofit and Voluntary Sector Quarterly* 24 (1995): 59–78.

Jacques, Roy. *Manufacturing the Employee: Management Knowledge from the Nineteenth to Twenty-first Centuries.* London: Sage, 1996.

Jaffee, David. *Organization Theory: Tension and Change.* Boston: McGraw-Hill, 2001.

James, Estelle. "Commercialism among Nonprofits: Objectives, Opportunities, and Constraints." In *To Profit or Not to Profit: The Commercial Transformation of the Nonprofit Sector,* ed. Burton Weisbrod, 271–86. Cambridge: Cambridge University Press, 1998.

Janoski, Thomas, and John Wilson. "Pathways to Voluntarism: Family, Socialization, and Status Transmission Models." *Social Forces* 74 (1995): 271–92.

Jeavons, Thomas H. "When the Management Is the Message: Relating Values to Management Practice in Nonprofit Organizations." *Nonprofit Management & Leadership* 2 (1992): 403–17.

Jenkins, J. Craig. "Social Movement Philanthropy and American Democracy." In *Philanthropic Giving: Studies in Varieties and Goals,* ed. Richard Magat, 292–314. New York: Oxford University Press, 1989.

Joulfaian, David. "Basic Facts on Charitable Giving." OTA Paper 95. Washington, D.C.: U.S. Department of the Treasury, June 2005.

Jovanovic, Spoma, David Carolone, and Cynthia Massood. "Voice and Community Engagement: A Report of Young Leaders and Philanthropy." University of North Carolina at Greensboro, February 2004.

Kaminski, Andrea R. "Women as Donors." In *Hank Rosso's Achieving Excellence in Fund Raising,* 2nd ed., ed. Henry A. Rosso and Eugene R. Tempel, 200–214. San Francisco: Jossey-Bass, 2003.

Katz, Alfred H. *Self-Help in America: A Social Movement Perspective.* New York: Twayne, 1993.

Katz, Michael B. *The Undeserving Poor: From the War on Poverty to the War on Welfare.* New York: Pantheon Books, 1989.

———. *In the Shadow of the Poorhouse: A Social History of Welfare in America.* 10th anniversary ed. New York: Basic Books, 1996.

Kaufman, Jason. *For the Common Good? American Civic Life and the Golden Age of Fraternity.* New York: Oxford University Press, 2002.

Kellner, Douglas. "Habermas, the Public Sphere, and Democracy: A Critical Intervention." Available at www.gseis.ucla.edu/faculty/kellner/papers/habermas.htm.

Kemmis, Daniel. *Community and the Politics of Place.* Norman: University of Oklahoma Press, 1990.

Kennedy, Maureen. "Clubs with a Cause." *Health,* December 2002, 72–75.

Kerlin, Janelle A. "Nonprofit Commercial Revenue: A Replacement for Declining Government Grants and Private Contributions?" Paper presented at the thirty-fifth annual ARNOVA conference, Chicago, November 16–18, 2006.

Kettl, Don. "The Global Revolution in Public Management: Driving Themes, Missing Links." *Journal of Policy Analysis and Management* 16 (1997): 446–62.

———. *Government by Proxy.* Washington, D.C.: Congressional Quarterly Press, 1988.

King, Samantha. *Pink Ribbons, Inc.: Breast Cancer and the Politics of Philanthropy.* Minneapolis: University of Minnesota Press, 2006.

Knight, Louise. W. "Jane Addams and Hull House: Historical Lessons on Nonprofit Leadership." *Nonprofit Management & Leadership* 2 (1991): 125–41.

Kong, Dolores. "Fortunate Seek Guidance in Giving Away Their Wealth." *Boston Globe,* November 18, 2001, F5.

Korelitz, Jean H. "Second Helpings." *Real Simple,* August 2002, 85–90.

Krugman, Paul. "For Richer." *New York Times Magazine,* October 20, 2002, 62.

Kvale, Steinar. *InterViews: An Introduction to Qualitative Research Interviewing.* Thousand Oaks: Sage, 1996.

Kwon, Hyeong-ki. "Associations, Civic Norms, and Democracy: Revisiting the Italian Case." *Theory & Society* 33 (2004): 135–66.

Lemann, Nicholas. "Kicking in Groups." *Atlantic Monthly,* April 1996, 22–26.

Lenkowsky, Leslie. "Foundations and Corporate Philanthropy." In *The State of Nonprofit America,* ed. Lester M. Salamon, 355–86. Washington, D.C.: Brookings Institution Press, 2002.

Letts, Christine W., William Ryan, and Allen Grossman. "Virtuous Capital: What Foundations Can Learn from Venture Capitalists." *Harvard Business Review,* March/April 1997, 2–7.

Levi, Margaret. "Social and Unsocial Capital: A Review Essay of Robert Putnam's Making Democracy Work." *Politics and Society* 24 (1996): 45–55.

Levy, Neil. "Against Philanthropy, Individual and Corporate." In *The Kindness of Strangers: Philanthropy and Higher Education,* ed. Deni Elliott, 159–70. Lanham, Md.: Rowman & Littefield, 2006.

Lewis, Danielle. "Blacks Build New Legacy of Giving." *Sacramento Observer,* February 23, 2005.

Lichterman, Paul. *Elusive Togetherness: Church Groups Trying to Bridge America's Divisions.* Princeton, N.J.: Princeton University Press, 2005.

———. *The Search for Political Community.* New York: Cambridge University Press, 1996.

———. "Social Capital or Group Style? Rescuing Tocqueville's Insights on Civic Engagement." *Theory & Society* 35 (2006): 529–63.

Lincoln, Yvonna S., and Egon G. Guba. *Naturalistic Inquiry.* Newbury Park, Calif.: Sage, 1985.

Logan, John R., and Harvey Molotch. *Urban Fortunes: The Political Economy of Place.* Berkeley: University of California Press, 1987.

London, Scott. "Teledemocracy versus Deliberative Democracy: A Comparative Look at Two Models of Public Talk." *Journal of Interpersonal Computing and Technology* 3 (1995): 33–55.

Loseke, Donileen R. "'The Whole Spirit of Modern Philanthropy': The Construction of the Idea of Charity, 1912–1992." *Social Problems* 44 (1997): 425–44.

Lubove, Roy. *The Professional Altruist: The Emergence of Social Work as a Career, 1880–1930.* Cambridge: Harvard University Press, 1965.

Lynch, Jill Bruckner. "Generosity Grows with Women's Fund Giving Circles." *Today's Omaha Woman,* August/September 2003, 16–17, 24.

MacDonald, G. Jeffrey. "Where Are All the Charitable Bequests?" *Christian Science Monitor,* November 19, 2007.

Macduff, Nancy. "Societal Changes and the Rise of the Episodic Volunteer." In *Emerging Areas of Volunteering,* ed. Jeffrey L. Brudney, 49–61. Indianapolis: Association for Research on Nonprofit Organizations and Voluntary Action, 2005.

Matson, Eric. "The New Face of Social Capital: Young 'Venture Philanthropists' Combine Targeted Donations with Tough-Minded Oversight to Build a New Model of Community Activism." *Fast Company,* October 1996, 54.

Maxwell, Joseph A. "Designing a Qualitative Study." In *Handbook of Applied Social Research Methods*, ed. Leonard Bickman and Debra J. Rog, 69–100. Thousand Oaks: Sage, 1998.

May, William F. "Introduction." In *The Ethics of Giving and Receiving: Am I My Foolish Brother's Keeper?* ed. William F. May and A. Lewis Soens Jr., xvii–xl. Dallas: Southern Methodist University Press, 2000.

McCarthy, Kathleen D. *American Creed: Philanthropy and the Rise of Civil Society, 1700–1865.* Chicago: University of Chicago Press, 2003.

McCully, George. *Philanthropy Reconsidered: Private Initiatives, Public Good, Quality of Life.* Boston: Catalogue for Philanthropy, 2008.

McGarvie, Mark D. "The Dartmouth College Case and the Legal Design of Civil Society." In *Charity, Philanthropy, and Civility in American History,* ed. Lawrence J. Friedman, and Mark D. McGarvie, 91–105. New York: Cambridge University Press, 2003.

McPherson, J. Miller. "A Dynamic Model of Voluntary Affiliation." *Social Forces* 59 (1981): 705–28.

McPherson, J. Miller, and Lynn Smith-Lovin. "Homophily in Voluntary Organizations: Status Distance and the Composition of Face-to-Face Groups." *American Sociological Review* 52 (1987): 370–79.

McSwain, Cynthia J. "Administrators and Citizenship: The Liberalist Legacy of the Constitution." *Administration & Society* 17 (1985): 131–48.

McSwite, O. C. *Legitimacy in Public Administration: A Discourse Analysis.* Newbury Park, Calif.: Sage, 1997.

Menninger, Roy W. "Observations on the Psychology of Giving and Receiving Money." In *The Ethics of Giving and Receiving: Am I My Foolish Brother's Keeper?* ed. William F. May and A. Lewis Soens Jr., 202–15. Dallas: Southern Methodist University Press, 2000.

Miles, Matthew B., and Alan Michael Huberman. *Qualitative Data Analysis: An Expanded Sourcebook.* 2nd ed. Thousand Oaks: Sage, 1994.

Milofsky, Carl. "Structure and Process in Community Self-Help Organizations." In *Community Organizations: Studies in Resource Mobilization and Exchange,* ed. Carl Milofsky, 183–216. New York: Oxford University Press, 1988.

Milward, H. Brinton, and Keith G. Provan. "Governing the Hollow State." *Journal of Public Administration Research and Theory* 6 (2000): 193–95.

Moody, Michael. "'Building a Culture': The Construction and Evolution of Venture Philanthropy as a New Organization Field." *Nonprofit and Voluntary Sector Quarterly* 37 (2008): 324-52.

Nagai, Althea, Robert Lerner, and Stanley Rothman. *Giving for Social Change: Foundations, Public Policy, and the American Political Agenda.* Westport, Conn.: Praeger, 1994.

National Association of Children's Hospitals and Related Institutions. "Different Strokes for Different Folks: Giving Trends among Minorities and Other Groups," 2007, available at www.childrenshospitals.net.

Nevarez, Leonard. "Corporate Philanthropy in the New Urban Economy: The Role of Business-Nonprofit Realignment in Regime Politics." *Urban Affairs Review* 36 (2000): 197–227.

New Mountain Climbers. Brochure, n.d., available at www.scribd.com/doc/425922/New-Mountain-Climbers-brochure.

Newton, Kenneth. "Social Capital and Democracy." *American Behavioral Scientist* 40 (1997): 575–86.

Nickel, Patricia M., and Angela M. Eikenberry. "A Critique of the Discourse of Marketized Philanthropy." *American Behavioral Scientist,* forthcoming.

Nielsen, Waldemar A. *The Big Foundations.* New York: Columbia University Press. 1972.

Nightingale, Demetra S., and Nancy M. Pindus. "Privatization of Public Social Services: A Background Paper." Washington, D.C.: Urban Institute, 1997, available at www.urban.org.

Nonprofit Sector Strategy Group. *The Nonprofit Sector and the Market: Opportunities and Challenges.* Publication no. 01-013. Washington, D.C.: Aspen Institute, Summer 2001.

Norris, Pippa. *Democratic Phoenix: Reinventing Political Activism.* Cambridge: Cambridge University Press, 2002.

Nunn, Michelle. "Building the Bridge from Episodic Volunteerism to Social Capital." *Fletcher Forum of World Affairs* 24 (2000): 115–27.

Odendahl, Theresa. *Charity Begins at Home: Generosity and Self-Interest among the Philanthropic Elite.* New York: Basic Books, 1990.

Olasky, Marvin. *The Tragedy of American Compassion.* Washington, D.C.: Regnery, 1992.

Olson, Mancur. *The Logic of Collective Action: Public Goods and the Theory of Groups.* Cambridge: Harvard University Press, 1965.

Orloff, Avril. "Social Venture Partners Calgary: Emergence and Early Stages." Canadian Centre for Social Entrepreneurship, March 2002, available at www.business .ualberta.ca/ccse/publications.

Osborne, David E., and Ted Gaebler. *Reinventing Government: How the Entrepreneurial Spirit Is Transforming the Public Sector.* Reading, Mass.: Addison-Wesley, 1992.

Ostrander, Susan A. "The Problem of Poverty and Why Philanthropy Neglects It." In *The Future of the Nonprofit Sector: Challenges, Changes, and Policy Considerations,* ed. Virginia A. Hodgkinson and Richard W. Lyman and Associates, 219–36. San Francisco: Jossey-Bass, 1989.

Ostrander, Susan A., and Paul G. Schervish. "Giving and Getting: Philanthropy as a Social Relation." In *Critical Issues in American Philanthropy: Strengthening Theory and Practice,* ed. Jon Van Til, 67–98. San Francisco: Jossey-Bass, 1990.

Ostrower, Francie. *Why the Wealthy Give: The Culture of Elite Philanthropy.* Princeton, N.J.: Princeton University Press, 1995.

Passey, Andrew, and Fran Tonkiss. "Trust, Voluntary Association, and Civil Society." In *Trust and Civil Society,* ed. Fran Tonkiss and Andrew Passey. New York: St. Martin's Press, 2000.

Pateman, Carole. *Participation and Democratic Theory.* London: Cambridge University Press, 1970.

Paulson, Amanda. "A Pooling of Funds to Boost Donors' Impact." *Christian Science Monitor,* October 1, 2001, 18.

Payton, Robert L., and Michael P. Moody. *Understanding Philanthropy: Its Meaning and Mission.* Bloomington: Indiana University Press, 2008.

Pearce, Jone L. *Volunteers: The Organizational Behavior of Unpaid Workers.* New York: Routledge, 1993.

Peters, B. Guy. *The Future of Governing: Four Emerging Models.* Lawrence: University Press of Kansas, 1996.

——. "Managing the Hollow State." *International Journal of Public Administration* 17 (1994): 739–56.

Peters, B. Guy, and Jon Pierre. "Governance without Government? Rethinking Public Administration." *Journal of Public Administration Research and Theory* 8 (1998): 223–43.

Philanthropic Initiative. *What's a Donor to Do? The State of Donor Resources in America Today.* Boston: The Philanthropic Initiative, 2000.

Phillips, Kevin P. *Wealth and Democracy: A Political History of the American Rich.* New York: Broadway Books, 2002.

Pierre, Jon, ed. *Debating Governance: Authority, Steering, and Governance.* New York: Oxford University Press, 2000.

Poppendieck, Janet. *Sweet Charity? Emergency Food and the End of Entitlement.* New York: Penguin, 1998.

Pozorski, Carilu. "Social Venture Partners: 'Venture Capital' Grantmaking in Practice." *Grantsmanship Center Magazine,* Fall 2000, 24–26.

Prasad, Monica. *The Politics of Free Markets.* Chicago: University of Chicago Press, 2006.

Pratt, Jon. "Bowling Together: Fund Raising Practices and Civic Engagement." In *Critical Issues in Fund Raising,* ed. Dwight F. Burlingame, 247–55. New York: Wiley, 1997.

Putnam, Robert D. "Bowling Alone: America's Declining Social Capital." *Journal of Democracy* 6 (1995): 65–78.

——. *Bowling Alone: The Collapse and Revival of American Community.* New York: Simon & Schuster, 2000.

——. *Making Democracy Work: Civic Traditions in Modern Italy.* Princeton, N.J.: Princeton University Press, 1993.

Putnam, Robert D., and Lewis M. Feldstein. *Better Together: Restoring the American Community.* New York: Simon & Schuster, 2003.

Putnam, Robert D., and Kristin A. Goss. "Introduction." In *Democracies in Flux: The Evolution of Social Capital in Contemporary Society,* ed. Robert D. Putnam, 3–19. Oxford: Oxford University Press, 2002.

Ramos, Henry A. J. "Latino Philanthropy: Expanding U.S. Models of Giving and Civic Participation." In *Cultures of Caring: Philanthropy in Diverse American Communities.* Washington, D.C.: Council on Foundations, June 1999. Available at www.cof.org.

Rawls, John. *A Theory of Justice.* Oxford: Oxford University Press, 1999. First published 1971.

Reddy, Richard D. "Individual Philanthropy and Giving Behavior." In *Participation in Social and Political Activities,* ed. David Hornton Smith and Jacqueline Macaulay, 370–99. San Francisco: Jossey-Bass, 1980.

Reis, Thomas K., and Stephanie F. Clohesy. "Unleashing New Resources and Entrepreneurship for the Common Good: A Philanthropic Renaissance." In *New Directions for Philanthropic Fundraising: Understanding Donor Dynamics,* vol. 32. San Francisco: Jossey-Bass, 2001.

——. "Unleashing New Resources and Entrepreneurship for the Common Good: A Scan, Synthesis, and Scenario for Action." Knowledgebase publication no. 810. Battlecreek, Mich: W. K. Kellogg Foundation, January 1999.

Rhodes, R. A. W. "The New Governance: Governing without Government." *Political Studies* 44 (1996): 652–67.

Roberts Enterprise Development Fund, available at www.redf.org/index.htm.

Roelofs, Joan. "The Third Sector as a Protective Layer for Capitalism." *Monthly Review* 47 (1995): 16–25.

Rose-Ackerman, Susan. "United Charities: An Economic Analysis." In *Community Organizations: Studies in Resource Mobilization and Exchange,* ed. Carl Milofsky, 136–56. New York: Oxford University Press, 1988.

Rosenau, Pauline M. *Post-Modernism and the Social Sciences: Insights, Inroads, and Intrusions.* Princeton, N.J.: Princeton University Press, 1992.

Rosenblum, Nancy L. *Membership and Morals: The Personal Uses of Pluralism in America.* Princeton, N.J.: Princeton University Press, 1998.

Rothschild, Joyce, and J. Allen Whitt. *The Cooperative Workplace: Potentials and Dilemmas of Organizational Democracy and Participation.* New York: Cambridge University Press, 1986.

Rothschild-Whitt, Joyce. "The Collectivist Organization: An Alternative to Rational-Bureaucratic Models." *American Sociological Review* 44 (1979): 509–27.

Rutnik, Tracey, A., and Jessica Bearman. *Giving Together: A National Scan of Giving Circles and Shared Giving.* Washington, D.C.: Forum of Regional Associations of Grantmakers, 2005.

Rutnik, Tracey, A., and Buffy Beaudoin-Schwartz. "Growing Philanthropy through Giving Circles: Lessons Learned from Start-up to Grantmaking." Baltimore: Association of Baltimore Area Grantmakers, October 2003. Available at www.abagmd.org.

Ryan, William P. "The New Landscape for Nonprofits." *Harvard Business Review* 77 (1999): 127–36.

Salamon, Lester M. "Holding the Center: America's Nonprofit Sector at a Crossroads." New York: Nathan Cummings Foundation, January 16, 1997.

———. "The Marketization of Welfare: Changing Nonprofit and For-Profit Roles in the American Welfare State." *Social Service Review* 67 (1993): 16–39.

———. "Of Market Failure, Voluntary Failure, and Third-Party Government: The Theory of Government-Nonprofit Relations in the Modern Welfare State." *Journal of Voluntary Action & Research* 16 (1987): 29–49.

———. *Partners in Public Service: Government-Nonprofit Relations in the Modern Welfare State.* Baltimore: Johns Hopkins University Press, 1995.

———. "The Resilient Sector: The State of Nonprofit America." In *The State of Nonprofit America,* ed. Lester M. Salamon, 3–61. Washington, D.C.: Brookings Institution Press, 2002.

———. "Social Services." In *Who Benefits from the Nonprofit Sector?* ed. Charles T. Clotfelter, 134–73. Chicago: University of Chicago Press, 1992.

Sandel, Michael J. *Democracy's Discontent: America in Search of a Public Philosophy.* Cambridge: Belknap Press of Harvard University Press, 1996.

Sargent, Lyman T. *Extremism in America.* New York: New York University Press, 1995.

Saxon-Harrold, Susan K. E., Susan J. Wiener, Michael T. McCormack, and Michelle A. Weber. *America's Religious Congregations: Measuring Their Contribution to Society.* Washington, D.C.: Independent Sector, November 2000.

Sbarbaro, Cory. "Social Venture Partners Replication." Electronic Hallway, no. F96, 2002. Available at www.hallway.org.

Schervish, Paul G. "Gentle as Doves and Wise as Serpents: The Philosophy of Care and Sociology of Transmission." In *Care and Community in Modern Society: Passing on the Tradition of Service to Future Generations,* ed. Paul G. Schervish, Virginia A. Hodgkinson, and Margaret Gates, 1–20. San Francisco: Jossey-Bass, 1995.

Schervish, Paul G., and John J. Havens. "The New Physics of Philanthropy: The Supply-Side Vectors of Charitable Giving. Part 1: The Material Side of the Supply Side." *CASE International Journal of Educational Advancement* 2 (2001): 95–113.

———. "The Mind of the Millionaire: Findings from a National Survey on Wealth and Responsibility." In *New Directions for Philanthropic Fundraising: Understanding Donor Dynamics*, 32:75–107. San Francisco: Jossey-Bass, 2001.

———. "Social Participation and Charitable Giving: A Multivariate Analysis." *Voluntas* 8 (1997): 235–60.

Schervish, Paul G., John J. Havens, and Mary A. O'Herlihy. "Charitable Giving: How Much, by Whom, to What, and Why." In *The Nonprofit Sector: A Research Handbook*, 2nd ed., ed. Woodrow Powell and Richard Steinberg. New Haven: Yale University Press, 2002.

Schervish, Paul G., and Andrew Herman. *Empowerment and Beneficence: Strategies of Living and Giving among the Wealthy*. Final Report: The Study on Wealth and Philanthropy. Boston: Boston College Social Welfare Research Institute, July 1988.

Schervish, Paul G., Mary A. O'Herlihy, and John J. Havens. *Agent Animated Wealth and Philanthropy: The Dynamics of Accumulation and Allocation among High-Tech Donors*. Boston: Boston College Social Welfare Research Institute, Association of Fundraising Professionals, May 2001.

Schudson, Michael. "What If Civic Life Didn't Die?" *American Prospect* 25 (1996): 17–20.

Schuller, Tom, Stephen Baron, and John Field. "Social Capital: A Review and Critique." In *Social Capital: Critical Perspectives*, ed. Stephen Baron, John Field, and Tom Schuller, 1–38. Oxford: Oxford University Press, 2000.

Schulze, Robert O. "The Role of Economic Dominants in Community Power Structure." *American Sociological Review* 23 (1958): 3–9.

Schulze, Robert O., and Leonard U. Blumberg. "The Determination of Local Power Elites." *American Journal of Sociology* 63 (1957): 290–96.

Schweitzer, Carole. "Building on New Foundations." *Association Management,* October 2000, 28–39.

Sealander, Judith. "Curing Evils at Their Source: The Arrival of Scientific Giving." In *Charity, Philanthropy, and Civility in American History*, ed. Lawrence J. Friedman, and Mark D. McGarvie, 217–39. New York: Cambridge University Press, 2003.

Selinsky, Debbie. "The Power of Giving." *News & Observer,* November 30, 2001.

Sharing the Wealth. Radio broadcast. Sound Money. Minneapolis: Minnesota Public Radio, December 10, 2000.

Shaw, Sondra C., and Martha A. Taylor. *Reinventing Fundraising: Realizing the Potential of Women's Philanthropy*. San Francisco: Jossey-Bass, 1995.

Shaw-Hardy, Sondra. *Creating a Women's Giving Circle*. Rochester, Mich.: Women's Philanthropy Institute, 2000.

Silver, Allan. "The Curious Importance of Small Groups in American Sociology." In *Sociology in America*, ed. Herbert J. Gans, 61–72. Newbury Park: Sage, 1990.

Skloot, Edward. "Evolution or Extinction: A Strategy for Nonprofits in the Marketplace." *Nonprofit and Voluntary Sector Quarterly* 29 (2000): 315–24.

Skocpol, Theda. "Associations without Members." *American Prospect* 45 (1999): 66–73.

———. *Diminished Democracy: From Membership to Management in American Civic Life*. Norman: University of Oklahoma Press, 2003.

———. "The United States: From Membership to Advocacy." In *Democracies in Flux: The Evolution of Social Capital in Contemporary Society,* ed. Robert D. Putnam, 103–36. Oxford: Oxford University Press, 2002.

———. "Unravelling from Above." *American Prospect* 25 (March/April 1996): 20–25.

Smith, Steven Rathgeb. "Managing the Challenges of Government Contracts." In *The Jossey-Bass Handbook of Nonprofit Leadership and Management,* 2nd ed., ed. Robert D. Herman & Associates, 371–90. San Francisco: Jossey-Bass, 2004.

Smith, Steven Rathgeb, and Michael Lipsky. *Nonprofits for Hire: The Welfare State in the Age of Contracting.* Cambridge: Harvard University Press, 1993.

Social Venture Partners Seattle. "History." Seattle: Social Venture Partners Seattle, 2008. Available at www.svpseattle.org/about/history.

———. "Partner FAQs." Seattle: Social Venture Partners Seattle, 2008. Available at www .svpseattle.org/become-partner/faqs.

Sørensen, Eva. "Democratic Governance and the Changing Role of Users of Public Services." *Administrative Theory & Praxis* 22 (2000): 24–44.

———. "Democratic Theory and Network Governance." *Administrative Theory & Praxis* 24 (2002): 693–720.

Sørensen, Eva, and Jacob Torfing. "Network Governance and Post-Liberal Democracy." *Administrative Theory & Praxis* 27 (2005): 197–237.

———. "Network Politics, Political Capital, and Democracy." *International Journal of Public Administration* 26 (2003): 609–34.

Staeheli, Lynn A. "Citizenship and the Search for Community." In *State Devolution in America: Implications for a Diverse Society,* ed. Lynn A. Staeheli, Janet E. Kodras, and Colin Flint, 60–75. Thousand Oaks: Sage, 1997.

"Start a Giving Circle." *Today's Omaha Woman,* August/September 2003, back cover.

Stivers, Camilla. *Bureau Men, Settlement Women: Constructing Public Administration in the Progressive Era.* Lawrence: University Press of Kansas, 2000.

———. "The Public Agency as Polis: Active Citizenship in the Administrative State." *Administration & Society* 22 (1990): 86–105.

Streisand, Betsy. "The New Philanthropy." *U.S. News & World Report,* June 11, 2002, 40–42.

Streeck, Wolfgang. "Inclusion and Secession: Questions on the Boundaries of Associative Democracy." *Politics & Society* 20 (1992): 513–20.

Szasz, Andrew. "Progress through Mischief: The Social Movement Alternative to Secondary Associations." *Politics & Society* 20 (1992): 521–28.

Tamir, Yael. "Revisiting the Civic Sphere." In *Freedom of Association,* ed. Amy Gutmann, 214–38. Princeton, N.J.: Princeton University Press, 1998.

Tobin, Gary A., and Aryeh K. Weinberg. *Mega-Gifts in American Philanthropy: Giving Patterns, 2001–2003.* San Francisco: Institute for Jewish and Community Research, 2007. Available at www.jewishresearch.org/PDFs/MegaGift.Web.07.pdf.

Tocqueville, Alexis de. *Democracy in America.* New York: Bantam Books, 2000. First published 1835.

Toussaint, Rachel G. "Giving Circle Finds a Way to Help." *Seacoastonline,* February 3, 2004.

Trolander, Judith A. *Professionalism and Social Change: From the Settlement House Movement to Neighborhood Centers, 1886 to the Present.* New York: Columbia University Press, 1987.

Urban Institute. *The Nonprofit Sector in Brief: Facts and Figures from the Nonprofit Almanac 2007.* Washington, D.C.: Urban Institute, 2006.

U.S. Census Bureau. "Poverty: Trends for Selected Groups." U.S. Census Bureau, Housing and Household Economic Statistics Division, 2006. Available at www.census.gov/hhes/www/poverty/trends.html.

U.S. Conference of Mayors. "Hunger and Homelessness Continues to Rise in U.S. Cities," City Mayors Society, December 23, 2006. Available at www.citymayors.com/features/uscity_poverty.html.

Uslaner, Eric M. "Volunteering and Social Capital: How Trust and Religion Shape Civic Participation in the United States." In *Social Capital and Participation in Everyday Life*, ed. Paul Dekker and Eric M. Uslaner, 104–17. New York: Routledge, 2001.

Van Til, Jon. *Growing Civil Society: From Nonprofit Sector to Third Space.* Bloomington: Indiana University Press, 2000.

Ventriss, Curtis. "A Substantive View of Ethical Citizenship in Public Affairs." *Public Performance & Management Review* 31 (2007): 38–53.

Verba, Sidney, Kay L. Schlozman, and Henry E. Brady. *Voice and Equality: Civic Voluntarism in American Politics.* Cambridge: Harvard University Press, 1995.

Vogel, Ann. "Who's Making Global Civil Society: Philanthropy and U.S. Empire in World Society." *British Journal of Sociology* 57 (2006): 635–55.

Wagner, David. *What's Love Got to Do with It? A Critical Look at American Charity.* New York: New York Press, 2000.

Walsh, Katherine C. *Talking about Politics: Informal Groups and Social Identity in American Life.* Chicago: University of Chicago Press, 2004.

Wang, Shaoguang. "Money and Autonomy: Patterns of Civil Society Finance and Their Implications." *Studies in Comparative International Development* 40 (2006): 3–29.

Warren, Mark E. *Democracy and Association.* Princeton, N.J.: Princeton University Press, 2001.

Weber, Max. *The Theory of Social and Economic Organization.* New York: Oxford University Press, 1947.

Weber, Edward P. *Bringing Society Back In: Grassroots Ecosystem Management, Accountability, and Sustainable Communities.* Cambridge: MIT Press, 2003.

Weisbrod, Burton, ed. *To Profit or Not to Profit? The Commercial Transformation of the Nonprofit Sector.* New York: Cambridge University Press, 1998.

Weisinger, Judith Y., and Paul F. Salipante. "A Grounded Theory for Building Ethnically Bridging Social Capital in Voluntary Organizations." *Nonprofit and Voluntary Sector Quarterly* 34 (2005): 29–55.

Weitzman, Murray S., Nadine T. Jalandoni, Linda M. Lampkin, and Thomas H. Pollak. *The New Nonprofit Almanac and Desk Reference: The Essential Facts and Figures for Managers, Researchers, and Volunteers.* San Francisco: Jossey-Bass, 2002.

Whittington, Keith E. "Revisiting Tocqueville's America: Society, Politics, and Association in the Nineteenth Century." *American Behavioral Scientist* 42 (1998): 21–32.

Wiebe, Robert H. *Self-Rule: A Cultural History of American Democracy.* Chicago: University of Chicago Press, 1995.

Wolch, Jennifer R. *The Shadow State: Government and Voluntary Sector in Transition.* New York: Foundation Center, 1990.

Wolpert, Julian. "Communities, Networks, and the Future of Philanthropy." In *Philanthropy and the Nonprofit Sector in a Changing America,* ed. Charles T. Clotfelter, 231–47. Bloomington: Indiana University Press, 1999.

———. "Decentralization and Equity in Public and Nonprofit Sectors." *Nonprofit and Voluntary Sector Quarterly* 22 (1993): 281–96.

———. "How Federal Cutbacks Affect the Charitable Sector." In *State Devolution in America: Implications for a Diverse Society,* ed. Lynn Staeheli, Janet E. Kodras, and Colin Flint, 97–117. Thousand Oaks, Calif.: Sage, 1997.

Wuthnow, Robert. *Loose Connections: Joining Together in America's Fragmented Communities.* Cambridge: Harvard University Press, 1998.

———. *Sharing the Journey: Support Groups and America's New Quest for Community.* New York: Free Press, 1994.

———. "The United States: Bridging the Privileged and the Marginalized?" In *Democracies in Flux: The Evolution of Social Capital in Contemporary Society,* ed. Robert D. Putnam, 59–102. Oxford: Oxford University Press, 2002.

Young, Dennis R. "Commercialism in Nonprofit Social Service Associations." In *To Profit or Not to Profit: The Commercial Transformation of the Nonprofit Sector,* ed. Burton A. Weisbrod, 195–216. Cambridge: Cambridge University Press, 1998.

Young, Dennis R., and Lester M. Salamon. "Commercialization, Social Ventures, and For-Profit Competition." In *The State of Nonprofit America,* ed. L. M. Salamon, 423–46. Washington, D.C.: Brookings, 2002.

Young, Iris M. "Social Groups in Associative Democracy." *Politics & Society* 20 (1992): 529–34.

Zimmerman, Brenda, and Raymond Dart. *Charities Doing Commercial Ventures: Societal and Organizational Implications.* Trillium Foundation, 1998. Available at www.cprn.org.

Index

formal organization giving circles, 61, *62,* 69–71, 73–75, 79–81, 84–88, 90–92, 94–98, 100, 102, 103, 105, 106–109, *110,* 112, 114, *115,* 118, 125, 130; activities, *62,* 70, 92; awareness of need, 108, 112, 114, *115;* characteristics of members, 84–86; decision-making, 70, 73, 87–88, 106; funding recipients, 96–98, 100; impact on members, 94–95, 103, 112, 114, 118; grant-making, 70, 73, 79, 87–88, 96–97; relationship between donor and recipient, 80, 98, 114; strategic practices, 103; structure, *62,* 69, 70, 72–73, 75; types, 70–71

Forum of Regional Associations of Grantmakers, 2, 10, 57, 85, 124, 129n2; New Ventures in Philanthropy Initiative, 2, 124, 129n2

foundations, 2, 18, 34, 35, 36, 37, 58, 81, 86, 96, 100, 129n4; community, 1, 10, *62,* 70, 73, 74–75, 124; compared to giving circles, 101, 107; corporate, 80; critique, 25–26; funding recipients, 49–50, 101; private, 19, 50, 73, 78, 80; university, 60; women's, 70

fundraising, 14, 19, 21, 34, 60, 103, 108, 123, 127–128; by giving circles, 58, *62;* from giving circles, 78–79, 81; professionalization, 35, 39

Fung, Archon, 15, 53, 55, 112, 116–117

giving circles: awareness of need, 94–95, 103, 105, 107, 114; capacity building, 2, 58, 72, 79, 89–91, 102, 107, 118; characteristics of members, 84–86; comparison with other types of philanthropy, 77–81; decision-making, 1, 58, 61, 63, 69, 87–88, 91, 106–107; definition, ix, 2, 57–61; democratic effects, 82–104, 113; democratization, 108–116;; dimensions, 57–61, *110–111;* distribution of resources, 58, 64; diversity and, 84–86, 106, 113, 117; effects on members' giving, 101–103; funding recipients, 96–101, *115,* 124; identification with others, 47, 91–95, 106; independence, ix, 60–61, 66, 68, 105, 117–118; member characteristics, *62,* 82–86, *82,* 113, 123; member engagement, 60, 112; political impact, 112; reasons for joining, 75–77, *77,* 114; recipient characteristics, 96–98, 107, 108; relationship between donor and recipient, 80, 98, 114; shortcomings, 112; social opportunities, 59, 113; strategic practices, 103; tensions in purposes, 116–120; types, 61–75; women and, ix, 1, 3, 59–60, *62,* 66–68, 70, 73–77,

83, *84,* 90, 92, 96, 100–102, 106–108, 112–113, 125

Giving Circle of Hope, 58

governance, ix, 4, 5, 6–7, 14–16, 27, 46, 56, 86, 89–90, 96, 98, 114, 121; beyond the state, x, 4, 5–6,8–9, 11, 27, 44, 104, 109, 114, 118–119, 120; minigovernments, 118; minipublics, 52–53, 55, 112, 116, 118; network, 5, 51

Gramsci, Antonio, 25

Habermas, Jürgen, 6, 31, 131n37

Hestia Fund, 96, 102–103, 124

individuals in need: 57–59, 86, 91, 94–98, 105, 107, 113–115

Institute for Jewish and Community Research, 19

International Society for Third Sector Research (ISTR), 35

Kettering Foundation's National Issues Forum, 53

Kiwanis, 2, 7, 39, 78, 130n4

Latino Giving Circle of Chicago, *62*

leadership, 8, 16, 38–39, 61, 90–91, 96, 107, *111,* 119; shared, *62,* 87, 106

League of Women Voters, 7, 39, 130n4

Lions, 7

loose network giving circles, 61, *62,* 66–69, 76, 78, 79, 94, 102, 106–109, *110,* 124, 125; activities, *62,* 90–91; awareness of need, 94–95 114, 118; characteristics of members, 84–86; decision-making, 87, 89; funding recipients, 96–98, 100, 114–115; democratic participation, 107, 108; strategic practices, 103; structure, *62,* 66, 68

Madison, James, 23

marketization, 35–37; effects on democracy, 40–42

Mill, John Stuart, 6, 23

modernity, 29–32, 45, 50

modernization, 7, 29–35, 37–40, 44–45, 52, 90, 105, 109

neo-liberal model, 5

network associations. *See* associations

New Mountain Climbers, *62*

new philanthropy. *See* philanthropy

New River Valley Change Network, 1, 58, 86, 119

new voluntarism. *See* voluntarism
network governance. *See* governance

Omaha Venture Group, x, 58, *62,* 70, 73–74, 88, 124
organizational models, 33, 36, 86–89; bureaucratic, 30, 34, 37, 39, 43, 51–53, 108, 109, 112–113, 118, 123, 125; collectivist-democratic, 109, *110,* 112–113; federated, 117, 119, 129; nonbureaucratic, 59, 66, 69, 76, 106, 108, 117
organizational sustainability, 36–37

Party with Purpose, *62*
Pateman, Carole, 6
philanthropy, x–xi, 6, 8–11, 12, 14–15, 31, 33–35, 57, 59, 64–65, 68, 75, 103, 109, 114, 120; antidemocratic effects, 18–27; corporate, 22, 25, 80; demand-side, 2, 60, 120; democratic attributes, 17, 44; democratizing, ix, 4, 44; demographics, 45, 48–50, *49;* failure, 8–9, 18; grassroots, 2, 69; organized, 34, 73, 83, 85–86, 98, 106, 124; modern, 2, 54; new, 2–4, 130n8; promoting, 60, *76,* 77, 129n2; role of, x, 9, 105; scientific, 7, 34, 54; supply-side, 3, 60; traditional, 2, 84, 98, 100, 106–107, 112; venture, 1, 17, 37, 70–72, 76; women's, 45, 84
postmodern, 44, 50, 53
posttraditional society, 3, 10, 44, 50–51, 54–55, 109, 116–117
public policy, xi, 1, 5, 15–16, 21, 23, 33, 35–36, 38, 55, 105, 112, 120
public sphere, 6, 16, 24, 31, 34, 40, 53, 112, 131n37
Putnam, Robert D., ix, 6–7, 16–17, 29, 41, 47, 52, 53–54, 91, 93, 113, 116

Quality of Life Giving Circle, 87, 95, 102

rational-bureaucratic model of organization. *See* organizational models
Red Heart Society, 87
redistribution of resources, 8, 17–20, 18–22, 48, 95, 105, 108, 113–116, 119
research methodology, 123–128
Roberts Enterprise Development Fund, 37
Rotary, 2, 7, 39, 78
Rousseau, Jean-Jacque, 6, 24

Sacramento Women's Action Network, 102
scientific charity movement, 7, 33, 34

Select Committee to Investigate Foundations and Comparable Organizations, 25
settlement house movement, 27, 34
Shared Giving, 62–64, 87, 97, 100–102
Silicon Valley Social Venture Fund, (SV2), 76, 102
small group giving circles, 61–65, *62,* 78–79, 95, *110,* 112, 117–118, 125; activities, 90; awareness of need, 114; characteristics of members, 84–86; bonding, 92; decision-making process, 61, 87–88; democratic participation, 90–91, 106–108; effects on giving, 101–103; funding recipients, 96–97, 102, *115;* relationship between donor and recipient, 94, 114; strategic practices, 103; structure, *62, 63*
small groups, 1, 3, 52–53, 55, 116
social capacity, 38, 45–46, 89
social capital, 4, 7, 17, 29, 41–42, 47, 91–93, 113, 116; bridging, 7, 47, 56, 91–92, 113–114, 116, 145n22; bonding, 7, 47, 56, 91–92, 107, 113, 116, 145n22
social change, xi, 1, 3, 25–26, 37, 40–41, 65, 112, 119–120
social control, 26, 33, *110*
social differences, 7, 47
social entrepreneurship, 36–37
social justice, 63, 100, 120
social movements, 7, 25–26
social transformation, 2, 10, 29, 44, 55, 109
Social Venture Partners (SVP), 1, 60, 70, 73, 75, 78–79, 102–103; accountability, 58; capacity building, 71, 79; Delaware, 88–89; funding recipients, 96–97; grant-making process, 71–72; structure, 70; Calgary, 124; Seattle, 1–2, *62,* 71–73, 88, 92–93, 101, 124
social welfare, x, 4–5, 9, 14, 24, 42, 49, 114, 129n4; services, 35
socioeconomic disparities, 13–14
street level bureaucrats, 35

Thoreau, Henry David, 23
Tocqueville, Alexis de, 7, 15–18, 24, 31–33, 38–39, 44, 46–47, 52, 86, 89, 91, 109, 117, 124n4

United Way, 2, 34, 49, 73, 80, 96

venture philanthropy. *See* philanthropy
voluntarism, x, 4–7, 10–11, 106, 112–113, 118; antidemocratic aspects, 17–18, 25, 26, 46, 105; beneficiaries, 95–98; benefits to democracy, 15–17, 95; democratic effects, 9, 29, 44, 48, 55, 104, 107; democratizing, 44–50, 82, 87, 91, 107–108; elitism, 52; failure, 8–9;

Philanthropic and Nonprofit Studies

Dwight F. Burlingame and David C. Hammack, editors

Thomas Adam, editor. *Philanthropy, Patronage, and Civil Society: Experiences from Germany, Great Britain, and North America*

Albert B. Anderson. *Ethics for Fundraisers*

Peter M. Ascoli. *Julius Rosenwald: The Man Who Built Sears, Roebuck and Advanced the Cause of Black Education in the American South*

Karen J. Blair. *The Torchbearers: Women and Their Amateur Arts Associations in America, 1890-1930*

Eleanor Brilliant. *Private Charity and Public Inquiry: A History of the Filer and Peterson Commissions*

Dwight F. Burlingame, editor. *The Responsibilities of Wealth*

Dwight F. Burlingame and Dennis Young, editors. *Corporate Philanthropy at the Crossroads*

Charles T. Clotfelter and Thomas Ehrlich, editors. *Philanthropy and the Nonprofit Sector in a Changing America*

Ruth Crocker. *Mrs. Russell Sage: Women's Activism and Philanthropy in Gilded Age and Progressive Era America*

Marcos Cueto, editor. *Missionaries of Science: The Rockefeller Foundation and Latin America*

William Damon and Susan Verducci, editors. *Taking Philanthropy Seriously: Beyond Noble Intentions to Responsible Giving*

Gregory Eiselein. *Literature and Humanitarian Reform in the Civil War Era*

Helen Gilbert and Chris Tiffin, editors. *Burden or Benefit?: Imperial Benevolence and Its Legacies*

Richard B. Gunderman. *We Make a Life by What We Give*

David C. Hammack, editor. *Making the Nonprofit Sector in the United States: A Reader*

David C. Hammack and Steven Heydemann, editors. *Globalization, Philanthropy, and Civil Society: Projecting Institutional Logics Abroad*

Jerome L. Himmelstein. *Looking Good and Doing Good: Corporate Philanthropy and Corporate Power*

Warren F. Ilchman, Stanley N. Katz, and Edward L. Queen II, editors. *Philanthropy in the World's Traditions*

Warren F. Ilchman, Alice Stone Ilchman, and Mary Hale Tolar, editors. *The Lucky Few and the Worthy Many: Scholarship Competitions and the World's Future Leaders*

Thomas H. Jeavons. *When the Bottom Line Is Faithfulness: Management of Christian Service Organizations*

Amy A. Kass, editor. *The Perfect Gift*

Amy A. Kass, editor. *Giving Well, Doing Good: Readings for Thoughtful Philanthropists*

Ellen Condliffe Lagemann, editor. *Philanthropic Foundations: New Scholarship, New Possibilities*

Daniel C. Levy. *To Export Progress: The Golden Age of University Assistance in the Americas*

Mike W. Martin. *Virtuous Giving: Philanthropy, Voluntary Service, and Caring*

Kathleen D. McCarthy, editor. *Women, Philanthropy, and Civil Society*

Marc A. Musick and John Wilson, editors. *Volunteers: A Social Profile*

Mary J. Oates. *The Catholic Philanthropic Tradition in America*

Robert S. Ogilvie. *Voluntarism, Community Life, and the American Ethic*

J. B. Schneewind, editor. *Giving: Western Ideas of Philanthropy*

William H. Schneider, editor. *Rockefeller Philanthropy and Modern Biomedicine: International Initiatives from World War I to the Cold War*

Bradford Smith, Sylvia Shue, Jennifer Lisa Vest, and Joseph Villarreal. *Philanthropy in Communities of Color*

David Horton Smith, Robert A. Stebbins, and Michael A. Dover, editors. *A Dictionary of Nonprofit Terms and Concepts*

David H. Smith. *Entrusted: The Moral Responsibilities of Trusteeship*

David H. Smith, editor. *Good Intentions: Moral Obstacles and Opportunities*

Jon Van Til. *Growing Civil Society: From Nonprofit Sector to Third Space*

Andrea Walton. *Women and Philanthropy in Education*

ANGELA M. EIKENBERRY is Assistant Professor in the School of Public Administration at the University of Nebraska at Omaha. In addition to her participation in giving circles, she has worked as a development and grant writing consultant.